Contemp

Contemporary Irish Plays

Freefall
Michael West

Forgotten
Pat Kinevane

Drum Belly
Richard Dormer

Planet Belfast
Rosemary Jenkinson

Desolate Heaven
Ailís Ní Ríain

The Boys of Foley Street
Louise Lowe

Bloomsbury Methuen Drama
An imprint of Bloomsbury Publishing Plc

B L O O M S B U R Y
LONDON • NEW DELHI • NEW YORK • SYDNEY

Bloomsbury Methuen Drama

An imprint of Bloomsbury Publishing Plc

50 Bedford Square	1385 Broadway
London	New York
WC1B 3DP	NY 10018
UK	USA

www.bloomsbury.com

**BLOOMSBURY, METHUEN DRAMA and the Diana logo are trademarks of
Bloomsbury Publishing Plc**

First published in 2015

British Library Cataloguing-in-Publication Data
A catalogue record for this book is available from the British Library.

ISBN: PB: 978-1-4725-7668-2
EPUB: 978-1-4725-7669-9
EPDF: 978-1-4725-7670-5

Library of Congress Cataloging-in-Publication Data
A catalog record for this book is available from the Library of Congress.

Typeset by Fakenham Prepress Solutions, Fakenham, Norfolk NR21 8NN
Printed and bound in India

Contents

Chronology

1994: During a trip to Australia, the Irish Taoiseach (Prime Minister) Albert Reynolds describes Ireland as a 'Celtic Tiger', drawing a comparison with the booming economies of southeast Asia. During the next ten years, that term will be widely adopted to describe the stunning transformation in the Irish economy: unemployment falls to less than three per cent, emigration ceases, and the country enjoys unprecedented levels of prosperity. Also in this year, legislation to decriminalise homosexuality comes into force, signalling a new liberalisation and secularisation of the society. A British TV documentary entitled *Suffer the Children* becomes one of the first public attempts to bring to light allegations of child abuse against Catholic priests in Ireland.

1998: The Good Friday Agreement is signed in Northern Ireland, seeking to bring to an end the Troubles. In New York, Martin McDonagh's *Beauty Queen of Leenane* wins four Tony Awards, signalling a global resurgence in the popularity of Irish drama.

1999: The Irish critic Fintan O'Toole argues that Irish drama has entered a 'third renaissance', following on from the Irish Literary Renaissance (1890–1926) and a second renaissance involving Brian Friel and Tom Murphy in the 1960s. Irish drama continues to thrive internationally, with major productions of plays by Sebastian Barry, Marina Carr, Martin McDonagh, Conor McPherson, Mark O'Rowe, and many others. In the same year, the Irish government establishes the Commission to Inquire into Child Abuse (CICA).

2002: Following the bursting of the dotcom bubble, not to mention the impact of the 11 September 2001 attacks in the United States, the Irish economy shows signs of slowing down. In order to return growth to the Irish economy, the government introduces tax incentives to stimulate the housing market. A major property bubble soon forms.

2004: The Irish economy continues to boom, but problems are becoming evident. A UN report warns that Ireland has one of the world's widest gaps between rich and poor – second only to the

United States. The Abbey Theatre celebrates its centenary year, but the festivities are severely undermined when it is revealed that the theatre has run up a considerable deficit. A major controversy about the future of the theatre erupts in the national press.

2005: The Irish government reluctantly agrees to bail out the Abbey Theatre. Some staff resign; others are made redundant, and the theatre is significantly restructured.

2006: *Forgotten* by Pat Kinevane premieres. It continues to tour in Ireland and internationally for several years.

2008: The global credit crunch has a disproportionately severe impact on Ireland. In September, the Irish government is forced to provide an unlimited guarantee of the country's five banks. That decision will ultimately come to be seen as signalling the end of the Celtic Tiger period. House prices plummet, unemployment soars, and mass emigration resumes.

2009: The Commission to Inquire into Child Abuse publishes its report, now referred to as *The Ryan Report*. It reveals that since the 1930s, more than 30,000 Irish children were abused in institutions run by the Catholic Church. Michael West's *Freefall* premieres. Major cuts to arts funding take place: several theatre companies lose their funding. A National Campaign for the Arts is initiated.

2010: As its economy collapses, the Irish government is forced to seek an emergency bailout from the International Monetary Fund, the European Union, and the European Central Bank. The bailout leads to the imposition of severe wage-cuts and tax increases. While the National Campaign for the Arts quickly gains a high profile, arts cuts continue.

2012: Premiere of *The Boys of Foley Street* as part of the Dublin Theatre Festival.

2013: The IMF/EU/ECB Bailout programme concludes, and Ireland regains its financial sovereignty. Premieres of *Drum Belly, Desolate Heaven* and *Planet Belfast*.

2014: As the year begins, modest signs of economic recovery are evident in Ireland.

Introduction

Symbols Adequate to our Predicament: Irish Drama, 2006–2014

Irish theatre seems to be at its strongest during times of national crisis. The first great movement in Irish drama came in the 1890s, when the death of the political leader Charles Stewart Parnell caused widespread disillusionment and division. The failure of Parnell's Home Rule movement led people to move in large numbers from politics to art – and that in turn led to the foundation of Ireland's national theatre, the Abbey, in 1904. During the following years, writers such as W. B. Yeats, J. M. Synge and James Joyce attempted to imagine the kind of country that Ireland could become. For those great artists, crisis and creativity were intimately interlinked.

Something similar happened in the 1920s, when the Irish War of Independence gave way to a brutal Civil War. Those painful events found direct expression in one of the masterpieces of Irish theatre, Sean O'Casey's 'trilogy' of *The Shadow of a Gunman*, *Juno and the Paycock*, and *The Plough and the Stars*. Then, in the 1960s, economic stagnation and mass emigration inspired the emergence of a new generation of writers, led by Tom Murphy and Brian Friel – while in the 1980s the Troubles in Northern Ireland were marked by the foundation of major new companies such as Field Day and Charabanc.

Upon first glance, the Celtic Tiger period might seem like an exception to this pattern. From roughly 1995 to 2008, Ireland experienced a spectacular economic boom: it became one of the world's richest countries, and was widely celebrated for its successful combination of low taxes with high rates of foreign direct investment. Added to that economic miracle, was the arrival of peace to Northern Ireland, with the Good Friday Agreement of 1998 proving a durable, if necessarily imperfect, solution to a conflict that had for decades seemed intractable.

Those social transformations were matched by the arrival of major new Irish playwrights: in quick succession, audiences internationally were introduced to Marina Carr, Conor McPherson,

Martin McDonagh, Enda Walsh, Owen McCafferty, Mark O'Rowe, and many others. As the new millennium arrived, critics were suggesting that the Celtic Tiger era had brought about a new golden age for Irish playwriting.

Yet, perhaps paradoxically, the theatre in Ireland did not prosper during that period of economic success. Yes, there were great new Irish plays – but most of them were being premiered in countries other than Ireland: many of the plays of Martin McDonagh and Conor McPherson opened in England, for example; and new works by Enda Walsh often premiered in Germany. Within Ireland itself, however, the major companies often struggled to produce interesting or innovative new plays – and there was a suspicion in some quarters that the Irish theatre was out of touch with everyday life in the country.

Perhaps the best example of the instability of Irish theatre during the boom years is the fact that the Abbey Theatre almost collapsed due to funding difficulties in 2004 – a remarkable occurrence given the country's prosperity at that time. The Abbey marked its centenary year embroiled in controversy about budgeting and mismanagement; it survived only because the Irish government agreed, very reluctantly, to bail it out.

What no one realised at that time was that the Abbey was merely the first of a series of national institutions that would be deemed 'too big to fail' by the Irish state. In September 2008, as the global credit crunch took hold, Ireland was forced to issue an unlimited guarantee of the deposits and loans of the country's five banks, using state funds to keep them in business. The decision to support the banks quickly eroded investor confidence in the Irish economy, which itself soon needed a bailout from the International Monetary Fund, the EU and the European Central Bank. By 2010, Ireland's reputation had been transformed again: where before it had been celebrated for its rapid enrichment, now it was being derided for its profligacy and fiscal ineptitude.

The impact of the economic collapse was quickly felt. Emigration resumed, unemployment rose to almost fifteen per cent, and the Celtic Tiger period was soon recalled with a mixture of embarrassment, shame and despair. Meanwhile, in Northern Ireland, the deterioration of the UK economy was also having an impact.

Austerity has led to the reassertion of some of the political divisions that had seemed dormant: there are a growing number of disputes about such issues as flags and national emblems, and so-called 'dissident' republican terrorists are becoming more active. So throughout Ireland today there is a great deal of uncertainty about the future – and about who is to blame for the problems that the island now faces.

And the economic problems have been accompanied by an even greater trauma. The collapse of Ireland's banks presented the country with a series of figures too large to imagine in everyday terms – €80 billion to cover the losses of property developers, €500 billion to guarantee the banks, and so on. But those numbers seemed inconsequential when, in 2009, an Irish government enquiry (published in a document called the *Ryan Report*) produced another statistic – that, since the 1930s, an estimated 30,000 children in Ireland had suffered sexual and physical abuse in institutions run by the Catholic Church.

The revelation that the abuse had been so widespread had a profound impact, producing feelings of revulsion, horror and guilt. The director Annie Ryan described the situation succinctly. 'Ireland was overwhelmed with grief and remorse', she wrote. 'It broke. It fell to its knees. Amidst job losses, the unknown future, the change in status, in life-style, [these revelations were] a shocking reminder of everyone's roots'.

This anthology aims to capture the state of Irish theatre in this moment of transformation. What we find in the plays gathered here is a mixture of hope and rage, and a strange combination of the old with the new. The six writers whose works are collected here often draw on the example of their predecessors: Synge, Lady Gregory, O'Casey, Friel, and so on. Yet they are also attempting to find new ways of making theatre, new ways of creating what Seamus Heaney called 'symbols adequate to our predicament'. Some of the new approaches to Irish theatre-making have undoubtedly been forced by economic necessity. Yet this book aims to show that the emerging forms of writing and theatre practice are broader, more ambitious, and more collaborative than has been the case for many years. It would be wrong to say that Irish theatre is thriving – but it is rising imaginatively to a variety of new challenges.

One of the major transformations in Irish life since 2008 has been a collapse of moral and social authority. Bankers and politicians are, as in other countries, widely reviled for having brought about an era of austerity – and in Ireland the Catholic Church has been greatly weakened by its failure to protect the children in its care. There has been a resultant suspicion of all institutions (the media, the public service, business), which has been accompanied by a pervasive cynicism about the motivations of people who occupy positions of power.

That collapse of authority has coincided with a change in the status of the Irish playwright. Even until the Celtic Tiger era, the dominant idea in Irish theatre was that the dramatist should be viewed as a lone genius whose words must be treated reverentially: this, certainly, was the approach usually taken to the plays of figures such as Beckett and Friel. That idea has now been largely overturned, as a new generation – identifying themselves with the more capacious term 'theatre-makers' – has emerged to create work that is collaborative, and which blurs distinctions between writers, actors, directors and audiences.

One of the leading figures in this development has been Michael West, a playwright whose output since the turn of the century has been dominated by collaborative work with Annie Ryan's company Corn Exchange. Partners in life as well as in the theatre, Ryan and West have worked together on several important productions such as *Dublin by Lamplight* (2004) and *Everyday* (2006). Their process is to bring an original concept into a rehearsal room, work-shopping with actors to refine and develop their ideas – so that the composition of words on a page is carried out with a detailed awareness of the movements of actors in space and time. The resulting plays are clearly the work of West himself, but they have been enriched by the input of many Irish performers, and by Ryan's style of direction.

That method of working allowed Corn Exchange and West to respond quickly to a transforming Ireland: not only to the collapse of the Irish economy but also to the *Ryan Report*. The resulting play *Freefall* is a generous and heartfelt lament for a country that, as Annie Ryan had said, had 'fallen to its knees'. West's exploration of mortality in this play makes his protagonist seem universally recognisable, but the life of this man – an everyman figure whose name we never learn – can also be seen as a metaphor for the state of Ireland. As he dies, the man finds himself haunted by two 'ghosts'. One is a workman who tells the man that his house is going to collapse due to the longstanding neglect of its structure (a possible metaphor for the Celtic Tiger property bubble). The other is a kindly priest who had urged the man to make more of himself when he was in school (a characterization that can be seen as representing a need to move beyond anger with the Church in the wake of the child abuse scandals). So the play is a lament for the end of an ordinary life, but it also prompts questions about what Ireland might look like in a post-Celtic Tiger, post-Catholic future.

Perhaps, though, *Freefall* is fundamentally about love. That theme is best articulated in one of the man's interactions with his son, who has asked for advice about how to live well. The man replies that people worry too much about trying to change: 'You, for example', he says to his son, 'You're perfect the way you are'. The simplicity of these words acts as a moving reminder that it is possible for us to leave something behind after we're gone, something as uncomplicated as parental love – something that cannot be put in economic terms, but which we all acknowledge as having lasting worth.

But we must also acknowledge that some children never experience such love. The man was raised by his uncle and aunt, and is haunted by the fate of his sister, who was placed in an institution run by the Catholic Church while still an infant. The man's inability to know what happened to his sister leaves a haunting void at the heart of *Freefall*, a space that is impossible to fill and impossible to ignore. As a metaphor for the impact of the *Ryan Report*, West's unanswerable questions feel painfully appropriate.

Another play that allows us to think about the death of a particular version of Ireland is Pat Kinevane's *Forgotten*, which explores the lives of a quartet of elderly people, aged between 80 and 100. As his play shows, the elderly should not be 'forgotten' – not just because they have value in their own right, but also because their past helps to explain our present. His play asks us to think about our roots, about how we got to where we are – and about how we can choose different pathways into the future.

This link between the historical and the contemporary is evident not only thematically, but also in the play's form, which is simultaneously traditional and innovative. Within Irish drama, many plays involve the direct address of the audience that we find in *Forgotten*: Kinevane's use of overlapping and interlinking stories may remind audiences of works like Conor McPherson's *Port Authority* or even Samuel Beckett's *Play*. What makes *Forgotten* seem comparatively inventive, however, is that all four roles are played by one actor – who, in its original production, was Kinevane himself. To watch the play is to be made aware of the versatility and skill of the actor on stage: someone who can cross boundaries of age, gender and social class with the simplest of movements and gestures.

Yet the requirement that the four roles be played by one actor has a thematic impact as well. The stories in the play interlink beautifully: the audience is in the privileged position of understanding the plot in ways that characters like Dora and Eucharia perhaps never will. But those stories also interlink in the physical performance of the actor, who uses one body to characterise four different personae. The actor thus embodies *difference*: the socially constructed differences in terms of age, class, and gender that distinguish the characters from each other. But he also embodies commonality, showing that people must be valued for what we share. Like Kinevane's characters, we all fear loneliness, we all want to be loved, we all wonder about what might have been – and none of us wants to be forgotten, especially while we are still living. *Forgotten* thus offers us a partial glimpse of our own futures: old age awaits us all, and the stories in this play are, on some level, our own stories.

Another actor who has turned to writing plays is Richard Dormer. His *Drum Belly* is set in New York, and is a thriller involving Irish-American gangsters. As such, at its premiere at the Abbey Theatre it earned immediate comparisons with the early films of Quentin Tarantino. Those identifications are certainly apt: the use of popular music, the tightness of the plotting, and the quirkiness of the characterization will all seem familiar to anyone who has enjoyed *Reservoir Dogs*. And the play's use of a harshly aestheticized violence will also recall some of the strategies used in HBO's fantasy series *Game of Thrones* – in which Dormer plays a small but important role. So *Drum Belly* seems very well attuned to recent currents in American global culture.

Yet Dormer's deepest debt is not to cinema or TV but, arguably, to an Irish play: Tom Murphy's 1961 *A Whistle in the Dark*. Exploring the lives of a group of young Irish men who had emigrated to England, *Whistle* shows how violence, ignorance and contempt for the law arise directly from the trauma of emigration – from the fact that, although the characters may physically have left Ireland, they still carry the country's worst aspects with them, psychologically and in other ways. Murphy's play is a deeply personal family tragedy, yet it is also an uncompromisingly brave exploration of the impact of emigration upon Irish life generally.

Something similar happens in *Drum Belly*, a play that has emigration at its core. We meet characters who are named for the Irish counties Wicklow and Antrim – even though the men so named appear to know little about those places. And we also see in the gang-leader Sullivan a curious impulse to fetishise 'home' in his construction of a garden comprised of turf from Kildare, trees from Armagh and Cavan, and lavender from County Down. Sullivan is attempting to recreate the entire island of Ireland in his New York home, flattening out diversity and distinction – and, significantly, also ignoring the existence of the border that places Armagh and Down in Northern Ireland and Cavan, Clare and Kildare in the Irish Republic. For Sullivan, this imagined version of home is a guarantor of his own identity, his own authenticity. His resultant sense of rootedness in turn allows him to forego responsibility for the violence that he inflicts upon people in his adopted home.

Yet Ireland – the real Ireland – can still make its presence felt. It does so in the form of Bobby, a young man from Northern Ireland who is fleeing some form of communal violence, and who silently observes much of the action in New York. That direct link between Ireland and America is important: the play is set in 1969, a year famous in America for the moon landing, but infamous in Ireland as the starting point of the Troubles. *Drum Belly* thus dramatises a time when each country took 'one giant leap' that would change it forever. By merging those two events, Dormer returns us to another time of transformation, a time when Ireland was (as in the present) facing a moment of forced re-invention. And by placing emigration at the centre of that re-definition, Dormer makes the argument that Tom Murphy made in *Whistle in the Dark*: we may think we can leave Ireland – or leave behind the past – but both will continue to exert a gravitational pull, tugging upon us like the moon drags upon the oceans.

The power of the past is also a central theme in Rosemary Jenkinson's dark satire *Planet Belfast*. By juxtaposing the local with the global, the play's title makes Jenkinson's intentions immediately apparent: she wants to show that, whatever Ireland's problems, the future of the planet requires attention too. But, again, a link between past and present drives the play forward.

Jenkinson dramatises a Belfast that is trying to change and develop, trying to determine how to move beyond the Troubles without forgetting those who suffered and died during that conflict. She allows the audience to have some good-natured if incisive fun at the expense of what might be called the 'trauma industry': her play sometimes implies that if Northern Ireland can't seem to 'move on' from the pain of the past, this might be because there are economic imperatives against doing so. Yet she also shows that trauma is real and inescapable: the problem is not that individual experiences have been repressed, but that they have been appropriated by state-funded institutions that seem more concerned with self-perpetuation than with helping people.

Importantly, however, the protagonist of *Planet Belfast* is attempting to move away from her past. As a member of the Green Party, Alice is willing to deal with the nationalist and unionist sides of the Northern Irish conflict; she identifies with neither grouping herself. Instead, her focus in on the future of the planet: the Troubles seem relatively inconsequential when put in the context of climate change, after all. Jenkinson's play takes in events around the world, showing that a catastrophe in China can have a palpable impact on Northern Ireland. And she also shows how global occurrences can have both local and personal manifestations. For example, the play's consideration of the ethics of genetically modified food is placed in the context of the Great Irish Famine of the 1840s, a disaster that arose partly as a result of dependence on a single crop. And that debate about genetics maps in surprising ways onto Alice's own preoccupations with reproduction. The play therefore raises serious questions about how parenthood continues to determine the identities of women – and, simultaneously, Alice's desire to have a child allows us to consider what kind of planet we want future generations to inherit. Throughout the play, then, personal and global imperatives are shown to be interdependent.

In dramatising the desire for a child, Jenkinson is both resuscitating and reinventing one of the most durable tropes in Northern Irish Drama. In plays about the Troubles, dead or dying babies abound – as seen in Brian Friel's *Translations*, Stewart Parker's *Pentecost*, and many others. In such works, the death of a baby acts as a metaphor for the health of society: those plays are often seen as expressing the idea that Northern Ireland had no future. Jenkinson uses this trope much more positively than writers like Friel and Parker did – but she is also more ambiguous. *Planet Belfast* shows that there may be hope for Northern Ireland (and for the planet), but it also leaves us with the obligation to consider how such a future can be realised.

Uncertainty about the future also haunts Ailís Ní Ríain's *Desolate Heaven*. Woven into the action are references to W. B. Yeats's 1889 'The Stolen Child', a poem that, like Ní Ríain's play, aims to blend a desire for escape with a deeply felt sense of loss. Yeats invites us to imagine his eponymous child's joy in fleeing to 'the waters and the wild' because ours is a world 'more full of weeping than [we] can understand' – yet he also shows that the child's disappearance is an occasion of horrendous sorrow. In a similar fashion, Ní Ríain gives us characters who are desperate to escape from a life they find unbearable, who are determined to shed their innocence. Yet they too discover that escape is neither achievable nor fully desirable.

By focussing on themes of innocence and loss, *Desolate Heaven* is not so much about stolen children as stolen childhoods. Its central characters Orlaith and Sive begin and end the play on a beach, a space that has neither the stability of land nor the fluidity of sea, but which is somewhere between the two. Similarly, these teenagers shift uneasily between the certainties of childhood and the freedoms of adulthood, without occupying either role fully. The indeterminacy of their identities is clear from the play's beginning. The

girls' interactions seem innocent if not infantile, yet their responsibilities are entirely adult: both are obliged to care for a parent who
has become disabled in some way. That reversal of responsibilities
with their parents has left both girls feeling 'weighted down' with
worry. It's scarcely surprising that they decide to run away.

Ní Ríain leaves open the question of whether the girls are
fleeing in order to prolong their childhoods, or if they instead wish
to achieve an adult-like independence; their motivations shift and
mature. The characters certainly use their freedom to experience
different forms of sexual awakening, exploring questions of sexual
orientation as well as sexual autonomy (an example of how one
of the most significant developments in recent Irish drama has
been a growing openness in the representation of LGBT lives and
concerns). Yet also of consequence to both girls is the question
of identity. As the pair journey through Ireland, they encounter a
series of women who have rejected the gender-based roles assigned
to them by their society. For example, one trims bales of hay,
another drives lorries, another is a butcher – all of which are jobs
traditionally associated with men. Given that Orlaith and Sive are
themselves in flight from roles imposed upon them by others, they
find comfort and inspiration in the freedom of such women, each of
whom is a 'law unto herself'. Ní Ríain's creation of these strange
role models draws the audience in irresistibly, forcing us to consider
the relationship between self-determination, gender and sexuality in
Ireland today.

A different kind of theatrical immediacy is created in Louise Lowe
and Anu Productions' *The Boys of Foley Street*, a play that inserts
the audience directly into the recent history of inner-city Dublin.
Devised as the third part of a four-play sequence called *The
Monto Cycle*, *The Boys of Foley Street* takes as its starting point a
radio documentary made in 1975 about four working-class Dublin
teenagers. The production asks what happened to those eponymous
'boys', using that question to explore the life of Foley Street over
many decades, and through the frame of several major events. We
witness the bombing of Dublin by Loyalist terrorists in 1974, the
visit of Pope John Paul II to Ireland in 1979 and, most painfully,
the heroin epidemic that devastated Dublin in the 1980s. By

focussing on bombing victims, drug addicts, neglected children, and despairing parents, Lowe and her company do something similar to Kinevane and Ní Ríain: they force us to acknowledge the dignity of people who have been ignored and forgotten, and they assert the value of lives that have been treated as if they are worthless.

But whereas the other writers in this anthology invite us to identify with their characters from the relatively safe distance of an auditorium, Lowe instead demands that we immerse ourselves fully into the production. As staged by Anu, *Foley Street* can only be viewed by two audience-members at a time. We do not merely watch the performance but are obliged to interact with the actors and the physical environment of the production – which is the real Foley Street itself. The production is mapped out in such a way that different audiences can have entirely different experiences of the performance. We might begin seated in the back of a car, listening to the documentary that gives *Foley Street* its title. From there, we might be driven to a council flat; bustled inside, we find ourselves encountering violence, deprivation, and squalor. As the action continues, other experiences present themselves: we sit in a bombed-out car, witness a young man being beaten, and are faced with the evidence of what heroin has done to thousands of Dublin lives. We move through different time periods, until forty years of this community's history blur into a kind of theatrical vortex.

And because we interact with the performance, we are obliged to make decisions. When a young woman asks us to pin her dress closed, we're confronted with our capacity for both horror and compassion. When we're asked to film an act of violence, we're faced with questions about our own agency as members of an audience. And when a character demands that we sit in the back of a car, we're reminded forcefully of the trust that audiences unthinkingly place in theatrical representation. *The Boys of Foley Street* makes clear that, even if we do nothing (*especially* if we do nothing), we have still made a choice – and must be judged accordingly.

The work of Anu may not seem to have much in common with the ostensibly more conventional dramas that dominate the Irish stage. But *Foley Street* shares with the plays in this anthology a demand that audiences confront their own choices. The community depicted in this play is complex and multifaceted – and it occupies a space that is only five minutes' walk from Dublin's main thoroughfare O'Connell Street. Why have these lives been so frequently absent from public consciousness? The problems we find in the production are real: why have they been ignored? And what is owed to the individuals in this play: people who have faced poverty, addiction, abuse and violence – largely alone? The audience at *Foley Street* have no choice but to consider such questions. And that experience forces us to experience the emotions of pity, empathy and terror that were at the core of Greek drama, and which are so rarely inspired in theatre today.

It is again significant that this work was created through a process of collaboration and devising. The words we hear are based on interviews with real people, and the design and stage management of *Foley Street* are as essential to its success as the script and direction. But what Anu wish to make most explicit is that the audience too are collaborators: meaning is created not for us but with us. In a country struggling to come to terms with its culpability – for the banking crash, for the abuse of children by the Catholic Church – this focus on personal decision-making feels urgent and essential.

These six new dramas all share a sense of questioning, specifically about issues of agency and responsibility. They are very different from each other, but all aim to shift their audiences' focus away from blame and towards a sense of what our responsibilities might be – for the care of our vulnerable citizens, for the future of our planet, for the dignity and integrity of our own lives.

These writers and companies also set out to retrieve the past, in order to show that times of crisis can lead to renewal and reinvention. If theatres cannot afford to stay open, one response is to turn the entire city of Dublin into a performance space, as Louise Lowe and Anu have done. If economic imperatives require us to make plays with fewer roles, Pat Kinevane shows that one actor can bring countless characters to our stages – including people who have never been seen there before. If *Drum Belly* demands that we face the truth about our roots, Michael West's *Freefall* begins the process of understanding how we might forgive ourselves afterwards. And if *Desolate Heaven* suggests that the legacy of the past has robbed our children of a future, *Planet Belfast* implies that it's not too late for us to do things differently.

We do not have certainty about the future in Ireland – but perhaps that insecurity means that we're no longer as complacent about the future either. The collapse of the Celtic Tiger has been met with a blurring of distinctions in our theatre: between devised and scripted work, between adaptations and originals, between the personal and the global, between Ireland and the rest of the world – between the actor, the director, the author and the audience – and between male and female, gay and straight, rich and poor. Those changes may arise from unprecedentedly awful events. But they have inspired a series of exciting new plays that reveal to us something worth admiring: an Irish theatre that is courageous, curious and, above all, resilient.

Patrick Lonergan,
Galway, 2014

Freefall

Michael West

in collaboration with the Corn Exchange

Freefall was first performed at Project Arts Centre, Dublin, as part of the Ulster Bank Dublin Theatre Festival 2009 with the following cast:

A	Andrew Bennett
B	Janet Moran
C	Ruth McGill
D	Louis Lovett
G	Damian Kearney
J	Paul Reid

Writer	Michael West
Director	Annie Ryan
Set Designer	Kris Stone
Lighting Design	Matt Frey
Composer	Conor Linehan

Characters

A
B
C
D
G
J

A Maker's Note

We set out to make what would become *Freefall* in late Autumn 2008, just as the world's markets collapsed. We knew that we wanted our new piece to be contemporary and to explore ways of theatrical transformation, deepening the style and practice of the company. When the fall happened, it became clear that change would become not just our means of telling our story, but the story itself.

In the face of change – even a change for the better – the psyche panics and resists. We want to know Who We Are, to be fixed as an identity. With each day, each year, the self we think we know passes away and another slightly different one takes its place. You could argue that your mental health depends on how well you deal with this never-ending process – these little deaths of the self. And after a while, we realised we were really making a piece about grief.

Not long after we started our research, we came across an extraordinary talk on ted.com by Dr Jill Bolte Taylor, an American neuroscientist who suffered a catastrophic stroke yet recovered to tell her story. Her experience was one of profound desolation and despair, coupled with awareness and bliss, having lost the language centre that connects our sense of identity to our past and future. It helped enormously that she was already a happy-go-lucky gal from the Mid-West in the best brain hospital in the United States, but crucially, that she also had a loving mother who climbed into bed with her and nursed her from infancy to adulthood again – who taught her how to eat, to sit up, to talk, to remember. She literally loved her back to adulthood. It took eight years. Hers is an amazing, uplifting, American story.

So, we thought, what if something like that happened to an ordinary Irish man? We knew he couldn't have quite the happy ending of Dr Jill Bolte Taylor, but despite the lack of support he might have, there was still something at the core of our exploration into character that was about acceptance, humour and ultimately compassion.

As our man's story began to unfold in the summer, the *Ryan Report* was released after a nine-year investigation into the systemic rape and abuse of 30,000 children in the care of Catholic orphanages and industrial schools in Ireland, stretching back to the 1930s. Stories poured into the airwaves and newspapers, on the streets, in our rehearsal rooms. Ireland was overwhelmed with grief and remorse. It broke. It fell to its knees. Amidst job losses, the unknown future, the change in status, in lifestyle, this report was a shocking reminder of everyone's roots.

Our play isn't overtly about the collapse of the Celtic Tiger or the Catholic Church, but it is our setting – Ireland 2009. Ours was the attempt at finding the human experience within all this confusion, corruption, darkness and denial. While we found this incredibly sad story on our hands, we also had the funniest actors you can imagine in the room. Irish actors are renowned for their playfulness and they are more or less allergic to sentimentality. And anyway, our ethos has always been one that works hard for precision, but at the end of the day, would do anything for a good gag.

This tension between rigour and play is very much at the core of what we do. Our company's name comes from an idea of creating an exchange of physical theatre techniques that empower the ensemble to make theatre. Our process has evolved to include an hour of yoga followed by voice training and ensemble work, after which we rehearse. The commitment to this practice greatly deepened our sense of appreciation for each other and the work. And the quality of this gratitude and flow infiltrated the story itself and made the production what it is.

Our intention is to shape the present moment for you to feel something. Change is our subject for this play, but it is also our method and at the very heart of the art form itself. Theatre seeks to transform space, to transform you. And then it's gone. You can't put it on a shelf, on a wall. It is experienced and then reverberates in you, as a memory. Perhaps we, who deal with the live form and ultimately its passing, might have a chance at capturing the sense of impossibility we all feel about our own passing, about change, the loss of ourselves as we grow and the anticipation of what might happen next.

Annie Ryan
Dublin, June 2010

A Writer's Note: The Naming of Parts

The playwright Tom Murphy has said that a play is a theorem which the actors try to prove in front of an audience.

Our initial efforts to understand the geometry of *Freefall* involved four characters around a table, A, B, C and D. We knew they made up two couples AB and CD; and we knew that the story would in some way map the distance between a husband and wife – or as it's known in Euclidean notation |AB|.

As A moved to the centre of the whole thing, it made sense that everyone else would double up as the significant others in his life. To keep the book-keeping simple the roles were identified by letter rather than character name. The number of performers at one stage grew to seven, comprising five actors and two live musicians who were to take on small roles. Along the way the musicians were recorded playing Conor Linehan's achingly beautiful score and we let the actors tell the story. But a legacy of their existence is the absence of the letters E and F in the cast list.

All of which is proof of a kind that artistic collaboration is as much about what is left out as what stays in.

This is particularly the case in our play, for although the character A is all over the script, it seemed right that our main character should remain unnamed. It quietly underlined his anonymity and unassuming nature, and it felt like a correct and entirely natural fit. For it to work, it had to slip by without drawing attention to itself; it gave a certain pleasure to think that someone would only notice they were missing such a crucial piece of information considerably after the fact – that it would create a tiny lack, a hesitation, a sense of something missing and yet on the tip of the tongue.

But of course all this was by way of discovery not strategy. Since he was known through the entire development process as A and embodied by the incomparable Andrew Bennett, we always knew who we were referring to. It certainly never occurred to us that any delicate, momentary unease in having no name to put to a face would be anything more than that. Until the first reviews appeared referring confidently to John or Gerry.

So what do you call someone with no name? Someone could probably clarify all this and show that A is really 'A', but I fear if we go that route we'll end up with Bertrand Russell telling us the set of all anonymous characters should itself remain anonymous and that the king of France is bald.

But back on planet earth it's probably enough to say that so many people worked so hard to make this production possible that it would be impossible to thank them all, even with all the letters of the alphabet. In addition to all the technical support and expertise that fleshed out the naked geometry, there is the generosity of funding bodies and audiences that invite us to keep trying to tell stories.

I am as ever indebted to the good humour and guts of the cast during all stages of this play's development and for making it come alive. It's a pleasure to acknowledge their contribution here – Andrew Bennett, Damian Kearney, Louis Lovett, Ruth McGill and Janet Moran – who all agreed to perform it before a scene was written and in one or two cases before a scene was finished. Thanks also to Tom French for an unwitting line which unlocked the play; to Christian Schiaretti and Clara Simpson, who provided refuge for the initial writing of this project; to Florence et Didier in Villemus, Eoin West and Etáin O'Malley; to Anne Bogart and SITI company for introducing me to the work of Dr Jill Bolte Taylor; to Loughlin Deegan and the International Dublin Theatre Festival, and to the Arts Council of Ireland/An Chomhairle Ealaíon. Lastly I have to thank Sarah Durcan, our producer, unstinting support and champion, and Annie Ryan who is beyond compare.

Michael West
Dublin, June 2010

A bare stage.

Spanning the entire width, there are curtains on a rail that can be drawn open and shut.

A screen on which film can be projected.

Two hospital beds on castors which can double as tables.

On either side of the playing space there are wigs and various props. (In the script, real objects are marked in CAPS; all other objects are mimed.) There are also a couple of microphones, which the performers use for the phone calls and all sound effects. There are some chairs and a sofa. These wings are clearly visible to the audience at all times.

There is a portable camera which becomes A's point of view in the hospital scenes, with the carers looking into it when they talk to him. In these scenes the actor playing A stands or sits to one side, watching himself, as it were. As the play begins, the camera is placed downstage centre.

Episode One

1.1

The company arranges the space for the performance. This includes drawing the curtains and setting one of the beds as a table bearing the leftovers of a party – some Indian TAKEAWAY TRAYS, wine-stained GLASSES and a couple of empty BOTTLES.

An image comes to life on the screen. It is a close-up of A, in pyjamas, sitting in his kitchen talking to Jack, his eighteen-year-old son. In the sequence that follows Jack is off-screen, holding the camera.

Film footage – Thursday morning

A   Well ok, but I'm not really going to say anything, because I've nothing to say.

Jack (*off-screen*)   Can you tell me a little bit about yourself.

A   You know everything.

Jack (*off-screen*)   I don't. Let's just start somewhere. Where are you from?

A   Limerick.

Jack (*off-screen*)   Ok, let's do that again. Where are you from?

A   Limerick.

Jack (*off-screen*)   But you were brought up in Cork.

A   I'm from Limerick.

Jack (*off-screen*)   And …?

A   And I've had a completely normal life.

Jack (*off-screen*)   In what way?

A   I've done all the normal things, I've been very lucky.

Jack (*off-screen*)   And is that normal? To think you're lucky. How are you normal?

A   I am normal. I went to school, got an education, I got a job, I got married. I had a son. Who should be in school.

Jack (*off-screen*)   And you should be at work.

A   Maybe that's how I'm lucky. (*Pause.*) I am lucky. I married your mother.

1.2

Kitchen – Friday morning

*The curtains open revealing **A** in pyjamas sitting at the table. **B**, as **Louise**, is dressed for work and has a dire hangover. She drinks a MUG of tea and watches him.*

Louise   Are you ok?

A   I've a headache.

Louise *places the MUG of tea beside him. He doesn't touch it but his heart with his left hand.*

A   I feel …

Louise   I know. I do too. I'm sorry. I'm sorry. But I have to go.

She pulls herself together.

Louise   I have to go to work. I'll call you later. What are we going to do about Jack?

A   Jack?

Louise   Will we tell him later?

A   What?

Louise   Jack. I want to tell him later. About us.

A   Ok.

Louise   What are *you* going to do?

A   With what?

Louise   With your life.

Exit **Louise**.

A   I'm going to … I'm going to put out the bins. And bottles.

He goes to clear the table of last night's remains and discovers his right arm isn't quite right. He drops a BOTTLE. He can't tear off a BIN LINER; he struggles to open it. He tidies away the FOIL TRAYS. He has a headache and needs a rest. He gets up and tries to walk and finds he is dragging his right leg.

A   There's something wrong with me. It must be my heart. It's breaking. I need to see a doctor. A doctor. I need help. I'm having a heart attack. It can't be. I had a check-up. Only last month.

1.3

Check-up – Last month

A GP's consulting room. **A** *is suddenly able-bodied again.*

D   Is it your leg?

A   No, no. That's an old …

D *reads a FILE.*

D   It's a while since your last check-up.

A   The fact is, Doctor, I don't know if there really is something wrong with me.

D   Well let's have a look, shall we? Sit up there for me.

D *makes a note.*

A   The fact is for some time now I feel as if there's something missing, something *I'm* missing, you know? I seem to be normal, but I'm not, I feel numb.

D   Where? In the hands or the face?

A   In … Inside.

D   Hmmm. Any history of heart attacks, sclerosis, angina, cirrhosis?

A   No.

D   Deformity, insanity, congenital abnormality?

A   No.

D   Syphilis, gonorrhoea, chlamydia, gout?

A   A little indigestion, maybe.

D   Impetigo, scabies, psoriasis, acting rashly?

A   No.

D   Depression?

Pause.

D   A history of depression in your family?

A   Well, my wife …

D   *Your* family.

A   O. Well I don't really … they're all gone. My mother, my sister.

D   Father?

A   My father died.

D   Aha. Of what?

A   Old age. Eighty something. I hadn't seen him since I was a child.

D   Maybe so, but what killed him?

A   A fall. I think.

D (*makes a note*)   History of falling.

A   Yes! I have the urge to fall down before women I don't know, women I pass on the streets. I want to fall down before them and kiss their knees, I want to hold them, hold them, hold them for the longest time. I see women and wonder when they were last held like that, if they've been loved and adored.

D   I see.

D *examines him. He unscrews a flap in the back of* **A***'s head and peers inside.*

A   I find myself in tears, I weep doing the simplest things, putting coins in a meter, looking for my keys, making a list. I weep over things I've lost, that I'll never do, over the enormity of things, their insignificance, or because I can't find them. I worry about my son, if he'll ever be happy, if he'll ever find January –

D   Sorry.

D *has inadvertently switched channels by poking his brain.*

A   February, March, April, May –

D *tries to get him back on track and pokes again.*

A   Spoons, spittoons, pots, pans, kettles, kitchen condiments –

D   Just a second.

D *gets him back to normal with a final poke and replaces the screws. While* **A** *talks,* **D** *clambers under the table like a car mechanic, and from beneath drills a bore hole to see what's wrong with* **A**'s *insides. Splinters fly, flies buzz.* **D** *shines a torch up there to make sure he hasn't missed anything.*

A   An indescribable longing, an intense longing, and a reduced capacity to do anything about it. I feel powerless and impotent, unable to respond to my appetites or desires. I feel somehow diminished, that I am less myself. A sense of being off-balance, of blindness, inward-looking pain and discomfort, an inability to recall significant events and thoughts and emotions, a general numbness and insensitivity to life.

D *finishes up his inspection, replaces everything as it was and emerges.*

D   Well nothing too serious. Nothing I could find anyway.

A   Nothing?

D   That's good, isn't it? Look, you probably have too much time on your hands. What you need is a nice long walk, a proper steak, a bottle of wine. And a good laugh.

He leaves, taking the MUG with him.

1.4

House – Friday morning

A *finds himself back in his hall.*

A   How long have I been standing here? The light is different. I can't remember what I'm doing. I'm in the hall. I'm looking for the phone. I'm sinking, turning, falling.

He falls to the floor. His image appears on the screen.

A   I'm looking at the … ceiling. I hear a strange hissing, like a leaking tyre or cylinder of gas. It's my breathing. I want to sleep.

The phone rings. The answering machine kicks in.

Louise (*voice coming over speakers*)   Hi. It's me. It's lunch, after lunch. I tried earlier but couldn't get through. Are you there? I'll wait a sec in case you're going to pick up. Are you going to pick up? You might be out. Anyway. I'm just … seeing how you are. And … You're not going to pick up. Ok. Bye.

She hangs up.

A   A sound, a rhythmic sound floods through me, apple apple apple apple, it is my blood, my life. I watch the shadow slowly climb the wall and part of me goes with it. I could be lying here for hours or days. I'm coming apart.

The doorbell rings during the above. The phone rings again.

G (*over speaker*)   Hello. It's dry rot. The fungal expert. There's no answer. I'll try one more time.

The doorbell rings repeatedly.

A   I'm here. I'm here.

Thumping on the door.

A   I'm here.

1.5

Rescue

*Two paramedics (**D** and **G**) break down the door and find him on the floor. They lift him on a gurney.*

A   … Apple apple apple apple. Thank you. Thank you.

A & E department – Friday afternoon

*A is wheeled in from the ambulance by the paramedics. The arrival comes as a violent shock. Two nurses (**B** and **C**) meet them and begin the triage assessment. It all happens very fast.*

D   You know what's nice with that? An egg.

C   Conscious?

G   In and out.

A   Ah! It's too bright. And loud.

B   What's he presenting?

D   Patient was found collapsed in his own home.

A   What's happening to me?

C   Heart attack?

G   No.

D   Suspected stroke.

C   Stroke.

B   A stroke?

A   What? I can't have a stroke. I have things to do. Dishes, bottles. I have to find Jack. I have to talk to him. I need a phone. Somebody get me a phone.

G   He needs a scan.

C   There's a backlog.

B   What's his blood pressure?

A   Can't you hear me? Why can't you hear me?

G   About 200 over 100.

D   You'd need to check that.

B   Will I check it?

C   Put down 200 over 100.

A   I need to talk to someone. I need to see someone.

G   I need to get a coffee.

D   I need my wheels. Where will we bring him?

B   O god. Not in there.

C   Put him here for the moment.

D   Yeah, but do you have a spare gurney, or …?

A *gets up from the trolley bed and watches them leave, unseen and invisible.*

A   Don't go. Don't leave me. I need help. I need to talk to my wife. I need to tell her … to ask her … Hello? Hello?

1.6

Hospital – Friday evening

Behind a curtain – and looking into a camera mounted on the bed so that their faces loom large on the screen – the doctors and interns hover busily, inserting an IV and taking his pulse, blood pressure and temperature. **A** *watches from the sidelines.*

B   Don't worry, you're going to be fine.

C   Now then, we're just going to take your blood pressure.

D   Hello? Can you hear me? How are you doing today? (*To* **C**.) Blood pressure? I can't read this. What have you got?

C   Blood pressure … 200 systolic, over …

She releases the cuff and listens with a stethoscope to his brachial pulse.

D (*reading*)   No trauma, medical event, vital signs stable.

B   We checked for hypoglycemia, but his blood sugar's fine.

D (*to* **A**)   Can you squeeze my hand? Ok, can you lift your hand? And this one? (*To* **B**.) Severe motor impairment to the right side.

B   A stroke.

D   An insult to the brain certainly. (*To* **A**.) Don't worry, you're in the right place.

C   106 diastolic.

C *has finished taking his blood pressure.*

D   Not a heart attack anyway. (*To* **A**.) You've very high blood pressure, we need to do something about that.

C   We have thrombolitics on standby.

D   No blood-thinning agents until we know if he's ischemic or haemorrhagic. Has he had a CAT scan?

B   He's down for one. They're busy.

D   We're all busy. It's Friday. People, we need to see the inside of his head.

B   I'll check about the scan.

Exit **B**.

D   Thank you. (*To* **A**.) We need to take a picture of your brain to see if your stroke is due to a clot or a small bleed. Very important that we know the difference. Then we can work out how to help you. Now let's have a look at your pupils.

D *shines a light in his eyes.*

A   You're hurting me … Ah!

D   What was that?

C   Sorry, that was me.

She's been inserting an IV into his arm. She checks the patient notes.

D   Pupils equally round and reactive to light. (*To* **A**.) We'll find out what's going on in there, ok?

C   There's no name here, and no next of kin.

D   Nothing?

C   No.

D   Nobody knows he's here.

Enter **G**.

G   Lads. You're needed. Two stabbings. One with a screwdriver.

C   He's married, he has a ring.

D   See if someone can find his wife.

Episode Two

2.1

House – Thursday afternoon

A is on the phone.

A   I need to speak to my wife. – This is … her husband. – Yes, I'd like to leave a message for my wife, Louise. – Well, she uses both names. – No, it's the same person, she just … Is my wife there? I think I can hear her. – Look the message is Denis is coming tonight. – Just tell her. She'll know what it means.

Doorbell.

A   Who's this? (*To phone.*) Hello, love. – What I said. Denis is coming tonight. I forgot to tell you earlier. – He said tomorrow didn't suit. – Hang on a second, there's someone at the door.

*A opens the door to find G as the **Fungal Man**, in overalls.*

Fungal Man   Dry rot?

A   I'm sorry?

Fungal Man   I'm here about the dry rot. The fungal expert? You arranged an appointment.

*Still talking to his wife, A tries to tell the **Fungal Man** he's almost done.*

A   Did I? Yes. Come in. (*Back on phone.*) Well he's coming. I've already said yes. And he's bringing his new girlfriend. – I did already. – And I hoovered. – I did that too. – I did them separately. – Don't worry, I'm cooking, everything's sorted. And could you get milk. I forgot. Hello? (*She's hung up. To **Fungal Man**.*) Sorry. My wife.

2.2

Fungal cave – Thursday

A *and* **Fungal Man** *enter the garage where he shines a torch up at the ceiling.*

Fungal Man   Technically it's a slime mould, but that doesn't begin to describe its genius. It's a completely different order of life to almost anything on the planet.

A   Dry rot is?

Fungal Man   *Serpula lacrymans*, yeah. See that? The trails, tendrils? Beautiful stuff. It sends out tendrils through concrete, plaster, wood, actually *through* it, looking for moisture. And when it gets it …

He graphically sucks up water.

A   And is it serious?

Fungal Man   It means business, I can tell you that. How long has it been like this?

A   I don't know. We haven't … It hasn't been a problem before.

Fungal Man   You should have called me a long time ago. People always leave these things until it's too late.

A   Can't we just stick some paint on it? Some anti-mould stuff and cover it up.

Fungal Man   No, look. You see that?

A   The brown folds there?

Fungal Man   That's a lovely specimen of fruiting *Serpula lacrymans*. Fruiting. Releasing *millions* of spores. And once it fruits … Once it fruits. Do you know a good plumber?

A   I do a bit of …

Fungal Man   Don't get the guy who did this. Or that. You know what this means?

A No.

Fungal Man You are sitting on a time bomb …

Louise (*off*) Hello? I'm home.

2.3

Hall – Thursday evening

Louise *enters after a long day at work.*

Louise When are they coming? Jack!

A Eight.

Louise I can't believe you asked Denis. I just want to go to bed. Jack!

A Have a shower. They come, we eat, they go. It'll be fine.

Louise We need to talk.

She goes into bedroom to change.

A We do. I had a man over to look under the stairs and he said we've a pretty serious problem. He says it's been there for years, and we haven't done anything about it.

Louise I know.

A How do you know?

Louise He's our son.

A I'm talking about the dry rot.

Louise What?

A That's what I'm telling you. We have a dry rot infestation and it's threatening the whole house.

Louise I don't care about the house. I'm talking about Jack. Where is he?

A Jack is off with Charlie.

Louise The school rang me today. He didn't go in again. Did he say anything?

A   I don't remember.

Louise   You don't remember?

A   He's got his camera gear, so I don't know when we'll see him. Actually, he's doing a video project. I'm in it. It's quite funny, really. He's so … He interviewed me and I found myself telling him …

Louise   You don't seem all that bothered that our son is going to drop out of school. What are you going to do about it?

A   What am I going to do about it?

Louise   Are you just going to do nothing?

A pause.

A   Will I ask them not to come?

Louise   It's too late.

A   No, look, I'll just call him.

Louise   We can't, love. They're practically here.

A   I'll cancel. I'll call him and explain.

Louise   We invited them.

A   He'll understand.

Doorbell.

Louise   Let's just try to be nice to each other.

A   Yes. Coming!

2.4

*Enter **D** and **C** in OVERCOATS as **Denis** and **Lydia**. They bear several BOTTLES of wine and a box of CHOCOLATES.*

Denis   We're not late?

A (*off*)   God no.

Lydia   Or early?

A   God no!

A *is handed two bottles of wine which he places on a table.*
Denis *keeps another for himself and heads off to the living room*
with it, leaving **Lydia** *alone.*

Denis   This one's mine. And this is Lydia.

Louise (*off*)   Hi Denis!

A   She'll be down in a …

A *returns and takes her box of chocolates.*

A   Let me take that.

A *receives her coat and hangs it up.*

A   Thank you.

Lydia *and* **Denis** *sit on the sofa.* **A** *joins them.*

Lydia   Denis has told me a lot about you.

A   None of it true, I'm sure.

Denis *laughs loudly.*

Denis   O it's all true. Isn't it?

A   I wouldn't know.

Denis   He wouldn't know!

Lydia   I believe you were terrible messers back in Cork. At least
that's what Denis says.

Denis   You don't believe me? Ask him!

Lydia   I think I better. Were you? Did you terrorise the place?

A   I wouldn't …

Denis   But look how things have changed. Look at us now. Both
orphans. Both married to bossy women. Luckily my wife is at
home with kids. (*To* **Lydia**.) Sorry love. I promised I wouldn't talk
about her and how she's bleeding me dry. Don't break up! You

can't afford it. But let's not talk about money either or someone will end up killing themselves. Let's have that drink!

Enter **Louise**.

Louise   Denis. I'm so sorry about your mother.

Denis   Very sad. But for the best.

They embrace warmly. **A** *nods at the bottle* **Denis** *is hoarding.*

A   Do you want me to open that?

Denis   No, no. That's for later.

Louise   Hello, Lydia. Nice to meet you.

Lydia   Hi. That's a lovely … dress, house you have.

Louise   Thank you.

Denis   Yes, I want to open it myself. Do you have a cork …

Denis *exits to look for a corkscrew.*

A   Drink! Yes. What's everyone having?

Louise   Yes please.

A   We've wine, we've beer. We've Denis's special bottle.

Denis (*off*)   Don't touch that.

A   Lydia. White or red?

Lydia   I'm not really drinking at the moment.

A   White, then.

Lydia   Just a small one, thank you.

A   Denis?

Denis (*re-enters*)   Who owns that car outside? It's not yours is it?

A   No, that's our neighbour.

Louise   It can't fit in their drive.

A   Something to drink, Denis?

Denis   I think I'll just start on my one.

A   Well we've actually got some nice …

Louise   O yes. It's a special occasion, Denis and … Lydia.

Lydia   It's lovely to finally meet you both.

Denis   Isn't it? I've told her all about you, about us. Now I need to open that lad. Let it breathe.

Lydia   Denis told me what happened to you and your sister. That's so sad. I didn't get to meet Milly, unfortunately, but she sounds like a very kind aunt, person. You were so lucky in a way. I mean, you weren't lucky. You were … I just meant you must miss her too. I'm sure you do.

Denis and **Louise** *exit silently.*

Lydia   I'll just stop talking, will I?

A   I'll go and get us all a drink. Something special for the guests …

2.5

Fungal cave

A *heads off down a corridor with several turns and stairs that lead into the cramped, dry rot-infested basement. He looks with fascinated horror at the place.*

A   *Serp. Serpula …*

Out of the gloom appears the **Fungal Man**.

Fungal Man   *Lacrymans.* The weeping snakes. That's their name in Latin.

A   Are you still here?

Fungal Man   All this will have to go. As well as the wet and dry rot …

A   The *Serpula …*

Fungal Man   *Lacrymans*, yes, you've damp, mould, and quite a nice fungal infestation behind the radiators.

A   But you can fix it, right? Everything's going to be ok?

Fungal Man   Well, we can try. But there's something I should …

A sees something in the wall.

A   What's that?

Fungal Man   That? Yeah, I found that earlier. You might want to have a look at it.

A finds a small door which opens into a magical cave.

A   I had no idea.

Fungal Man   People don't. And it's just under the surface. Go on.

Fungal Man *ushers him on and slips away.* **A** *looks about him.*

Some Christmas tree lights flicker unseen. He finds a present. He checks it's for him and that he's alone and shakes it. He shakes it again and listens to its forlorn cardboard rattle.

A   A jigsaw …

He drops it to the floor.

2.6

Cork – 1971

C and G embrace. They are **Milly** *and* **Gus**. *They fall into bed and pull up the covers.* **A** *stands watching them wriggle and giggle under the blanket. He is seven.*

Gus   Chinese, Japanese, look at *these* Christmas trees.

Milly   Gussy!

Gus   Jingle bells, Jingle bells, let's go all the way. O what fun it is to ride, on a big, fat—

They are suddenly aware of being watched.

Milly   Happy Christmas. Was Santa good to you?

Gus   Go down and play, would you?

A   Well that's what I was thinking, that Santa mightn't actually know I'm here.

Milly   O?

A   Yes, he might think I'm still living with my Dada and have left my presents there.

Milly   And who gave you your presents?

A   The jigsaw? Well, I don't know.

Milly   And the annual.

A   Yeah, the annual. But Denis got an Action Man and toys and stuff, and I was thinking Santa probably left me my real presents in my old house because he didn't know I'd be here, and the jigsaw is probably from my Dada, because he knows I don't like jigsaws. So I was just wondering if we could call him and see if my presents are there. Can we phone him?

Milly   We'll ring him later, pet.

A   We can't ring him now?

Milly   Later.

Gus   It's, what? Seven in the morning! On Christmas!

A   Maybe he'll bring them round.

Milly   Maybe.

A   Ok. Thanks, Auntie Milly.

Milly   Now go down and play.

Gus *thinks they're back on.* **A** *doesn't move.*

Milly   What is it?

A   I was thinking the same thing maybe happened to my sister. Because if I don't know where she is, Santa mightn't either, so that's probably why our toys are back at our home. She's not coming, is she?

Milly   No.

Gus　Close the door.

A *leaves. The mood is ruined.* **Milly** *stares after him.* **Gus** *looks at the ceiling.*

A *listens from the hall.*

Gus　Will he stop asking about her.

Milly　He *has* stopped asking about her.

Gus　Isn't he lucky enough that we took him in in the first place?

Milly　He *has* stopped asking about her.

Gus　And how long are we supposed to have him?

Milly　For a while. Until he's settled.

Gus　He's settled, hasn't he? It's weeks now. He'd be better off with his sister, if he keeps asking for her.

Milly　He's stopped asking, I told you. Anyhow, they wouldn't be sent to the same place, so they wouldn't be together anyway. And besides I promised Eileen.

Gus　*I* didn't make any promise.

Milly　*I* did and I already broke half of it, so I'm not breaking the other half.

Gus　You were the one who didn't want another baby.

Milly　I promised my sister.

Gus　It's better that she has a clean start somewhere.

Milly　We should have taken the little baby.

Gus　She'll have more chance of finding somewhere on her own.

Milly　I hope so, Gussy. But he's staying.

Gus　If he puts one foot out of line, one foot.

Milly　We're keeping him.

Denis, *aged eight, approaches* **A** *and stands defiantly before him. He holds out an ACTION MAN before going into a spectacular battle sequence with sound effects from which* **A** *is pointedly excluded.*

Denis (*at imaginary enemy*)   Hand in hoch, hand in hoch!

A *tries to join in, sound effects and all.* **Denis** *looks on witheringly and repeats his attempts back to him.*

Denis   Pachew, pachew? Spa.

Milly (*off*)   I heard that, Denis Looby.

Milly *comes by and makes* **Denis** *give the Action Man to* **A**.

Milly   Give it to him.

Denis *complies with ill grace. It won't be for long.*

2.7

Caravan, Cork – 1974

*In a cramped caravan with steamed up windows, waiting for the rain to ease. The kids (**A**, **D** and **B**) are playing Monopoly with* **Milly**.

Enter **Gus** *from the tiny bog.*

Gus   I wouldn't go in there for a while, if I was you.

He watches them play for a bit.

Gus   Buy. Why don't you buy?

Denise   I don't have enough money.

Gus   Borrow it. Who's the bank?

Milly   We've run out.

Gus   Write it down.

A   And we've no houses, or only five or something, and he's taken them.

Gus   Good lad.

Denise   I wish we were back in America.

Gus   Denise, we had to come home and help the people in Cork.

Milly   But for our holidays? O Gussy, why are we here in Courtmac when we could be anywhere where there's sun.

Denise   Somewhere warm.

Milly   Can we please go to a country that has weather and not only feckin rain?

Gus   And how are we going to afford a plane for *five* of us, Milly?

Milly   Don't start with your budgeting talk, you'll have me up the mouldy caravan wall.

Gus   Yea, well, money doesn't grow on ...

Milly   Didn't you get the new car?

Gus   That's part of my work! I *have* to drive a Ford, Milly, I *want* to drive a Ford. I work for Ford.

Milly   You didn't have to buy a stupid yellow ...

Gus   Mustard. Mustard.

Milly   Yellow.

Gus   Ford is a beautiful company and I am proud to call myself a Ford man.

While their argument continues inaudibly, **Denis** *rubs the window clear of condensation.*

Denis   I can see your father.

A   Can you?

Denis   Yes. Look, there he is. He's come to spy on us.

A   Where?

Denis   Maybe he's come to take you back.

A   I can't see him.

Denis   There. Over there behind the hedge.

A   Near the donkey?

Denis   Is that a donkey? I could have sworn …

A looks back at the game in shame.

Denis   Hee-haw.

Denis *brays, getting louder and louder, as the argument comes back into focus.*

Milly   … talking about money, you mean, cold-hearted man. Stop it, Denis. Some things are more important than money.

Gus   That's easy for you to say, since you don't have any.

Milly   Like family. Shut up, Denis.

Gus   This *is* my family.

A   I want to go home.

Gus   Well you *can't* go home! We're on holiday now, so we're going to enjoy it.

They leave.

A is back in the fungal cave unsure of whether he is alone or not.

A   Hello? Dry Rot Man? Anybody there? I'm getting a drink. Something special for our guests.

Uncertainly he takes a bottle and returns to the party to find everyone is gone, the table abandoned. He sits on it.

Episode Three

3.1

Hospital – Friday evening

Louise (*voice over speaker*)   Hi, it's me again. Are you there? Jack? Are you back? It's about five. Anyway, I'm working late and

I'm going to have to talk to someone here when I'm done. So I don't know, eat without me or … There should be a bit of Indian from last night. I hope you're ok. That's all. Ok, bye.

Sitting on the table, **A** *is carefully wheeled down a corridor by a nurse* (**C**)*. She talks to the camera and her face appears on the screen.*

C   Now how's that? Aren't you grand and comfy?

A   I can't move, I can't speak. Am I still alive?

C   Of course you are. There isn't a proper room ready for you just yet, now is that all right? So we're just taking you down here to a quiet place so you can get some rest, ok?

A   My head, my head is throbbing. The lights are too bright. Breathing hurts my ribs. All I can hear is the blood pumping through my veins, apple apple apple apple, the pressure in my head.

C   Good man. Now here we are. It's only temporary, nothing lasts forever.

She gently tucks him in.

A   Don't leave me. I'm afraid. Talk some more. Tell me I'm going to be all right. Am I always going to feel like this? … Are you still there? Is anybody there?

The nurse slips away, pulling the curtain to reveal …

3.2

Schoolyard, Cork – 1976

Denis   I have a photo. Anybody want to see a photo?

A thirteen-year-old **Denis** *shows the lads* (**A** *and* **G**) *a picture, carefully torn from a magazine. They are amazed and drink it in.*

Denis   And look at that. And see that? That's a wicker chair.

G   Look at her tits.

A *can't take his eyes off her. Through the following he manages to get a hand on one edge of the picture.*

Denis   'Tits.' Look at the whole thing.

G   Hole thing.

Denis   You're not appreciating the quality, lads. That's called backlighting. She's backlit. See the aura around her hair?

G   That's like your mother's hair.

Denis *slaps him expertly.* **Denis** *unfolds the picture again and* **A** *resumes his quest to hold it.*

Denis   See that? That is bamboo. That's a rubber plant. That is a house in America.

A (*reading*)   Penthouse.

Denis   That's right, yeah. And I was in it.

G   No way.

Denis   Yep. I was in America.

G   Was she there?

Denis   Who do you think took the photo?

A   Brother Laurence!

The bell clangs loudly and they look around in alarm. **Denis** *shoves the photo at* **A** *who pockets it.*

Denis   Don't tear it, don't tear it. Hi, Brother Laurence!

3.3

The classroom

D *and* **C** *set the chairs.* **A** *sits and surreptitiously inspects the photo.* **B** *is doing an impression of the teacher.*

B   In poetry, the line is divided into metrical units called … What are they called?

G *enters as* **Brother Laurence**, *wearing a black SOUTANE and carrying a CANE. He paces the classroom.*

Laurence   In poetry, the line is divided into metrical units called … What are they called? Feet. Feet. And what's this one? Well? Well?

He holds up a long finger.

C   A finger, sir.

Laurence   *This*, you ignoramuses, is a dactyl. A finger. The Greek for finger. And why is it named after a finger? Because it resembles the joints of a finger. (*He counts off the joints.*) Long, short, short. Like what? Like Oliver Gogarty. Like Malachi Mulligan. Like savages. Savages savages savages savages. Give me your hand, boy.

Denis *stretches out a hand in fear and braces for the pain.*
Brother Laurence *lightly taps the meter on the open palm.*

Laurence   ONE two three, ONE two three, do you feel it? It's a waltz, boys. Hickory Dickory, Higgledy Piggeldy. You hear dactyls in the roll call, we are blessed with dactyls in this class. Anthony Finnegan, Cassidy, Halligan, Christopher Comerford, Mickeleen Lonigan. Now what's a trochee? Well?

Denis   A foot.

Laurence   A foot, is it? What kind of foot? Short, long, long, short?

Denis   A trochee is a … short and a long.

Laurence   No! You fucking savages. A short and a long is an iamb. What's an iamb? An iamb is a short and a long. Di dum, di dum, di dum, di dum. And át my báck I álways hear, Doreen O'Dea begin her tea. I wandered lonely as a cloud, away alone alas along begob. But a trochee is its opposite, a long and a short. Like … like *trochee*, a little example of itself. Like, like, give me something else.

Denis   Finger!

C   Foot.

A   Apple.

Laurence   Apple, good. Apple apple apple apple. Say it.

Denis (*to* **A**)   Spapple.

The class say apple softly through the following.

Laurence   Trochees in your educational horizons include chicken licken, henny penny, cocky locky, ducky lucky, turkey lurky, foxy loxy and Father Gerard Manly Hopkins. Trochees in this class include Andrew, Colm, Denis Looby, Dermot, eejit, Eamon Carney, Peter Casey, Peter Farrell, Peter Piper Pumpkin Eater, Michael Collins, DeValera, fitter faster bigger longer, langer, bucket—

He swoops on **A** *who is looking at his photo again.*

Laurence   And what is that you have in your sweaty little hand that means you cannot pay attention to our class? What is it? Show me.

A *refuses.*

Laurence   Stand. Give it to me.

A *stands and hands over the folded photo.* **Brother Laurence** *carefully holds it.*

Laurence   And what is this? Who is this?

He slowly picks a corner and unfolds the image.

A   It's … my mother.

Hysteria. The bell goes.

Laurence   Everybody out. Not you. Everybody out. Close the door.

The pupils leave. **A** *is absolutely terrified.* **Brother Laurence** *looks at him seriously, still holding the picture.*

Laurence   I'm disappointed in you. Why is that, do you think? You're not like the rest of those savages. But you've stopped working. You've stopped trying. And if you don't apply yourself, how else are you going to get out of here? You still have your whole life ahead of you. You can't always think about what you've lost, you know. And you may be a bit young for this, but you're also free of a lot of things that hold people back. So I want to put you forward for the Entrance Exhibition. The Scholarship exam for getting into college.

A   Is that my punishment?

Laurence   Is that your punishment? If you like. But I think you've probably had enough punishment as it is.

Laurence *hands the picture back to* **A**.

Laurence   Burn that.

Laurence *leaves.*

3.4

House – Thursday

In the kitchen, **A** *smells something burning. From the dining room we can hear bits of a heated conversation.*

Denis   Well it's gone.

Louise   Yeah, but who's paying for it?

Denis   Louise. I'm sorry, but …

Louise   We are. We all are.

Denis   It's not that simple.

Louise   And Jack, and your kids, and all our kids will be paying for it for the rest of their lives.

Lydia   And how many kids do you have?

Louise   What?

A *realises he is burning the dinner and closes the door to the hall. Their voices become muffled. He wafts the air behind him and opens a window to let out the smoke. He goes into the hall – we* *can hear their voices again – and finds a phonebook and a sheaf of take-away menus which he hurriedly scans. He picks one and locates the phone.*

Denis   … Look, we are where we are. We're all responsible and we're in it together. The sooner we accept it the better.

Lydia   Denis is writing a book.

Louise   No way.

Denis   Lydia.

Louise   You're not. Are you? Are you really writing a book?

Lydia   He is. I'm helping him order his thoughts and, and chapter headings and some of the concepts. I've a lot of books.

Louise   Is it a self-help book?

Denis (*together*)   No.

Lydia (*together*)   Yes.

Denis   Sort of.

Louise   What's the title?

Denis   I haven't …

Lydia   *Good Change, Bad Change*, is the working … It's really how to adapt to the global warming of emotional and economic ecosystems.

Louise *guffaws as* **A** *ducks back into the kitchen and closes the door, shutting out their voices once more.*

A   Hello? Yes, I'd like to order … Can you hear me? I can't talk any louder. I'd like to order a meal for four. I don't actually care what type of food as long as I can get it immediately. What's quickest? Do you do French, or Italian? You're an Indian! I just need dinner for four … No, forty-five minutes is too long. It has to be now. How about if I pick up? I'll pick up. Great, I'll pick up. Thank you.

A *hangs up and goes to join them.*

Denis   It's a shock, I agree with you. It's been profoundly disturbing – but for the best!

Louise   How can you say that, when people are losing their livelihoods, their …

Denis   Change is always disturbing, but we have to embrace it, because we are changing all the time.

Lydia   Everything is changing.

Denis   As Lydia says. And that's the point of my book. You'll have to read it. I'll give you one.

They notice him standing there.

Louise   Are we ready?

A   I'm afraid the potatoes are still not done. I don't know why but they're rock hard.

Lydia   We can wait.

Louise   Please. I have to eat something.

Lydia   Can we help?

A   No, everything is … It's just the potatoes.

Denis   Potatoes! Even the potatoes have turned against us.

Three bags of CRISPS drop onto the table. They open them, reluctantly at first, and tuck in.

A   There, that's just a … while we're waiting. I hope everyone likes Indian.

Louise *chokes on a crisp and coughs violently.*

Lydia   I love Indian!

Denis (*to* **A**)   Is it going to be spicy?

Lydia   I hope so. Hot food makes me … you know.

Denis   I'm only asking because this is a very expensive bottle of wine and I want to know if I should drink it all first.

A (*to* **Louise**)   Are you ok?

Denis   That's a bad cough. You should have someone look at that.

Lydia (*searching for water*)   O yes, here.

A   If you … arms up.

Louise (*coughing*)   No, I'm fine.

Lydia   Water. I don't have any.

A   Put your arms up.

Louise   Get off.

Louise *gets up to leave.*

A (*to* **Denis**)   I thought, arms up.

Louise *coughs away.* **Denis** *raises his arms.*

Denis   Hand in hoch! Don't shoot. It's a stick up. Give her the Heimlich!

Louise   Excuse me.

Denis   Some air. This woman needs air. Clear this lady's passage.

Louise   Stop!

Exit **Louise**, *still coughing and laughing, accompanied by* **Denis**.

Lydia   He's funny, isn't he?

A   Gas.

Lydia   I just don't know how to talk to him sometimes. You just never know if he's … You never know how he's going to react. He's so angry most of the time, with his wife, with his work, and he's going away and for how long, and is he, I mean is he, this is a weird thing to ask, but do you think he's changed? I know he's had lots of women, *lots* of women, but do you think he'll …?

A   I have to check something.

He tries to slip away but she follows him.

Lydia   Of course you don't know, do you? How can you answer that? I mean, how did you and Louise know you were meant for each other? Was it love at first sight?

3.5

Dorm room, Dublin – 1986

Night. **A** *is studying at his desk.*

A   Gross Domestic Product or Yd equals Consumption plus Investment plus Government spending plus Exports minus Imports. Yd equals C + I + G + N. GDP equals GNP minus the net inflow of labour and property incomes from abroad.

Denis (*twenty-three*) *arrives in full flight, carrying two BOTTLES of wine.*

A   Denis?

Denis   Is Gerry in?

A   No. What are you …? What time is it?

Denis   Time for you to meet some friends.

A   No, no, I'm studying. I have exams tomorrow.

Denis *talks to some unseen girls.*

Denis   Come on in girls. Louise. Ciara.

A   I'm sorry, but you can't stay.

Denis   Of course we're not staying.

A   I have to study.

Denis   Study us! We're fascinating. Aren't we, girls?

A   I have my finals tomorrow. Tomorrow morning and I can't—

Denis   It's an amazing threshold. We stand on the threshold of the rest of your life. This is Ciara. Louise.

Clara   Clara.

Denis   Who's having what? Who's having who?

He presents two young girls, **B** *and* **C** *(aged seventeen), and they troop past* **A** *into his tiny room.*

Clara   Come on, Louise.

A   You have to go, take them somewhere else.

Denis   The fact is … (*whispers*) I can't bring them anywhere else.

A   Why? Are they … No, Denis. You can't. (*To girls.*) Are you two still in school?

Denis   Now, glasses. Ciara, *Clara*, you follow me.

Clara *follows* **Denis** *off into the adjoining room.* **A** *and* **Louise** *are left alone.*

Louise   Hi. I'm Louise.

A   Do you know him?

Louise   No.

A   You can't stay.

From the other room, **Denis** *uncorks a bottle with a cheer.*

Half an hour later. **A** *and* **Louise** *sit silently while* **Clara** *and* **Denis** *have audible sex next door. Long pause.*

A   Do you like school?

Louise   Can we please open that bottle of wine?

A *and* **Louise** *an hour later.*

Louise *pukes and pukes.*

A   Are you ok? You'll be ok.

Louise   Sh. I'm ok now. I feel better now. I'm sorry about your books.

A   Would you like a drink?

She certainly does not.

A   Of water. Have some water. Sip it.

Louise   I feel better. Do you want to kiss me?

A   You should drink something.

Louise   Kiss me.

A   I'm not sure that you're …

Louise   Don't you want to?

A   It's not that I want or don't want.

Louise   Come here.

A   You should sit down for a second. Have a rest.

Louise   Yeah. Sit here with me. Don't go.

Denis and **Clara** *begin making noise again.*

A   I'm not going anywhere. Denis is. Denis! You've got to go. I have to study. Denis, that's enough. You've got to take these girls home. Their parents will be …

Louise   Can I stay?

A   No.

Louise   Hold me.

A   Ok. How's that?

Louise   I've got the spins. You're nice.

A   So are you.

Louise   No. I'm a very bad girl.

A   No, you just had a bit too much …

Louise   No, I'm a very bad girl. Why don't you kiss me? Is it the … Does my breath smell?

She lays a hand in his crotch.

A   What are you doing?

Louise   Saying thank you. For saving me.

A   I don't think …

She starts grappling with his flies and dips her head in his lap.

A   No, no, no. O my god.

She abruptly comes upright.

Louise   I've got the spins again. Spins.

A   Are you ok?

She steadies herself and then heroically returns to work.

A   Stop, stop, stop. Please.

He fights her off. She struggles onto the bed.

Louise   I'm just going to … lie down for a minute. Ring my mum. Actually, she's not even my mum. I'm adopted.

And she passes out. He watches her sleep and gently tucks her in. He chastely lies down beside her.

3.6

Dublin – 1998

Grey, post-coital moment. He sighs.

A   Thank you, love.

Louise   That was the worst sex I have ever had, anywhere, at any time. Including college. Including you.

A   I'm sorry. I …

Louise   I just mean that it was *disappointing*.

A   Sorry.

Louise   Not you. Not only you. I mean me. I should be at my sexual peak. It's all right for you, you're well past yours, but I don't want to give up yet, I want to *feel*. I want an earthquake.

A   I'll try harder, I promise.

Louise   It's not about that. You and me, we could try all night, all year, all our lives, and I'd never get there.

A   Well, not *never*, just not that last time.

Louise   O look, it works, it doesn't work. There's not much difference any more. You must feel that too.

A   No. I'm always … grateful.

Pause.

Louise   You're welcome.

A   But I am.

Louise   I know. But that's not … drive. It's not … raw.

A   Do you want me to shout a bit?

Louise   God no.

A   Or say things?

Louise   No, forget it.

A   I'll do anything. I'll do sexy.

Louise   Love, you couldn't do sexy if your life depended on it.

A   You be sexy then.

Louise   I'm really not in the mood.

A   Dance for me.

Louise   I'm getting sad now.

A   But you said you wanted to spice it up.

Louise   I don't think we can. It's just feels too weird. Is that Jack?

A   We could try.

Louise   No. It'd be like … It's like we've become brother and sister. We don't have a normal sexual relationship, just a slumbering, over-familiar one that sort of sadly strays over into mild incest every month or so. Or longer.

A   I wouldn't mind if it turned out you were my sister.

Louise   I'm not sure that's …

A   I think it would be amazing if after all this time we found each other and took care of each other.

She is looking at him.

A   I only mean that it would be a happy ending of a sort.

Louise   In what … *How*?

He shrugs.

Louise   I mean, I hope your sister, wherever she is, did ok, is ok …

A   Forget it.

Louise   But wishing that you'd married her. And had a child with her.

A   I said forget it.

Louise   And not happily married either.

A   Look, leave it. I shouldn't have mentioned it.

Louise   O my god.

A   Just leave it. I never said it.

Louise   How long have you been fantasising this? Have you thought that all along?

A *gets up and leaves. He goes into the bathroom and looks at his reflection.*

3.7

Bathroom, Cork – 1977

A (*aged thirteen*), *brushing his teeth, mind wandering. The following action is mimed, supported by live sound effects. He lifts off the lid of the laundry basket. And sees them. His brushing slows and stops. He spits into the sink and drops his brush. He bends and carefully retrieves a pair of* **Denise***'s knickers. He stares at them, holding them taut between his fingers. He inspects them gently, then delicately sniffs them.*

B (*off*)   Mum! Denis is being a complete prick.

D (*off*)   Like you'd know.

B (*off*)   Prick.

C (*off*)   Denise! Denis. Everyone. Time for Mass.

B (*off*)   He is. Stop it! You prick!

G (*off*)   Watch your mouth. There's no need for language.

B (*off*)   You didn't see him, Dad.

Instinctively **A** *looks around to make sure he is unobserved. He hurriedly stuffs them into his pocket and goes outside.*

In a quiet part of the garden, **A** *checks he is alone. He reaches into his pocket and produces the KNICKERS – now tangible and perfect. He sniffs them and then greedily inhales.*

Enter **Denis**.

Denis   What you doing?

A *stuffs them back in his pocket.*

A   Nothing.

Denis   What's in your pocket?

A   Nothing.

Denis   I saw you.

A   Just a hanky. I've a cold.

Denis   Show me.

A   Fuck off, Denis.

Denis   Show me, or I'll tell. Mum!

He shows **Denis** *the knickers, holding them limply before him.*

Denis   Put them on. Put them on.

A *gives a tiny shake of his head.*

Denis *makes to tell.* **A** *gives in and bends and tucks up a leg.*

Denis   No, not like that. On your head.

A *puts the knickers on his head.* **Denis** *is pleased.*

Denis   Spa.

Episode Four

4.1

Hospital – Friday night

A *is alone again in a corridor.*

Medical personnel pass by and ignore him. The sound of their movements is amplified.

Louise (*voice over speaker*) Hello, are you there? Hello? I know you haven't called. And I've no way of reaching you if you don't pick up. Are you going to answer? Where are you?

Cars pass and drown out her voice. Other voices are audible.

Louise   Jack? Jack, are you there? I don't know what to do now. I was going to stay out for a bit, but I wanted to know if you'd heard from Jack.

A woman's voice can be heard asking if she wants another drink.

Louise   (*away from phone*) In a minute. Actually, no. (*Intimate.*) Maybe you're in bed. I'm just going to come home then. (*Away from phone.*) No, I'm not staying, I have to—

She hangs up.

4.2

Hall door – Thursday

A burst of laughter from **B**, **C** *and* **D**, *off.* **A** *enters, still wearing the knickers, followed by* **Denis**, *laughing.*

Denis   Relax, come on. We're just having a laugh. I'm sorry. I couldn't help it.

This sets him off again.

A I have to get the food.

Denis I'm coming too. Leave them. They want to talk about us anyway.

A You don't have to …

Denis But I do, I do. Let me buy the dinner.

A No, no, you can't.

Denis Nah-ah. I insist.

A You're our guests, we invited you. You can't be buying us …

Denis Why not?

A Because I burned the food!

Denis Hey, hey! It doesn't matter. None of it matters. All these attachments, they mean nothing.

A What?

Denis I'm telling you, you have to let go of everything – the past, the future. Because we're all going to die.

A The food will be getting cold.

Denis It's true. Losing everything, my job, my house, my wife, my family – it's the best thing that ever happened to me.

A I'm happy for you. Now we should …

Denis Because you don't have these things anyway, and holding on tightly like I did, like you do … I mean, wouldn't you like to walk away, leave all this behind?

A I'm not quite at that stage yet.

Denis She'd probably thank you for it. You'd be doing her a huge favour …

A Denis, you may think it's ok to walk away from your responsibilities …

Denis I'm just winding you up. You're right. I am walking away. There's nothing to keep me here any more. That's why I'm leaving.

A Have you told Lydia?

Denis What?

A Have you told Lydia.

Denis Ah, Lydia. Lydia's been good for me. Helped me see things. Helped me let go of my attachment to things. That's a nice car. Is it your neighbour's?

A I, em …

Denis They just leave it out here? You know what these cost? Look it's not locked. Let's get in.

A Don't, you'll set off the alarm.

Denis Why don't we go? Right now. You and me.

A Denis, it's not yours, you'll set it off.

Denis We'll just borrow it. We'll bring it back. Let's do it. Get in.

A What?

Denis Get in.

A No.

4.3

Cortina, Cork – 1979

Denis Get in the car, get in the car.

A We'll get caught.

Denis I dare you. We're just going to sit in it.

They sit and savour the delights of **Gussy**'s *Cortina.*

Denis You know what I'm thinking?

A Starsky and Hutch?

Denis   Not in a Cortina. You know what I'm thinking?

A   What?

Denis   Angela McCarthy.

A   Angela McCarthy, yeah. I love her.

Denis   Imagine if we turned up at Angela McCarthy's. Hi Angela, we're just dropping by. You want to hop in?

Denis *is holding the key.*

A   That's not the key.

Denis   Stick it in.

A   I'm getting out.

Denis   If I took it on my own, you'd just tell.

Denis *reaches across and inserts the key.*

Denis   I'm turning it on.

A   Stop it.

Denis   Push your left foot down on the pedal.

A   No.

Denis   The clutch, step on the clutch.

A *complies and* **Denis** *turns on the ignition.*

Denis   Feel the power. Baby! Let's go. Let's go!

A *drives off nervously.*

Denis   Put it into second. Now third. Watch out, watch out!

A *panics and* **Denis** *laughs delightedly. They drive on.*

Denis   Sorry, sorry. You looked so ... You're doing well. Don't crash!

He laughs again.

A   I don't know where we're going.

Denis   Just drive.

Denis *tugs the mirror so he can see his hair.*

Denis   Angela McCarthy will let you drop the hand.

The excitement drains out of the adventure for **A** *and he turns for home.*

Denis   Why did you turn there?

A   I'm driving.

Denis   Go straight here.

A *turns again.*

Denis   What are you doing?

A   We're going home.

Denis   Home? Coward.

A   Yes! Yes and we're going home.

Denis   Well it's hardly your home, is it? Your home is some boggy field with your Da humping sheep, pretending they're your sister.

A   Shut up.

Denis   Your poor baby sister. Baaaba. Baaabaa.

A   Shut up.

Denis (*sings*)   Your poor little sheep who's lost her way, baa, baa, baa.

A *brakes sharply.*

A   Get out of the car.

Denis   What, thirty yards from our house? Sorry, my house.

A   Get out.

Denis   If you'd driven to Angela McCarthy's then at least you could have dumped me at the side of the road. Like your sister. Like your baabaa –

A punches **Denis** *suddenly in the head.* **Denis** *is astonished and then rouses to action.*

Denis   Don't you touch me, you filthy –

A punches him again. They grapple in the car. And don't see that **Gus** *has slunk up beside them.*

Gus   The fuck do you think you're doing?

Denis   Hi Dad.

Gus   Get out of the car.

They obey.

Milly (*off*)   Gussy! Did you find them?

Denis   Sorry, Dad.

A   Sorry.

Denis   But we weren't going anywhere ...

Gus   Don't be smart! You've driven it to here, didn't you?

Milly *arrives to cool them down.*

Milly   Gussy, we don't beat them, remember? We shout at them.

Gus   I am shouting. Now, go into the house.

Milly   Be nice to your father, boys. Your daddy's upset.

Gus   I'm not his fucking father.

Milly   They're closing the factory.

Denis   Ford is closing?

Gus   Think they can treat people like that. Welcoming them into the bosom of the family for how many years? And they turn around and drop you. I will not stand for it. I will not stand for it.

Gus *has a violent turn, trashing the car to the astonishment of the boys. He breaks down in tears.* **Milly** *comforts him.*

Gus   That was my car. I loved that car.

Milly   Gussy.

Gus   What am I going to do, Milly? What are we going to do?

Milly   It's all right, Gussy, we'll manage.

They depart. **Denis** *and* **A** *share a look and* **A** *takes the knickers off his head. Exit* **Denis**.

4.4

Hospital

A *gets onto his bed and lies down.* **B** *and* **C** *make the rounds. They can barely be heard. Music plays over the scene.*

C   Is he ready for a scan?

B   Are they taking him now?

C   The machine was down earlier. Anyway, they're ready. He hasn't eaten or drunk anything?

B   Doesn't look like it.

C   They want him to have contrast. Will you fit it? The back of the hand.

Enter **D**.

C (*to* **A**)   You have to lie still, otherwise they won't be able to do the scan.

D   Is he ready? I'm to take him down.

C   Bring him down.

They wheel the gurney into the corridor and down to Radiology.

C   Administer a mild sedative through the IV. If he's restless they can clamp him. It's very quick. They just need to keep the head still while they do the scan.

A *is fed into the CAT scanning machine. His image appears on the screen as the lights pass over him.*

A porter (**G**) *then wheels him into the next scene.*

4.5

Dinner party – Thursday

*With **A** still lying in state on the table, the others eat their takeaway around – and possibly including – his remains.*

Denis   Lydia's qualifying as a homeopathist.

Pause.

Louise   Good for you. I think herbal medicine is really important.

A   It's not herbal medicine.

Denis   And she cured a baby of … what was it, darling?

Lydia   Croup.

Denis   I was going to say meningitis!

Louise   Well, who knows? I mean there's things in plants we haven't even begun to understand.

A   Yes, but it's not herbal medicine.

Denis (*drinking*)   You know, I can't taste this at all.

Louise   I envy you, actually, helping people, and so naturally.

A   Homeopathy is not herbal medicine.

Louise   Isn't it?

A   No, it's nothing.

Lydia   No.

A   Sorry. Tinctures of nothing.

Louise   I can't believe you just said that.

A   Sorry.

Denis   You can't just dismiss alternative healing practices like that. (*To **Lydia**.*) Can he?

Louise   What do you know about herbal medicine anyway?

A   Homeopathy is not herbal medicine.

Louise   It is.

A   I'm just pointing out a fact.

Louise   It's herbal medicine.

A   It isn't. Tell her, please. Is it herbal medicine? Is it herbal medicine?

Lydia   They're extracts.

Louise   Ha!

A   Reduced to nothing.

Lydia   No.

A   Diluted to nothing.

Lydia   No.

A   They *were* extracts, maybe, before they're diluted a million times, to nothing.

Louise   They're extracts.

Denis   Can't taste a thing.

A   Parts per million! Parts per million! Even if there *was* rosemary or thyme or mint in it a hundred years ago there isn't any more. *I* contain more rosemary than those pills.

Louise   I can only apologise for my husband. Did everyone have enough?

Lydia   It was very nice, thank you.

A   I'm just saying.

Louise   More wine?

Denis   No thanks.

Lydia   No.

A (*to himself*)   Dispersed molecules.

Louise   Anyone for coffee? Tea?

A   Trace atoms.

Louise   Coffee, Lydia?

A   That's all.

Lydia   No, thanks. It doesn't agree with me.

Denis   Neither does Professor Penthouse there.

Louise   Tea, then? Herbal, maybe?

Denis   Herbal!

Lydia   Maybe, yes.

Louise   How about you, Denis?

A   Denis, what do you think of it?

Denis   Hmm?

Louise   Tea or coffee?

A   Is this part of the new Denis, the new changed Denis?

Denis   I don't know, I'm just … It's Lydia's …

Louise   Leave him alone. What are you having, Denis?

A   Of course, you're supporting Lydia. I mean, that's right, you should support Lydia.

Louise   Leave it, please, we're having a conversation.

A   You wouldn't want to leave her twisting in the wind. But she's a right to know what you think, more than any of us, doesn't she, don't you? So I'm only asking …

Louise   Don't answer him. More wine?

A   What do you think, Denis? Is there something to it, or do you think it is complete and utter donkey pizzle?

All turn to **Denis**.

Denis   The mind … is a powerful tool.

Long pause.

Louise (*claps*)   Well said.

A   Do you mean placebo?

Louise   Gone. Done. Tea, coffee.

A   Denis. Are you talking about the placebo …

Louise   It's over! Denis, what do you want!

Denis   I'm trying to make up my mind.

Louise   Well at least you haven't closed yours off.

Denis   Why don't I help you?

Louise   You don't have to do that.

Denis   I want to.

Louise   Do you?

Denis   Watch me. A cup of tea, a cup of gall, and how about …

Denis *deliberately spills a drink on* **Louise**. *She looks at him and then at the spill.*

Denis   Look what I've done.

Louise   I'll have to change.

Denis   Don't change. I love you just the way you are.

She laughs.

Denis   I do. I love the colour, the cloth, the cut.

Louise   The cut of it.

Denis   And look, it's easily cleaned.

He dabs the spill very gently.

Denis   There's a little bit. And there's a little bit. And there's a little bit. And there's a little bit.

Louise   I'll have to soak it.

She looks at him and walks away.

Denis   I'm going to make some coffee.

Denis *leaves* **A** *and* **Lydia** *alone.*

Lydia   My father died of cancer.

He smiles helplessly.

Lydia   It was very unpleasant for him. They couldn't do anything
for him. But they gave him chemo anyway. And they killed him.
I really believe that. But I don't believe in suffering. Pain is a
reality. But suffering is what you allow to happen. To yourself. To
others. And for my father, dying, I know that iced water, anything,
a walk, a quiet conversation, were better for him than what they
did to him. That's all. Do you have a bathroom?

A   Yes. No. Look, I apologise for going on like that, before. I'm
sorry. I'm terribly sorry. Would you like anything?

Lydia   I'd like Denis to love me. Because I love him. I love
him.

A   The bathroom! The bathroom. The small one is downstairs,
but the flush is … there's a kind of knack to it. And there's a
bigger one … Shall I show you?

Lydia   I don't know what to do. I mean, nothing, obviously. He
says he loves me and I want to believe him but I just don't, isn't
that weird? That I want the man I love to say he loves me and
when he does it isn't enough. And now he's going away and I'm
worried that he's not coming back and I don't know what to do.
Should I follow him or give him an ultimatum or just let him do
whatever he wants. Is that what love is?

A   Like I said. Down the hall. Or upstairs. I'm just … I need a
whiskey.

*He steps out and finds himself back in hospital. He lies down on
the bed.*

Episode Five

5.1

Hospital – Friday, 11p.m.

Enter **Louise** *escorted by a doctor* (**D**). *She is in shock.*

Louise   Where is he? What's happened to him?

D   Well he's had some kind of stroke, but we don't yet know how severe the damage is to his brain.

Louise   He has brain damage.

D   We're waiting for a consultant to confirm the results of the scan, but it seems he has a brain tumour and it's caused a small bleed.

Louise   Is he ok? Can he talk?

D   Not at the moment.

Louise   Can he move?

D   His body is in shock and it may recover some or part of its function.

Louise   Or it may not. That's what you're saying, isn't it?

She sees **A** *lying completely still.*

D   It's really too early to say how permanent the damage will prove. The consultant may decide to operate, or he may not. We're just going to have to wait and see how your husband responds. Now, when did you last see him?

Louise   When? This morning. I went to work.

D   Can I ask you, did he exhibit any symptoms?

Louise   What?

D   Headaches, nausea, problems with vision.

Louise   I don't know.

D   Did he complain of numbness or dizziness?

Louise   No, not that I was aware of.

D   Is there any history of stroke or aneurysm or brain attack in his family?

Louise   I don't know.

D   Is there any way we could find out?

Louise   I don't know his family. He doesn't have one. He doesn't have any family.

D   I'll leave you alone with him for a minute.

Exit **D**.

Louise *looks at him without saying anything.*

Finally she sits by his head and strokes his hair.

5.2

Flashback – 1969

A   Mum. What do you look like when you're dead?

B   You look like you're asleep, dear.

A   I mean in Heaven. What does everybody look like?

B   They look like themselves, dear.

A   Can you recognise everyone? Will Granny look like Granny? Will she be old? And Grandpa, he died when he was young, so will he look young? How do we know?

B   You'll just know.

A   How do we know?

B   It's like wearing a different hat, or something. Or different clothes.

A   I'll know what you look like and you'll recognise me too?

B   Don't worry, you'll always know it's me.

A   How?

B   Because I'll come up to you like this and give you a kiss like this.

He winces.

A   I don't like kisses. Will we have lips?

B   Even if we don't have bodies or shapes –

A   Or hats or clothes.

B   We'll always know each other, and when I come up to you I promise you'll know it's me. Now, go to sleep. Go to sleep or your Dada'll be getting cross. Good night.

A   Good night.

She leaves. In the dark, **A** *whispers ...*

A   Mum? Mum? Are you there? Mum? Mummy?

5.3

Fungal cave

A *gets up and goes down into the cave. The* **Fungal Man** *is packing up his stuff.*

A   What are you doing?

G   Finishing up.

A   Don't go. Stay for a drink!

G   Ah, no. I can't.

A   You will.

G   I shouldn't.

A   Do. Stay for a drink. You must.

G   You know, I will.

A   Good. Come up and say hello.

G   Will they mind?

A   No, no. In fact I doubt they even miss me.

G   Am I ok like this? Should I change?

A   No, no. It's casual. Very relaxed. I just came down to get another bottle. It's quite nice in here, isn't it? Very nice, actually. I should have some good whiskey. And some glasses. You know we might just stay here for a bit. There's no rush.

G   It's your house.

A   It is, isn't it?

He goes to find his prize whiskey.

A   How's it all going?

G   Well you'll have to strip everything back to the foundations. The plaster, the insulation, most of that concrete will all have to come out. There's chemical treatment, you can't stay here during that and then it's new stairs, rewiring, replastering. It's going to cost you a lot of money. You are insured, aren't you?

A *runs off and fetches* **Brother Laurence***'s SOUTANE.*

A   Would you mind terribly changing after all?

G   Sure.

G *gets dressed as* **Brother Laurence**.

G   Do you want me to say anything?

A   No. (*Pause.*) I'd hoped you'd be able to help me. But it's … I was looking for something.

G *shuffles off.*

5.4

Nursing home – a few months ago

A *finds a nurse.*

B   And have you been before?

He shakes his head.

B   Well she wouldn't remember it even if you had. She will remember things from far back. But be gentle and calm.

A *turns around and sees* **Milly** (*seventy-six*).

A   Hello, Milly. It's me. You remember me?

Pause.

A   It's nice and … cosy. Nice tree.

Milly   I love Christmas!

A   Yes. I always think of you at Christmas. My first Christmas with you. You're looking well. Are you happy here? Are they … Are you happy?

Long pause.

Milly   I love the smell of pine trees.

A   Me too. Anyway. I wanted to ask you about your sister. Your sister, Eileen.

Milly   My sister?

A   Yes. Your sister, my mother.

Milly   My sister is dead. Very sad.

A   That's right.

Milly   Poor Eileen. So young.

A   That's right. But before she died, she asked you something. What did she ask you?

Milly   Ask me?

A   When she was young.

Milly   She asked if I'd … be her bridesmaid. She's very pretty. Do you know her?

A   I need to know where my sister is. I've tried. I've looked everywhere and there really are no records. Can you help me, Milly? Do you know anything about my sister?

Milly   My sister is dead. Very sad.

A   *My* sister. The little baby. Remember the little baby?

Milly   The baby?

A   Yes, there was a baby. A baby girl. And you gave her up.

Milly   The baby.

A   You must have heard something. You must know something, Milly. I need you to tell me.

Milly   I can't.

A   You can.

Milly *is frightened and upset.*

A   You have to think. I need to find her.

Milly   We wanted to take the baby.

A   Yes, but you didn't.

Milly   A baby girl.

A   Yes.

Milly   Where is she?

A   I ... don't know.

Milly   We should have taken the little baby. We should have taken the little baby. We should have taken the little baby.

*Another nurse (**D**), comes over and attends to a distraught **Milly**.*

D   Now look what you've done. Milly, calm down. Milly, calm down. Be quiet. There's no baby. No baby. There is no baby. Everything's ok. Look at the tree. See the decorations? Look at the Christmas tree.

She looks up in delight.

Milly   Nobody told me it was Christmas.

A   Thanks, Milly.

Milly   Thanks a million.

A   Thanks a million.

Milly (*to* **D**)   I love the smell of pine.

Episode Six

6.1

Hospital bedside – Saturday

From afar, **A** *watches* **Louise** *talking into the camera where his body used to be. Her face is projected onto the screen.*

Louise   Where's that nurse? I can't find him. I've left messages, on his phone, with his friends, but nobody knows where he is. You know what he's like. They're supposed to be taking you for another scan. And there's a consultant, somewhere. I don't know when they're going to see you. It's very hard to see you here like this. I don't know if you can hear me, though that might be a blessing after everything I've said.

A   Just keep talking to me.

Louise   I've been thinking about you all day. How kind you've been, from the moment I met you. You've been such a good man.

A   No.

Louise   Such a good husband and father. And I've been a terrible wife.

A   No, no.

Louise   I've become so hard. So dissatisfied. I've always wanted more, I always wanted something else, and it's made me sick, sick to the point I want to throw up my life. And I know it's a ridiculous thing to say in the circumstances, but it doesn't have to be like this any more.

A   Hold my hand.

Louise   Because if this is who we are now, if this is our lives, then I want you to know I'm here. I'm here for you.

A   Stay with me.

Louise   I'll help you. You don't need to be afraid of anything. Everything will be all right.

A   Yes.

Louise   Everything is going to be ok. I don't want you to worry. I don't want you to suffer. You don't have to take care of us all any more. And if you don't want to stay … If you want to go, go.

A   No, I …

Louise   Don't let us hold you back.

A   No, I haven't finished.

Louise   Because we'll be fine.

A   No, look. I'm still here. I'm still here.

Louise   That's all I wanted to say.

A   I'm not ready to go anywhere.

She gets up and makes to leave.

Louise   I'm going to try Jack again.

A   Don't go. Listen to me. I need help. Why can't you hear me.

Louise   He won't be able to find …

A   Look, I can move my toe. Look! I'm moving it.

She has seen the tiniest movement in his foot.

Louise   Did you do that?

A   Yes!

Louise   Can you hear me?

A   Yes!

Louise   Can you understand me?

A   Can you understand me?

Louise   If you can understand me, move your foot.

With great effort he twitches his toe.

Louise   O my god. You're still here ...

A   Yes. I'm going to get better. I'm going to get out of here.

Louise   I have to call someone. Nurse! I need a nurse. Doctor! I'll be right back.

She leaves and starts to hunt down some hospital staff.

Louise   Nurse! Doctor! Help me! I need help! Somebody help him!

A *frantically starts putting out all the remains from the night before on the gurney.*

A   We can start over again. Let me show you. We can make a fresh start. Let me show you.

He sets the table the way it was at the top – BOTTLES, TAKEAWAY TINS, GLASSES. The others glide on and assist him.

A   Thank you. Thank you.

6.2

Thursday – late

Louise *slumps into the sofa, laughing wearily at herself.*

Louise   It's like I haven't been here. I've been away and missing my life. I've become so hard, hard and fat. And ugly. I'm so ugly.

A *starts to move towards her but is overtaken by* **Denis**.

A & Denis   You're not ugly.

Louise   Ugly. Gross. Disgusting.

Denis   You're not disgusting.

Louise   What are you, some kind of compliment machine? Look at me, I'm disgusting.

Denis   You're not.

Denis *sits beside her on the sofa.* **A** *looks helplessly on.*

Louise   What am I then?

Denis   Angry.

Louise   O yes.

Denis   Disappointed. Frustrated.

Louise   What? Don't.

Denis   Guilty. Sad. Passionate.

Louise   I know what you're …

Denis   Warm, alive.

Louise   No I'm not.

He takes her hand.

Denis   How about here?

She takes it back.

Louise   No, you.

He takes her forearm.

Denis   How about here?

She doesn't respond, but neither does she take her arm away. He continues his search for life, touching her gently in her palm, the crook of her elbow, her inner arm, her shoulder, her neck, her nape.

Denis   How about here? How about here? And here?

Louise   Maybe a little.

Denis *slowly, slowly moves in for the kill.*

Lydia *is sitting, rather drunk, at the table, telling* **A** *how it is.*

Lydia   The thing is, the thing is, if you love someone, you love them. And there's nothing you can do about it. Is there? Because if you can help yourself, then you're not helplessly, you know, in love. And if it's all … control. If it's all … deliberate. Then it's not … free. Am I right? And if you love someone, you would do anything for them. Anything. That's what it means, am I right? So I've decided. I've decided, I'm letting him go.

Denis *and* **Louise** *embrace. He pulls her towards him, but she gets an arm up under his chin to keep him at bay. He keeps wrapping his arms around her as she twists and struggles to escape. They clamber over each other as if they were determined to get past a particularly inventive and resilient octopus. They roll onto the floor.*

A   What are you doing?

Louise   Me? I'm … entertaining.

A   What am I supposed to do?

Louise   Talk to Lydia. Tell her something.

Denis *and* **Louise** *resume their struggle. They are swimming across the floor, past furniture and obstacles, knocking things over, taking things with them as they travel.*

A *begins his story, getting sadder and sadder the further he goes.* **Louise** *and* **Denis** *get correspondingly more animated.* **Lydia** *watches impassively.*

A   There was this donkey, an old donkey, and it died on the side of the road, and some lads thought it would be funny to cut off its mickey and use it for a football. So they kick it around in the dust and then they throw it over the wall of the convent, and it lands there where a young nun sees it and picks it up. And the young nun brings it to the Reverend Mother, because she knows everything, and shows it to her and the Reverend Mother looks at it and says,

'Oh no. Father McCarthy.'

He is weeping. **Brother Laurence** *is having a* WHISKEY *in the wings and laughs heartily.*

G   That's a good one.

Lydia   Another drink.

Denis　Haven't you had enough?

Lydia　No. I want another drink.

Louise　Give her another drink.

Brother Laurence *moves to the table and pours himself another drink.* **A** *picks up a BOTTLE.*

A　This is dead.

Lydia　Minother drink.

Louise　Get her another drink.

G　That's a good one, all right.

Lydia　I don't want to be alone. I don't want to be abandoned. I don't want to get old. I don't want to be ugly. I don't want to give up my life.

A　Yes. Life is precious.

A *pokes* **Lydia** *as the music picks up in tempo and volume.*

Louise *and* **Denis** *climax.*

A　Get up. We have to dance.

Lydia　I couldn't.

A *hauls her up and whirls her round. She squeals in protest and staggers off.*

Lydia　O no, I'm going to … I'm going to throw up.

She throws up off-stage.

A　Is she ok? Is she going to be all right? Is she going to be all right? Is she going to be all right?

6.3

Hospital – 1971

His trauma makes him appear vulnerable and young. Up on the screen, **C** *slowly approaches the young boy as* **Milly**.

Milly   Would you like to say goodbye to her?

Clearly he doesn't.

Milly   Will you say goodbye to your mother?

He gives the tiniest shake of his head.

Milly   You're going to stay with us for a little while, ok? Denis is about your age. You like Denis, don't you? That'll be fun, won't it?

Denis *gets up from lying with* **Louise** *and walks past him to the sofa.*

6.4

Sitting room

Lydia *re-enters.*

Lydia   I'm sorry, I think I made a bit of a mess in there.

A *gets their COATS.*

Lydia (*to* **Denis**)   Did I make a show of myself? Will you forgive me? You're not going to leave me are you?

Denis   Come on. We're going home.

Lydia   You're not going to leave me, are you?

Denis *and* **Lydia** *leave.*

6.5

Thursday night, Friday morning

Dawn is slowly breaking. **Louise** *lies on the sofa.* **A** *sits at the table.*

Louise   I'm done. Look at me. It's gone. If you want to go, go. (*Pause.*) I want to go. You live here with Jack. You're not going to say anything, are you?

She leaves.

A   Do you think we should get a DNA test?

Louise (*off*)   What?

A   To be sure.

Louise (*off*)   Don't do this.

A   So that we don't have to keep wondering.

Louise (*off*)   No, no, no, no. I'm too tired.

A   If there was even the slightest chance that we were …

Louise (*off*)   Imagine if … I can't believe you'd even *say* that to me.

A   Don't you want to know?

Louise   No!

She comes back on.

A   You should find out, maybe your family are still …

Louise   They're not my family, they're birth parents, they're gone.

A   But they mightn't be, you don't know, they might be looking for you.

Louise   They gave me away. They put me up for adoption for a reason.

A   They might need to find you, they might have to tell you something.

Louise   That's *my* business. Maybe one day I *will* want to find them, but at the moment I don't, and I certainly don't just to please you.

A   I'm only trying to help you find …

Louise   But you're not trying to help me, you're obsessed with making me somebody else. Why do you persist with this fantasy? Why? How do you think me being your sister would save our marriage?

A   I don't.

Louise   I'm not your sister! Why do you keep at it? I can't bear it! Why do keep at it?

A   Because it would mean she was loved. It would mean somebody loved her. Not very well, not like she deserved. But somebody loved her. And didn't just leave her. Abandon her. And it would mean I didn't let her down. I didn't let her down.

She regards him for a while and then leaves.

Brother Laurence *tries but fails to say something before he, too, departs.*

Kitchen – Friday morning

Louise *is dressed for work and has a dire hangover. She drinks a MUG of tea and watches him. He has a headache.*

Louise   Are you ok?

A   I've a headache.

Louise *places the mug of tea beside him. He doesn't touch it but his heart with his left hand.*

A   I feel …

Louise   I know. I do too. I'm sorry. I'm sorry. But I have to go.

She pulls herself together.

Louise   I have to go to work. I'll call you later. What are we going to do about Jack?

A   Jack?

Louise   Will we tell him later?

A   What?

Louise   Jack. I want to tell him later. About us.

A   Ok.

Louise   What are *you* going to do?

A   With what?

Louise   With your life.

Exit **Louise**.

A   I'm going to … I'm going to put out the bins. And bottles.

He starts to clear the table as he did before and drops a BOTTLE. The others come on and take over from him. They strike the set. The lights are very bright.

6.6

Final consultation

D   I think we're done.

A   Really?

D   Yes. You're finished.

A   That's it? I'm done?

D   Yes, you just have to leave.

A   O, sorry. Should I thank you?

D   Some people do. Some people are not at all happy. You are one of the quiet ones.

A   Is that good?

D   It makes absolutely no odds.

D *resumes his tidying, with* **B**, **C** *and* **G**.

A   Do I have to sign, or pick up a form, or …

D   No, no.

A   It's just I feel like there's something I'm supposed to have done, something I should have …

D   Well … You should have thought of that earlier.

They're almost done. Music.

A   No, wait, it's important. There are things I haven't said.

Things I want to say again. I need to think. I need more time. My son, I haven't seen my boy. I have to see my boy. I have to see my boy. I need to see him one more time. I'm not ready. There's too much I haven't done. It's not time. I don't want to go!

The others step away into the darkness. **A** *softens with pleasure as the lights begin to dim around him.*

B (*over microphone*)   Talk to him. Say something.

Jack (*voice off*)   Hi Dad. I'm here.

A   Jack! You came. I knew you'd come. Talk to me.

Jack (*voice off*)   Are you ok?

A   Just keep talking. I want to hear you talking. Even when I can't hear what you're saying.

The light is getting fainter.

A   That light is too bright. Wait, I'll close my eyes, I don't even need to see you, just to hear you, to know you're there. I'm so glad you're here. I'm still here, I'm still, it's still too bright. It's so bright! There's too much noise. It just needs to be quiet. Listen. Apple apple apple apple. Sh, almost. Apple apple almost. Apple, sh. Apple. Ap. Ap. Ap. Free.

The last syllable turns into the continuous beep of a heart monitor as it flatlines.

Blackout.

Film footage – Thursday morning

The screen comes to life with an image of **A** *laughing.*

A   Well I don't know.

Jack (*off-screen*)   You must know something.

A   I don't, I really don't. That's something you'll have to work out for yourself.

Jack (*off-screen*)   But your experience must … What lessons, what advice would you like to share with me, then?

A   With you? Be nice. Be nice to your mother. (*Pause.*) All this thing about change … I think it's hard for people to change. But sometimes it's not about changing at all, it's letting go of trying to be something you're not, I don't know. You, for example. You're perfect the way you are. Is that it? Am I done? Are we done?

He smiles at his son. Fade out.

Lights come up on the empty space.

Forgotten

Pat Kinevane

For my darling and beautiful angel, Kez

Forgotten was first performed by Fishamble: The New Play Company in the Bank of Ireland Arts Centre, Dublin, on 25 May 2006 during the Bealtaine Festival.

Written and Performed by Pat Kinevane

Director	Jim Culleton
Producer	Orla Flanagan
Composer	Brian Byrne
Designer	Catherine Condell
Lighting Design	Pat Kinevane and Jim Culleton
Stage Manager	Gerard Blanch

Characters

Women: **Dora**

   Eucharia

Men: **Flor**

   Gustus

The action takes place now.

All characters are between eighty and one hundred years old.

They live in separate retirement homes and care facilities.

Music plays.

Darkness. The clacking sound of the Tsuke. First two, then four, then eight, then a gathering of pace until they gallop to a punctuated slam of a door crashing shut. A baby cries loudly. Music rises. A cacophony of voices, barely distinguishable, mixes with the melody. The lines overlap and echo. Light. A fully robed actor appears and sheds various items during an initial dance ritual, also revealing various spaces on the stage with dignified movement. The music and chorus continue ...

Flor   Twas ...

Gustus   To look at me now ...

Lights up slowly.

Eucharia   Ye'd never think I was once ...

Flor   Seventeen ...

Dora   Twenty-one

Flor   See you in three!

Gustus   Twenty-two.

Eucharia   Sixteen ...

Gustus   Golden ...

Dora   With my whole life ...

Flor   Shpread in front of me ...

Eucharia   Like ... like ...

Gustus   A beauteous meal ...

Dora   But now.

Flor   Now!

Eucharia   Most of the time ...

Gustus   These days ...

Dora   I feel.

Eucharia   I'm feeling …

Gustus   And I'm not even …

Three pools of light come up as cloths are lifted off three tables, two downstage and one upstage. The actor hangs up the kimono. Lights fade up and music stops.

Eventually, we focus on …

Flor … *Meticulously cleaning throughout, polishes, spits and shines the entire area, even the floor and the pros-arch with a cloth. Before speaking, he finds a specific point in the auditorium … and utters …*

Flor   Twas the likes of me made this basterin country what it is today. No politician nor party can take credit for that. Twas the likes of mise and me brothers built it up from the civil war rubble, and vwhat do I get for me crownin fuckin years? Pigswill dinners on plastic plates and a dirty oul candlewick spread what whiffs of all the gumsy hoors that croaked it in this kip of a home afore me. And the butterscotch icing on the cake?

I'm shomewhere in the arsehole of Limerick!

(*shouts off*) Does no one clane anythin anymore? Filthy Tarts and Trollops! …

(*upbeat*) That's the end of part two. I'll be back in a couple of minutes.

They loooove to chat, Ginuine Irish gurls just waiting to natter. Text 'Panties' to 57 69 69! Formoo-lated and controlled by L'Abatoire Garnier Paris – it could be you! Because ou're worth it. Don't touch that dial! Shove a watch up oour hole and pass the scutterin time.

(*Polishing and travelling.*) Nathin' bugs me, now, bugs me more, to be honesht with ou now, than the reek of a dirty lady. No soap used at all. Cover it up the shtink with perfume de toilet and roses. These are not just Roses. These are long-lasting velvet-petal gran prix roses. These are M and S roses. Vwhat the fuck is a gran prix rose hah?

(*shouts off*) Dirty Maids!

Half of the nurses walkin with germs and grime. The oul wans in here with no teeth and moustaches! Not a lady way to be not a lady-way.

Loud music.

The large sound of a gong.

Music stops.

Welcome back to me, Flor! And I'm joined by my guesht Sargent – oh camera 9 – so, ask me arse agus failte air ais agus tonight.

Flor *sings his Macra na Feirme version of Copa Cabana ... ending in ...*

> Combines and thrashin'
> Were always the fashion,
> They have polish for tractors
> It's new from Max Factor
> At the Macra ...
> Don't fall in love.

Music. Dora's Theme as **Flor** *throws his towel to the floor. Music stops.*

Dora *draws flowers on a large white pad. She drinks from a delicate cup. A small doll stands next to a modern telephone on her table.*

Dora   So Much Love. His name, Flor. A sculpted country-man. Flor. Father had hired him to plough the slopes at the rear of the Hermitage. I was compelled to watch him from the parlour window, every hour of Monday and the entire Shrove Tuesday! Wednesday, I simply had to go outside and offer him refreshment. Delicious! Eucharia, my scullery maid, had been forwardly coy with him at elevenses up to this. I sent her to town for starch. Then, *I* carried the silver tray across the furrows, in my best goloshes. Up close, a creature. He said very little. Small smile, but, huge eyes, the biggest I'd ever seen, or, maybe the most hypnotic – for I could see my lashes, Battenburg and the teapot

– all reflected in his shiny pupils. And … Absolutely … I felt
ready to smile back. He told me he travelled … contract work,
all over the southwest. Stag's eyes and a mini smile. So, such
insanity, I asked him to meet me, that night. He suggested the
picture hall. *The Song of Bernadette*. Shockingly, I agreed. It was
just, experimental!

Mother was busy with her tapestry. I looked … quite … nineteen,
touched cologne behind my lobes. No make-up. Never did, but
I spent hours, nothing changes, on my hair by copying a print
of Dorothy Lamour that I'd cut from *Harper's Bazaar*. Piled up,
rolls here and in there, and under. That spring! I told Mother I was
taking a stroll to Rushbrook's, for a chat and cake with Ottaline.
Mother believed me, sewing industriously, for the charity bizzare.

Flor was on time outside the Ormonde – hair oiled. He smelt of
apricots. Curiously breathtaking, for a hand. But I was flattered he
had gone to all that effort. For me. We went inside … the labourer,
and I. It all felt, outrageously wicked!

Jennifer Jones was most stunning as Bernadette. I hooted and
loved the way she said that. 'I am the Immaculate Conception.' I
did love it. Not sure about Flor. The perfect gent for the duration
of the programme! No tricks! He left me home, on his bicycle!
A first for me. Lifted me from the crossbar and suddenly, danced
me, controlled me, for a full ten minutes, swept me into a fever by
the Hermitage gates. This Horseman of the Apocalypse. He kissed
like a rustic sultan. I walked the lane to the house alone. I was
instantly and completely spellbound by his body. Just that!

Music. **Flor** *dances … Then speaks … Music stops.*

Flor   And our Minister in Brussels oooooooo! Eighteen-carat
prick. 'Wouldn't mind if he spent some of his budget on his teeth.
A dope like that, nepresentin' us abroad the land, and not an ounce
of enamel left in his burnt-out fusebox of a Mullah gob. Then he
gives us a shpare tenner 'o pension for good behaviour, for not
givin out or shittin on the floor. Sure my teeth are better than his
oul Caa-bog cake-hole, and I ancient. Wouldn't ou think he'd get a
grant for himself from the Euro-what crowd to buy some soda and

scrub the bejaysus scum from his gnashers. And him nepresentin us in Turkey and Belo Horizonte! Oooooooooooooo!

(*shouts off*) Filthy tight-arsed Bollocks.

Flor *throws towel. Music. A Sting.*

Music stops with three twangs.

Dora   Eucharia was at the foot of the bed. Mother gasping for breath. A flock of candles, like the film. The Rector, mumbling. She looked as if she'd been a patient for years, and yet it was only three hours since I'd last seen her, sorry thing. How beastly the whip of a changing wind! The Rector, more mumbling, giving her communion. Eucharia trying to force a gently lit candle into her fist. Father in a chair ... sobbing.

Last year's beetfields had been harrowed. And the exodus of rats must have fled t'ward the house. At dusk, Mother had noticed a swarm of ten on the lawn and tried to telephone Rushbrooks to warn me, on my return. As she wound and dialled, a stray one at her feet. It jumped, bit her viciously and locked on. Father killed it with a poker. But it must have been a putrid vermin, for she reacted fatal-fast, fine at first, and washed her wrist. Gathered herself and ate a slice of sunflowerbread. But within an hour, she brought that up, thrust into roars and ravings. Quivering and scratching her last, I saw merely the tail-end of her suffering – guilty of my night at the pictures. (*Whispers.*) I should never have gone. Never have lied.

Sound cue. Harp glissando ...

Sound cue stops.

A suddenly furious **Dora** *...*

Observing her passing, I thought ... that rat. That rat had a kinder death. How unfair. But Eucharia held her hand, and made her quiet, all the while begging her serenely 'Let go now Mrs Venister, let go, go to the light, and let the beams, the beams take you home.' I thought it extraordinary. I ran to the gatelodge and fired Flor immediately. The next day, he had vanished.

Sound cue. Harp glissando.

Sound cue stops.

Father was devastated. He demanded nothing but omelette from the moment she died. Nothing else. For months. I could not leave him alone for any period of lengthy time but he'd pine like an urchin puppy on a wet lost day.

There's always that onus on just an only child. He … he was a burden, honestly. Eucharia became ill also and had to leave that summer. I had little time for anything – he needed constant care until, he yearned, pitifully, and I buried him too, the following dark Boxing Day.

Sound cue. Harp glissando.

She dials a number on her phone. She waits. Then speaks …

Sound cue stops.

Front desk, good afternoon. Room 336 here. May I speak to Matron please.

A short pause.

Yes. I'm holding for Matron thank …

Another pause.

Matron yes. It's Dora. Fine yes. I'll have my chowder in twenty minutes. If you would thank you. Oh and just to let you know … I shall be absent from bloom arranging henceforth. The woman is inept. I have learnt nothing new in six weeks. I was by no means troublesome. She said. Did she? Well I am eighty-three years old and I refuse to have this conversation. Au revoir.

Music. The News Anthem!

Flor   I'm back! RTE. News every hour on de-hour, read by me – a big fat heifer! Wance upon a time there in England there was a terminally ill woman who couldn't face the horrors of her death ahead, the slow rotting liverspotted countdown to the coffin so she travelled to Switzerland to a swanky clinic where they let her, all above board, let her drink a concoction and take her own life and she did and she stopped suffering and could you slow the autocue please and by God isn't she the luckiest lucky lucklady to eshcape this torturous garden of shite-hole and she lay down happily ever after. Agus anois an aimsir.

Get back ...

I'll bath myself ! I'll bath myself I don't want none of your nursey hussey hands on my Pelt. I am the clane-est buck in here and yet ye scald me with suds and sudo-cream. That water is scalding. Please! Don't! Don't touch my buttons! I'll bath myself. Has nobody a shkitter of dignity left?

(*shouts off, with a gesture to his hair*) If anyone is going to the dairy get me some Brilliantine?

Thanks Nurse.

He takes a tablet from the imaginary nurse.

He swallows.

He puts his hand in his pocket.

Music as introduction to **Gustus**.

Lights up on **Gustus**.

Gustus *sits. A cake stands beside a white cardboard box on his table. He can only move his arms henceforth ...*

His words are a voice recording.

Gustus   Three years back. A stroke. Me daughter – useless. Couldn't cope with me after the rehab. Would ya credit that? A stroke. Released 20 per cent of the equity of me gaff. I got meself a bed in here. Amn't I better off ? Truth be told – she frightens me, something bleedin horrible. I did me best for her and so did Georgina. And all babies are born with their own personality, I know, but twelve weeks and she was a trial beyond compare, even then. Don't get me wrong, we were thankful to have her, but determined, don't be talkin to me. She tore me own nipple off trying to suckle a feed, many's the night ... any port in a storm for her. And every man that came into the house, she'd charm him with a particular goo or gaa – no time for women, ever, and signs on she gave Georgina a woeges life – wore her out. Still does, well, me in any case. Maybe she'll call later on. God now, the awkwardness of that I hate. I hate it God! But it's my day. Tis, and she'll not spoil my day, me ninety-fourth day of sorts, and still suckin air.

Refers to cake ...

Didn't even deliver it herself. And she only livin only up the road in Kimmage. A taxi left it at the desk, and 'Gustus' written on the side. Would she not even write 'to Dad'? Poxy so and so! God forgive me. The vixen. Bad school reports, short skirts, empty bottles of Bass out the back toilet. She even sold me Frankie Laine records to buy fags. Stop now Gus. Happy thoughts come on, come on, come on.

'More Doctors smoke Camels than any other Cigarette'! I remember that ad when I was young – There was, let me see it now, a picture of a doctor on the telephone, just woken up in the middle of the night and he in bed. His bag ... am, spectacles and watch were on his locker, alongside a ... a ... pen, and blank paper . And next to his head was a bubble like, a caption, what's this it was now again ... oh yeah ... 'I'll be right over.' 'I'll be right over!' As much as to say – 'Although I haven't had much sleep, this packet of Camels will give me the particular kick I need to do my doctorly duty during the night' ... And a pyjamas on him ... fancy now!

'Clare ta God. Twenty-nine and still she was dog lazy. Nayra job so she got a course. Trainee chef. Hotel. Kildare town. Away from us. Hau! Paradise. Oh! A Letter from her boss. Rumours. Galavantin. Suggested Parental intervention. By meself. Bus to Kildare. Check up on me bould lassie!

Lights up on **Flor**.

Flor speaks, whisking his duster cloth and chopping his hands. Music for Cookery Time! plays under dialogue.

Flor   Welcome back! Here's one I prepared ten years ago! I always throw in a extra packet of butter to taysht. I'm a hoor for the butter, and to season I use a bottle of vodka and eight ounces of paprika pepper. Now, cabbage is an underestimated food, so, I've shtuffed this with a pork stir-fry, left it to soak for four days, and finally – I like to serve it, as I do everything, in a cold coolee of raspberry sauce. I do love the cold coolee. Sometimes I boil myself up in a bag and pour cup-a-soup all over me body – and throw in an extra packet of butter to taste. No, gas mark seven. Tis on our fuckin website www.cross yer eyes and dot yer tees dot ie. and always wash your services in case ou get the bird flu and end up swinging out of oour wire-tray with delirium. Oh, and a shprinkle of coconut will always look very festive if ou have a dis-ayse – Bone Appetite !

Flor *gesticulates and animates his story. Music out.*

Holy Mary is under me bed. She is, under. I saw her last Monday, over there in a long white coat and a blue band on her neck. Snowy skin, and a head of the darkest hair. She was crying like a girl and kept saying she was lonely. The tears were blue and had trails of gold like a snail had travelled her nose – and she knee deep in watery weeping. Down at her feet two swans swam and kept looking up to her like they was asking for food. One of them shtuck his head under the waves a sorrow and pulled up an oyster shell. Mary the divine and beautiful mother of us all and our saviour, took, took the clam in her hand and burst it open. It blasted the whole ward and a sparkly cloud flew all over the patients. I asked her vwhat it was. She crawled back under my bed, and the swans went through the ceiling. Bone Voyage! Got me welfare travel pass. I will arise and go now, and go to Ennis … Free!

Music. Eucharia's Theme.

Music stops. Lights up on **Eucharia**.

Eucharia *sitting at a small table. A mirror stands thereon for her use. She opens a jar of cream for her face and applies it gracefully throughout the following …*

Eucharia   I gets a day out of here on Saturdays – and when I
come back all the others ask me how I look so well. See, Saturday
is a very special day for me. Saturday is my time to start all
over again, like most people's Mondays like. Ya have to have a
start-over day, every week, or ye'd maybe stall, and never start
again. And I'm shagged if I'm gettin addicted to crayons and
paper doilies, like the others. Shure most of them are spastic from
art and crafts! I couldn't hangle dat!

Anyway, Saturdays! I gets the first bus to O'Connell street, in
Dublin. There by lunchtime and back to Cork by seven that night.
I loves the smell of Arnotts. And I have to laugh every time at the
jackeen wans behind the separate cosmetics. It's mental ... orange
faces, tide marks cut off at the jaw-line and neck. You've been
'tango'd'. Haven't a clue. So, in the main door and I starts ... first
to the creams to moisturise my face. I do a different counter-rotate
every week, so they don't get questiony with me, d'ye know.

Time to start on the foundation. My favourite is oul reliable
Elizabeth Arden. No smudging, and the tester pots are always
well topped up. A small walk till that settles on. Have a gawk at
the Hosiery! So then I powder at the Dior counter, do my eyes
– wherever, soft colours, an oul lippy will finish me off, mostly
cherries or wine ... and I'm anyone's shu god help us!

Done and dusted in twenty-five minutes ... can't bate it, all for
free with the tops of products. I was always like that growin up
– only the best for Eucharia's skin – tis no wonder I look farty
and not my eighty-nine! It's a pity they don't do tester hairdos,
but ye can't win um all, and that gorgeous nurse in here from
Granabrather does a deadly set for me whenever I do need a treat.
In fairness the staff in here are amazin. They don't just do things
for ya like. They ask if you would like them done.

D'ya know what I loves then after my overhaul? A nice drop of
coffee and a confection in the first-floor cafe ... It's got a clear
view of the whole ground floor, everyone comin and lookin and
leavin, even liftin. I gets a great sconce from the table near the
balcony. Last ah ... about a month back, I saw a classy lifter. This
lanky wan, plain enough, pushin a blue pram – not a buggy now.

So there she goes, my madam, potterin around the men's socks and ties. Oh, talkin all the time to her baby – then, as she'd round a corner, the hand would just shoot into action. At one stage I saw her scoop four sets of underpants, two umbrellas and cuff links, all in one fell. Fantastic! and the nerve of a matador!

Chatting all the while to her imaginary infant, who, oddly enough has doubled in size since she came shopping half an hour ago.

More women lift ... Funny.

Better at hiding the signs. The men blush and bluster – But the lady-tea leaves! Slick. Some people can just bite and chew their shame away ... amazing!

Music. **Flor** *in Concert!*

Lights flash (as per rock concert) as **Flor** *picks up towel.*

Flor I'm back! Shops. Peoples in shops. Well well well well well well well well. It seems to have got frantic and cold, like none of dem assistants want to 'assist' you anymore. All chat between umselves, never even look to see if it's man, woman or gasur they're servin. Is it only me it happens to? Did they see me coming? Is it too shagging much to say 'can I help you sir' or even 'fresh day outside' ... but no. No time to talk or entertain a body, specially an oul codger like you, senile old man, who has brown fingers and a brown feel about ya. My father was a beautiful dancer.

Music increases in volume as **Flor** *joins in with soundtrack. Music out.*

Flashing lights stop.

Eucharia The ladies' fashions are a scream from my angle. Ah ... a panic!! Classic day last December 8th ... all the country wans comes up for the annual spree. It's mental. Fine big lumps of Mary-Jo's and Bridins. Doors burstin open, dozens of bags and flamin red cheeks ... can't see them for bags! Stocky blocky wans, baytin themselves into pleated skirts and fitted trouser suits! NOOOOOOOOO! I do feel like shouting down to them!

The best ever was this roundy wan, farmer's wife, no doubt in the world, arms of a soldier and a teeny head. She tried on a floral three-piece and when she came out through the fitting curtains she looked like, a bed settee, and I was weak watchin her sashay around as lady muck ... and she bought it! She was happy, and I had entertainment. It was a distraction from my angel in the shoe department.

I made, enquiries years back, like.

Three Chimes.

Selling the shoes. She's always there ... Glad to say ... good attendance record thank God. She wears knits a lot. Taupes and Gold. Suits her colouring. I marvel at her like. She'll be sixty-four in Jang'ry. Really looks after her hair, as straight as rushes, and her cheeks catch the light of a Goddess. I don't mind a sayin it – a true beauty.

Last Saturday ... I got the nerve, finally. I was saving for a while for a court shoe I saw from the cafe ... nice patent in the distance ... no carticular occasion or plan ... just – I suppose, an excuse to have a look at the girl proper, face to face, like any other ordinary shopper ... to say ... 'excuse me miss, you wouldn't have these in a size six please thanks awfully'. No, instead, with me nerves I made a sow's ear of my opportunity. She approached me – great charisma God bless her. Clear voice. 'Anything you see you like Mam?' (*Pause.*) That shook me. The way she said it – but of course she meant missus, or you, person, maam, as in 'yes maam'.

I fumbled with the display and said ... 'oh maybe, this one', holding up the shoe! 'This is, I like ... it's rawder massive'! Rawder massive! What was I like? That's all I could manage to form, 'Rawder massive'! I went scarlet! Almighty and everlasting God!

She was so sweet. Sold me the pair eventually.

Music.

Flor (*retreating*) I'll bath myself ... Get yer fingers off my hide – the big fat stern of you, yo floosy bitch! Stop shovin me. Shtop it!

Please give me a bit of privacy and let no one in – and look – Who
are you? Did I say this already? – (*mimes clearing strands of hair
from his face*) Barely look to say … 'Leave the shoppin now, old
man, old curse to the country, oul dyin thing that the state drags
along like a leper's limb. Trapped and lingerin in your decripid body.
If twas legal, we'd chop ou off and bury you on an offshore island
for geriatric odds n'ends.' Where's decency? Where's manners?
Where's patience and grace? Who's takin the horse to France?

Music out.

So if you want to join the support group for the Alzheimers
Association you have to learn the slogan and r'payt after me.

Vwhat do we want?

We don't know?

When do we want it?

Who?

Small pause.

Music. Dora's Theme.

Music stops. Lights up on **Dora**.

Dora   So much love. Centrepieces were my speciality, primarily
Christmas and Easter. Exactly twenty-one years old. I meandered
through my elms on the morning of Good Friday and the idea
struck me like a muse. All the rooks flapping overhead, in the
thrust of making and bedding their young. And what a sight on the
grove's floor! Hundreds of jet feathers. Eucharia thankfully came
back to me that February, so I got her to gather the entire treasure.
I used a scattered dressing of lavender and applemint amongst the
black wings and vermilion camelliae. A wonderful result – so high
off the table, so wide, a perfect decoration for the holy time of
year, and a mournful wreath for the death of Jesus … the King of
the Jews. *Up to pour wine.*

We served pheasant, plum sauce and a harvest of honey-glazed
carrots. No potatoes, too vulgar I thought. It was, by far, the best

birthday I ever had ... set off by my splendid craft of purple, green and pitch plumes. And what gifts I received! Randal Wilson ...

Randal Wilson gave me fresh chutney. Pots. Adored them. Lasted till October. Kirsten Anderson brought lace, was it, it was, exquisite napkins. Oh, and the worst gift imaginable from Petra Hanville – two stuffed pine-martens! Horrid creatures. I believe she always envied my balustrade and Osaka wall hangings. Certainly those, and my reproduction of Whistler's *Caprice*. She wanted them all. But I – I wanted her husband.

Music. To whom it concerns!

Music stops.

Flor   Florence, but you can call me Flor. Well Gay, I bought this old crock of a mirror, am, it was cracked ... oh, like myself Gay! You're gas, gas man. Am ... I, as ya can see from the before photo, oh huge craic in it ... like yourself Gay ... and only a smidgen of the original frame intact. Well ... oh very hard work Gay ... three months in toto! Oh yes, I did it all myself, with a little help from an antique book ... yes, the whole job cost me seventy pounds Gay. Yep ... A simple Victorian mirror and I made it into this beautiful ... oh a lot of polishing ... Gay ... yes ... it's now a chaise- lounge, with a matching sideboard. Thanks Gay ... oh all my own work ... except for the castors – I got them from a priest in Sneem, Co. Kerry ... oh very expensive, I let him have his wicked way with me gay and as well as the castors, he threw in an Elizabethan commode, which I changed into a shtaircase ... oh I beeswaxed them all Gay. My wrist is like putty. Isn't everyone's says you!! Roll it roll it roll it dare Collette! I'd like to say hello, to everyone below, especially my Mother ...

Thanks nurse.

He takes a tablet from the imaginary nurse.

He swallows it.

He puts his hand in his pocket.

Music.

Music stops.

Dora (*drunker*)   Jonathan Hanville – desired by most in the town. She was well well well well well aware of this, and, to the poor man's demise, kept him locked up for years. He seldom ventured out. She constantly reported his 'weak heart' and assured him of his invalidity daily. He swallowed her concern, pity and lies. How can a wife do such damage? No sicker than the rest of us was Jonathan, but she persuaded him so to keep him to her. The night of my party – a rare night for him to appear in public, he positively altered the hue of the spaces about him. Absorbed everything. A piece of chess. Soot hair. Hands unspoiled. Face, flawless. But she teased him down the path of middle age and emptiness. Expertly.

After the trifle, he poured me a Limoncello. Just did it, no 'will you', 'might you' or nodding question. He did not look at me directly. Petra was … guffawing to Otty Rushbrooke about her past Palm Sunday hunt, all teeth like her hounds, gold siphoning from her crevassed neck, not noticing what came next! Eucharia had left pencils and notes for after-dinner games on the damask. He held up a message he had scribbled. From nowhere. 'Happy Birthday, dash, you'. Later he quipped that he liked my centrepiece! How naughty was that! I needed air right then … out to the conservatory – suffice to say, private place. He followed. Cavalier.

In ecstasy.

Lent was finished. Touches. Rubbing. Wet mouths. My thigh … My God!

Tsuke beats.

Light fades to spot on **Dora** *which pulses in time to the beats.*

She freezes a Mie. Fist in mouth.

This melts.

Tsuke stops.

I met him nightly by the Arboretum. Times to talk, times for
nothing but raw pleasure. And, there was, so much Love.

Pause.

Through the summer he grew away from her – rows. August
came. The liberation of Paris. Plans were made. November – he
would take me to Orleans! For good. He had friends unknown
to her there. Money no object. I had but to sign and everything
would be sold. As for him – a staged robbery of his own house
– he actually organised this! His mad scheme. The Eve of our
elopement, he telephoned, and told me it was done. A man was
suitably paid to scatter the Mansion about and feign a pillage.
Meanwhile, the money was hidden – some his, most of it, hers.
Bundles of loot, let us say, stashed for the night under an old
discarded bath, somewhere out in the countryside. He said it
was once a trough for ponies. My lover. And after he comforted
her, post-crime, told her to calm and stroked her crevassed neck,
'Relax Petra! Thank Goodness nobody was hurt, et cetera.'
They went to bed. Their ultimate intimacy. Tomorrow, my silent
Valentino would collect the booty and whirl me up and off to
France. We would live happily, unchaining him, fulfilling me. I
packed my portmanteau. I even took the last pot of chutney and I
slept what I thought would be my final night at the Hermitage.

Music.

Flor   The grey mare at the post office I used to cash me book
at. Oul silver capall she was, wouldn't get a kick in a horny
shtampede! And her chain on her specs! Why is everyone wearing
chains? Isn't there enuf … chains … hah? And she'd take my
pension book and scrutinise it, and shtamp it, with her chainy eyes
on me, as if I wasn't me, but an imposter – I ask ou. Who'd want
to dress the shit-up as me!? Then she'd dump my spondulicks like
an oul bulldozer inta a metal trough and I could never grasp the
small one pences and the queue behind me sayin 'hurry up', in
their heads, layabouts and unmarried mothers and blackies and …
Drug addicts. 'Hurry up you dirty oul appendage man.'

Music stops.

At least I'm not gone mad, touch wood. (*He knocks.*) Is that the front door or the back door?

Music.

Lights up on **Gustus**.

Gustus *puts candles in cake* ...

Gustus   Arrived at her flat's address, middle of Kildare town – a Saturday morning. It was over a butcher shop – sawdust on the steps . She had no idea I was comin. I hope she'd be there, maybe sleepin off her week's work. I planned to take her to the Japanese Gardens – just the two of us. Climbing up, I remembered a spotless time when she was seven, and she won a school talent contest and she wrapped in a curtain! Georgy dressed her as a geisha girl and she sang this song. Rehearsed for months ... how could I forget ...

Red spotlight.

Music continues.

This fan that I am using,

Has come from quaint Japan ...

He rises and dances demurely with a fan ... dreamlike.

Where dainty fans are fluttered – By every maid and man

The dignified sam ... oor-I – They wave them in the air

White pretty little geishas – We wear them in our hair

Now dares a crowd. The Japanese. Treat their elder lemons with the utmost respect. See it as their duty.

In Japan, quaint Japan,

Where the fan is used by every maid and man

Maid and man.

In Japan ... quaint Japan.

Spotlight off.

He is back in his chair. Infirm.

Then I found number flat number seven.

I heard laughing through the doorframe. Her high giggle, and shrieks of fun, but then, other laughing, boys joined in, young men. I made to go back down the stairs. Then I heard breaths, and, Lord save us, moans. And whatever way I put my hand on the door, in panic maybe, it opened, and there she was. And five lads! I'll say no more. Brazen. One tried to continue. 'Me oul fella', she said. They half dressed themselves – all jockeys, young brats from the Curragh and I stood outside on the landing as they passed me by, no remorse, smoking little farts, Pips, and she, Gladys Knight incarnate, she put on a dressing gown, and made some tea.

Hated the course. Brought her home. Months later, up the pole. The stress. Poor Georgy. Rest her soul. Just me. Forty a day. Couldn't stop her. Toby. Nine pounds. All I could. Nursin the infant. Wondered. Which jockey? I set her up with a job in Arnotts as well. I went to school with the manager. She's still there, fundin his drumkits and footwear. Waste o' space the lummox, and he old enough to be crucified. All he knows is rock bands and trainers. She gets him a cut on them, oh, she's great!

I don't, deep worry about the pair o' them though. Probably because she was adopted by us. Fifteen years married and nera sign of a sprog. I never really, soldered my love for her, to my heart – ye know. Less so her son, odd fish. Not a drop of my veins in him. There's strangers in my home now, drawing my curtains and turning my key – her painted – perfect nails – that would reef the face of a grown man. They fight cat n' dog. Regard for them? Yes, sure I can't throw them on the street. Can I?

I miss ya Georgina. And to look at me now, look at me now.

Follows into music. Eucharia's Theme. Music stops.

Eucharia *begins to apply pale and eastern make-up foundation …*

Eucharia   C'mere I want ya. I felt a hint from me nephew Robert visitin a week ago. He wants the furniture. 'You can take it when I'm toast son,' says I, 'but let the arguments be on your

head, with yer sister', 'cos Lilian loves my fire brasses I got
from Dora Venister years back. It's a big pressure really, I mean,
they're all well set up in life, comfortable, six times a granaunt,
God protect them and their lovely minds, but, it does, unsettle me
at four in the mornings – who'll get what? Who is deserving of
which? Will they rip the pusses off each other and I gone? Wills
and testaments! They're all the wan – trouble with a capital R.I.P.

Good fettle all the same myself. Hannah Roche over there is due
to die any day, and, if ye ask me 'tis cos of the lorryload of tablets
they shovel inta her – cocktails! Demented is Hannah, talks back
to her Rice Krispies, calls the doctors Langers and told the bishop,
last week when he was doin his rounds, to get back to his bastard
children in London! So they had ta sedate her – poor incontinent
unfortunate. Hello, Hannah Banana, Hannah Banana, Hannah
Banana.

Nelly Dentures died this morning. Always suckin her teeth. I
heard her behind the curtain – the suckin stopped for the first time
since she came in here six years ago. I called the domestic nurse
and they found her curled up in her suitcase! Ah! She was always
sayin she was goin to sneak home. Tormented. All she had on was
her big knickers. Died trying to escape. Talk about packin it in hah
… Sure her family were all here within the hour, riflin through her
wardrobe over there. Near scalpin each other claiming her stuff –
a few trinkets. And do you know what's hilarious? Her twin sister
died in Accident & Emergency last Tuesday on a trolley. A trolley!
– God rest and redeem their souls shu God help us!

Tsuke beats.

Lights fade to spot on **Eucharia** *which pulse in time to the beats.*

She freezes a Mie.

Tsuke stops.

Amazing how families fall out though. It's mental. And if there's
land involved – things go spare altogether. Some folk think of
nothing else. Over eighty and all they want is your belongings,
slap ya in a box, snottin over your grave. Crocodile snot!

D'ya want a marshmalla? What? Ah, yer like a stick gurl!

I do fear dyin ... I do. Biggest fear? That there'd be no one
around to say goodbye – more so for their sakes – and the kids
... it's important to know what a corpse looks like. I hope it
happens in my sleep though. And me mask! Will I kick it like
this? Or this? Please not this! I'd like to see tunnels and beams
of promise. I want Technicolor, the lot, big strappin Gabriels
takin me by the hand, a Thora Hird chairlift through the clouds to
spare my hips, and at the top, someone like, I dunno, Mae West!
Cool as a breeze in a Kimolo, with a Babycham, maybe a few
Consulate, a welcome bit of a chat, get a map and a starter pack
for paradise. Yes, a stylish cross-over, luxury ... yeah ... beams,
beams, beams.

Music.

Lights flick against back wall in time to the music.

Flor   Don't touch my buttons. I'll bath myself. *Music stops.*

Flor   Apparitions can get no better than the Mother of God. For
years ...

I have had them. My dependable Virgin. My Mother of the pure
eyes, help me now.

Thanks nurse.

He takes a tablet from the imaginary nurse.

He swallows the tablet.

He puts his hand in his pocket.

There y'are again girl. There's somethin I'm confused about and
been meaning to ask ya. How come when we arrive, no babby is
better off than the other. Neighbours and presents and sentiments
o' welcome ... Ye little special precious little novelty. Same fuss,
same swabs, same blankets and bottles for all. Spick and span.
Musha the in between bit passes, then the wind down starts. None
of us is aqual then. Better fuss for some, others left to bake in the
sand of no care – No bottle no palm to rub your brow ... ye little

special precious little novelty. Come back to me on that one. I'm
not lookin for your pity. I just need your help girl.

Music. Acapella.

*He sings, harmonising to his own pre-recorded voice, in three-part
splendour ...*

> Hail Queen of Heaven the Ocean star,
> Guide of the wanderer here below,

Light gets brighter and music gets louder as **Flor** *stands*

> Thrown on life's surge
> We claim thy care
> Save us from terror and from woe
> Mother of Christ, Star of the Sea,
> Pray for the Wanderer, pray for me.
> But each time I go out with someone new
> You walk by, and I, fall to pieces ...

Music continues. A Sting.

Music stops.

Eucharia   Darkness would scare me alright. That's why I pray
for a bit of illumination, on me way. And the pain wouldn't bother
me cos I would insist on every narpotic ever invented to ease
me, why not? No one should suffer if we can fly to the moon.
Childbirth was a fecker on me, so I can't imagine death pangs
could be any worse than shovin a melon out my bum! It couldn't
possibly be.

The Man upstairs? I imagine him ... Middle-eastern like-swarthy,
loads of languages, and a degree in mental nursing to deal with all
the nutters the earth is returning up to him these days! Poor man,
how does he cope? Maybe he doesn't cope at all! Maybe him and
the divil are all the one, and he goes down the Styx for a bit of
passion and craic. Most culchies do!

I look forward to the bird's eye view though. Well, I presume I'll
qualify for it ... we'll see. A gift to be able to look down from
Eternity and see all the living continue, all their private moments,

read their thoughts and know their secrets. All the secrets we keep
from our friends, and only the dead can see … with wonder. Hope
me headstone is padded so I can sit up and read in the middle of
the night!

There'll be no truck with my will. They'll get a surprise no doubt,
when my extra savings … come their way and they can spree and
splash out, the way I never could. A nice surprise for them.

I used to take out a bit every now and then for needy times, that's
all. I was scared of being caught. Twas always a comfort to know
it was there daw, in case, like … like having prayed all your life,
the tickets to Heaven are easier to come by. It's mental.

Music. Strange sounds.

Flor   Inside this Sunday's *News of the Week* get your free
DVD and a bucket of piss and a copy of my new novel entitled
'Every nice girl I ever courted left or lurched me'. Like that
other apparition, the other vision I'd seen, and met, once on an
Ash Wednesday, a vision that … dismissed me! And I never saw
her, really again, because … posh fuckin country Madam fuckin
Butterfly! So once upon a time that night, I went on a bender with
a bottle of Hennessy in the Venisters' hay loft and was disthurbed
by the servant gettin eggs, all dolled up, painted doll, and she was
willin, so I humped the hole off her and came back wesht and our
Lady's been mindin me all the while since. Watchin me taste.

Music fades out.

Did ou ever taste the waste? The wasting? Not the coirp, but this,
up here turned to sludge. Seepin thru the skull to the upper nose
and down the tonsil. A taste of copper crossed with nutmeg and
milk. Savage milk. It hauls ya down, thru the thistles, the layer
of grass, on thru the pebbles, the rocks, past the kingdom of
millipedes and beetles, to the empire of husks. The Land of over.
The wasting is ferocious.

*He freezes a Mie. The cloth is in his mouth. Beats. Continues into
Harp glissando …*

Sound cue stops.

Dora   Next morning. Clandestine Mistress. Ears cocked for the hum of his Bentley.

Vite! Vite! Je n'en peux plus – Je n'en peux plus!

Strange. I believe I saw a rat, climbing the Orrery.

Eucharia came from town with apples at breakfast. 'Mornin, miss'. 'Good and a very good morning Euchee'. 'Pippins, miss?' 'In the basket, there, Euchee thank you'. After more pleasantries, by the way, she requested I sit and told me of early news up the town. Somebody, she said, had died in his sleep during the night. 'Peacefully miss … Mister Hanville, peacefully'.

Gustus   … Bony, muscles frozen. The lion's share of me shuttin down. But the flashes upset me more, flashes of meself, a strappin fine young man, of eighteen, strong, prime and golden, with me whole life spread in front me like a beauteous meal. And I have to admit, most of the time, these days, I feel … I'm feeling …

Eucharia   Wads of damp cash, under an oul bath. A windfall just peekin out. Found on an afternoon stroll. Thank someone. Scullery maids need blessings too. I think one of these Saturdays, I'll leave her some, in an embelote, anonymous, in Arnotts. For the attention of …

She definitely applies the finishing touches to her Geisha make-up, brows, liners and lips …

Handing me me change, no wedding ring … she touched my knuckles – I'll never let it down – her painted, perfect nails – like me at that age. Stag's eyes, like her fath … I wanted to cradle her then and there … She never knew who I was. Never will! My Angel. I was twenty-seven when I had her. I wasn't a child like. If I'd have known I'd find that money, maybe, I'd have held on to … Why did I give up an Angel like her? (*Gets upset.*) Sorry about this now. (*Recovers.*) But d'ya know what? Any day your feet hit the ground is a good wan.

The large strike of a gong.

Flor I'm back. And for the deaf dumb and blind, a Summary. A body should never grow old alone. A body should have a mate. But a lady – not a made-up walloper – a lady to mind a body. Oysters and chains in what was once the richest republic from here to Bi-aff-ra an' I'm left with fuck all in the end. Twas the likes of me. (Ore-datta) Twas.

He takes a fistful of tablets from his pocket. He eats them.

Music.

Lights fade until there is only the red spot of the sun.

The final cacophony of voices rises as he dances alone ...

Flor Twas.

Gustus To look at me now ... Ye'd never think I was once ...

Eucharia Seventeen ...

Flor See you in three.

Dora Twenty-one ...

Gustus Eighteen.

Eucharia Sixteen ...

Gustus Golden ...

Dora With my whole life ...

Flor Spread in front of me ...

Eucharia Like ... like ...

Gustus A beauteous meal ...

Dora But now ...

Flor Now!

Eucharia Most of the time ...

Gustus These days ...

Dora I feel. I'm feeling ...

Gustus   Forgotten … And I'm not even …

All   Gone.

A baby cries. The door slams shut.

Darkness.

Drum Belly

Richard Dormer

'Exile is a dream of a glorious return. Exile is
a vision of revolution … It is an endless paradox:
looking forward by always looking back. The exile
is a ball hurled high into the air.'
Salman Rushdie

Drum Belly was first performed at the Abbey Theatre, Dublin, on 10 April 2013, with the following cast:

Harvey Marr	Liam Carney
Walter Sorrow	Gerard Byrne
Johnny 'The Fox' Rourke	Ciarán O'Brien
Willy 'Wicklow' Hill	Ronan Leahy
Daniel 'Antrim' Malley	Phelim Drew
Chief Marion O'Hare	Gary Lydon
Thomas 'Lumpy' Flannegan	David Ganly
Mr. Gulliver Sullivan	Declan Conlon
Bobby Boy	Ryan McParland
Mickey No-No	Karl Shiels
Director	Sean Holmes
Set Design	Paul Wills
Lighting Design	Paul Keogan
Costume Design	Eimer Ní Mhaoldomhnaigh
Sound Design	Christopher Shutt

Characters

Harvey Marr, *sixties*
Walter Sorrow, *sixties*
Chief Marion O'Hare, *fifties*
Johnny 'The Fox' Rourke, *twenty-five*
Willy 'Wicklow' Hill, *thirties*
Daniel 'Antrim' Malley, *thirties*
Thomas 'Lumpy' Flannegan, *forties*
Mickey No-No, *thirties*
Gulliver Sullivan, *fifties*
Bobby Boy, *sixteen*

The play is set in Brooklyn, New York, July 1969.

Dedicated to the memory of
Robert Anthony Welch
1947–2013
Poet, Novelist, Playwright, Black Belt Shodan

Prologue

Darkness.

John F. Kennedy's voice rings out. It is the recording of his 1961 address to the American nation from Texas.

JFK (*voice-over*)   We choose to go to the moon …

Applause and cheering.

JFK (*voice-over*)   … We choose to go to the moon, we choose to go to the moon in this decade and do the other things, not because they are easy but because they are hard, because that goal will serve to organise and measure the best of our energies and skills. Because that challenge is one we are willing to accept, one we are unwilling to postpone and one we intend to win … and the others too.

A roar of an appreciative crowd, deafening.

Music: '1969' by The Stooges. This fades to silence.

The dark continues.

Gently, a baritone male voice begins to hum the hymn 'Abide with Me'.

Then, the soft wet sound of someone sawing meat.

After several long moments the lights come up slowly on …

The basement.

The bowels of a ten-storey Brooklyn tenement building. A sturdy wooden table upstage centre. A naked hanging light bulb dimly illuminates the scene. It is so dark that the walls are barely discernible. The table and floor are covered in sheets of cellophane plastic. There is blood everywhere. The bulk of an old furnace water-heating system lurks in the shadows. **Walter Sorrow***, a big bald man in a bloodied white butcher's apron over a blue pinstripe suit, stands with his back to us. He is cutting up large lumps of some unidentifiable hairless animal with a handsaw. Every now and then he disposes of a piece*

*of meat and bone in one of the several metal buckets beneath
the table. Another man stands nearby in an ill-fitting black
suit and a pork-pie hat smoking a cigarette: the weathered but
irrepressible* **Harvey Marr**.

Walter *hums the hymn while he works. He continues throughout
the following.*

Harvey   … We work a goddam miracle, and what thanks? We
go to the moon, we paint the Sistine Chapel, we put a bullet
in a guy's face. It's work. Extraordinary things happen every
day. We get up. Go to bed. Unfuckinbelievable. All the things
in between? Even more extraordinary. We do it. Huh? We do
it. We keep doin' it. Man's gotta eat. I gotta grand-daughter.
Mother's a junkie. Kids gotta eat. You're OK, Walter. Yes you
are. Sullivan? He's a good man. Best pal. Johnny? Good kid.
Yes. But some people? These rip-shits? Get treated like normal
people? Where's the sense in that? Hunks a' shit. Some people?
Don't deserve to live. Take up too much space. (*To the buckets
under the table.*) Ya fuck. (*To* **Walter**.) Wanna smoke? (*To
the buckets.*) Pig fuck … (*To* **Walter**.) I'll bet he had to break
his shit up with a fuckin' pole. Size twelve feet. European
measurement. You know what they say? Big feet? Big shits.
Details. That's life. The devil's in it. Wouldn't flush. Yes sir,
Mr Sorrow. The world's a better place. How's your mother? …
That bad … I'm sorry, Sorrow. Fuck that. Life is … poof …
She a religious woman? … It'll see her through. Yes. Take me,
I ain't religious an' all or anythin' but I get moments. Clarity.
You could say I have epiphanies. Dizzy Jesus. What a day. Tits
on 'er like wet paper bags. Idiot! You're an idiot, Harvey! The
day I've had, Walter, you wouldn't believe. Everything, it's …
The fuckin' day. *Postmen*? Let me tell ya. You wouldn't think to
look at me but today I had a skin full. A belly full a' bourbon,
Walter, Kentucky fire water. Two bottles, maybe fuckin' three.
Broad liked her bourbon. Christ. Told me she was forty-nine
… she wasn't. (*Pause.*) Her daughter might a' been. I told her
as much. She starts screaming the place like bejesus. Ya know?
Hysterical, like her fanny's on fire. I gotta get outta here. Spill
on to the sidewalk like a bucket of sick. I'm a shambles. I'm

staggering about the street like a fuckin' prophet. I'm arguing with myself. 'S true.

I'm convinced now that I'm my own father, God rest the mick son of a bitch. I never knew the bastard, but he must have existed. And I'm havin' a pop at him for turning out such a fuck-up of a human being, which is me. So I'm both, you see? It's fuckin' *epic*. It's … at one point I'm actually, I may have been crying. Shameful. I know. It's fucked-up. And then I'm loosing control of my bladder, Walter. A piss buster's comin' on. A loo-loo. I'm feeling a trickle. The beginnings of a gush. So I run to the side of the street, ya know, dignity an' all, I run to the side of the street, into an alley, under this tree or somethin' or a lamp post or somethin' and I whack it out, ya know. Out comes Johnny Thomas. Zzzipp. Flumpff. Whoosh. Ahhh. It's good. Fucking notable. So. So far so so-so … an' during this little interlude I look down and see what I'm zizzin' on. An' ya know what it is? … It's a gnome. Ya know? Those fuckin' garden things? Those things that people do? And it's big. It's a monster. About so high. Up to my nut sack. What's that about? People are fucked. Generally. Fuckos. But fuck that. I'm good. Man's landing on the moon, for Christ sakes.

Pause.

I hope you're getting all this, Walter?

Walter *becomes silent. He stops sawing meat and looks at* **Harvey***; a dead-eyed stare.*

Harvey   'Cause there's times I know you don't listen. I hope I'm not just talking to myself here?

Walter *stares at him.*

Harvey   What? What? What's that look for? What? You never do somethin' unpredictable? Well excuse me, Miss Perfect. You're flawless. I don't know whether to kiss your feet or nail you to a fuckin' tree. Look, I'm sorry I got you outta bed. But gimme a break, will ya? I'm explainin' myself here. Jesus Christ.

Harvey *continues and* **Walter** *begins sawing again, but he does not resume the hymn.*

Harvey   … So I'm standing there with my dick in my hand
pissing on a three-foot gnome. And it's good. *Yes.* Worth living
for. And then, then I take a look down and I realise … I see what's
happening. I'm pissing on a *leprechaun*. OK? The gnome? The
thing? Turns out a fuckin' leprechaun. It's true. Bright green.
Singing with his mouth open like this (*Stretches open his mouth.*)
and I'm pissin' on him. In his mouth. In his little red painted
mouth. BOOM! I think of St Patrick's Day. BOOM! Those big
proud barrel-chested bastards banging their drums. Every eye
in the crowd streaming, all goose bumps and jubilation, crying
out to Christ and his buddy the patron saint of Ireland. Then,
BAM! I'm offended. Back comes my heritage. *Bam.* It hits me
in the belly like a .38 slug. BAM! My heritage. A true-blood
second-generation mother-fucking Irishman. And I'm there. I
can hear those drums again. I'm right there. I'm thinking of a
hundred generations of suffering and oppression; a race of people
persecuted like the fuckin' Jews and it comes to *this* … In the
Land of the Brave, the Home of the Free, a bright green, three-
foot-high singing leprechaun, and I'm pissing on it. In its *mouth*.
And I start to feel the beginnings of *rage*. It's rising up in me like
sick, like fuckin' bile. I'm offended and *outraged* now. Who in
the name of sweet holy fuck would be so callous as to do such a
thing? To have this here? Who? I'm affronted. I'm angry. 'You
racist mother-fuckers! You racist fuckin' white-trash pig-suckin'
scum!' I'm screaming up at the windows now. Through no
fault of my own I'm pissing on a symbol of my ancestors. You
understand? *Our* ancestors. 'You racist fuckin' prick! You white-
trash piece of shit! Why don't you just come right out and fuck
me up the ass? Come on! Fuck me up the ass like you did the
home of my ancestors. Come on and fuck me, you trashy piece
of shit!' Then, then I glance over my shoulder … and there's this
guy standin' there. And get this: a postman. It's true. A fuckin'
postman? And all of a sudden … I'm *self-aware*. I'm seeing
what this guy's seeing: a bellicose drunk getting a blow-job from
a midget. A guy getting sucked off while hurling abuse at the
suckee. A midget dressed as a friggin' leprechaun. And from his
point of view I'm thinking that he could construe this as some
tramp in a suit being racially offensive to the Irish. Which was

not in fact the fuckin' case. And this … it's the opposite … And this guy's just watchin' me. And in his face I see *disgust*. In his eyes I see disgust and *pity*. *PITY?!* A postman is pitying *me*? A fuckin' deadbeat, rainy-day *postman*? I get to where I am today walking in these shoes, and this guy is takin' time out of his petty little fuckin' life to pity *me*? Now my temper is going in another direction *entirely*. Now I'm thinking 'You self-righteous little shit. Ya little … You pond-life, you bottom-feeder, ya fuckin' troglodyte!' So I turn to him and look him in the eye: 'Fuck you lookin' at, asshole? Wanna piece of this, huh? Want me to blow you away?' Then, *self-awareness* hits me again and I realise that I'm sayin' these words to him with my *dick* in my hand. And he sees this. An' ya know? Ya know what the cocksucker does now? He starts to laugh. Tha' fuck. And I know by the sound of that laugh that he's *German*. I just *know it*. An' you know how I hate the Germans? Especially one in a uniform. And he sees quite fucking clearly the change in me now and he stops laughin'. *Yes.* Even though my Johnny Thomas is hangin' out danglin' like a fat fish and there's piss all down my trouser leg, he's stopped laughing. *Yes.* He's not laughin' any more. *No.* No more shall that Nazi supercilious fuck laugh at a decent man caught in the moment of a small indiscretion. (*A small, sudden violence.*) BAM! Pops 'im clean through the forehead. Drops like a side of beef. BUMPF. His face is gone. BAM! One more in his fat ass just for good measure. BAM! I shoot the leprechaun, put my piece back in my pants, put my dick back in my johns and take a leisurely stroll over to the call box. Dial your number like I'm in a dream. I tell ya, I felt better. I released something. And it wasn't just a bladder full of piss. I felt different. Better. Elevated … Something … ya know? I did the world a couple of favours in the space of a few heartbeats and I didn't get paid a fucking *dime*.

Pause.

Harvey Huh?

He lifts a bundle at his feet: a large pair of shoes upon a crumpled blue uniform and a postman's mail sack. He goes to the furnace and throws them into the flames.

Free will. *Yes.* That's what that is. Yes. *Free will.* It's not all about money. Sometimes ... sometimes you just gotta do what you think is right.

Beat.

I'm hungry.

Blackout.

Music: 'Bad Moon Rising' by Creedence Clearwater Revival.

Act One

Scene One

The Shamrock bar.

Late morning. A Brooklyn Irish bar. The men occupy this space as if it's their own. For the moment there is no drink being taken. There is a palpable restless male energy in the room.

'Bad Moon Rising' continues to play on a jukebox at the end of the bar. **Rourke** *dances in front of it.* **Wicklow** *and* **Antrim** *dance near him. As the music finishes,* **Rourke** *punches the jukebox and laughs.*

Rourke   Takin' it to the church!

Wicklow   I'm outta breath.

Rourke   Love that fuckin' song.

Antrim   It's good.

Rourke   We're goin' to the fuckin' moon!

Antrim   It's a good song.

Rourke   I'm gonna play it again.

O'Hare   No. I'm sick listening to it.

Rourke   C'mon. 'S great tune.

O'Hare   Not after the third time.

Rourke   C'mon, Mary.

O'Hare   Don't call me that.

Rourke   What's a matter?

O'Hare   I'm fuckin' serious.

Rourke   Keep your hair on.

Wicklow *begins to sing.* **Rourke** *and* **Antrim** *join in.*

Wicklow
> Oh sugar, sugar, do do do do do do
> Oh honey, honey, do do do do do do
> You are my candy girl,
> And you got me wanting you …

Rourke   Who sings that one?

Wicklow   Fuck knows. Good tune though.

O'Hare   What time you got?

Rourke   Quarter past.

O'Hare   What time he say he'd be here?

Rourke   Fifteen minutes ago.

O'Hare   Should we be worried?

Rourke   Probably just runnin' late.

O'Hare   What do ya call that stuff, anyways?

Rourke   What?

O'Hare   That fuckin' stuff on the ceiling?

Rourke   Blood?

O'Hare   Nah. That twirly shit up there?

Rourke   Where?

O'Hare   Round the light. The swirls and stuff?

Rourke   The decorative stuff?

O'Hare   Yeah.

Lumpy   Filigree.

They all look at **Tom 'Lumpy' Flannegan**, *who is eating a foot-long hotdog.*

Rourke   Guy's a regular thesaurus.

O'Hare   A what?

Rourke   Thesaurus.

O'Hare   Fuck's that?

Rourke   It's Greek.

Wicklow   Fuckin' Greeks.

Rourke   Means 'house of words'.

Wicklow   Faggots.

Rourke   Guy's a house of words.

Wicklow   Guy's a house.

Lumpy   Filigree. Definition: 'ornamental art'.

Rourke   See?

Lumpy   Synonyms: fretwork, lattice, interlace, arabesque, braid, curlicue, finery, frill, frippery, furbelow, garniture, gewgaws, gilt, spangle, tinsel, trinket … wreath.

Beat.

Antrim   Fuck.

Wicklow   Curly-cue?

Rourke   Impressive, ain't he?

O'Hare   Still doesn't tell me what that is?

Rourke   He just said.

O'Hare   He said a lotta stuff.

Rourke   And it all means pretty much the same thing. Don't it, Lumpy?

Lumpy   Kinda.

O'Hare   Where'd you learn all them words anyways?

Lumpy   *Reader's Digest.*

Rourke   I'm thirsty.

O'Hare   Must have a good memory.

Wicklow   Stores it in his fat.

Rourke   Ignore 'im, Tommy.

O'Hare   Fili … filla – what the fuck is it?

Lumpy   Filigree.

O'Hare   OK.

Lumpy   My favourite word? Lately?

Antrim   I can remember the day I was born.

Wicklow   Crap.

Lumpy   'Fulminate'.

Wicklow (*generally, indicating* **Antrim**)   Yous hear what this guy just said?

Lumpy (*speaking through the following dialogue*)   'Fulminate'. Definition: criticise harshly. Synonyms: berate, castigate, declaim, denounce, rage, rail, reprobate, thunder … vituperate.

Wicklow   Says he can remember bein' born.

Antrim   Like it was yesterday.

Wicklow   You can't remember two minutes ago.

Antrim   I remember plenty.

Wicklow   Go shit yourself a new brain.

O'Hare   An' that all means the same as, the same as the word that you said?

Lumpy   Fulminate. They relate to it, yeah. They're synonyms.

O'Hare   Cinnamons?

Lumpy   Synonyms. Means 'synonymous with'. Alternatives.

Antrim (*quietly*)   Syn – on – yms.

Rourke   I need a drink.

O'Hare   Fuck me. That's crazy.

Wicklow   What is?

O'Hare   As if there aren't enough fuckin' words in the world as it is an' then along comes all these other words that mean the same thing?

Lumpy *nods.*

Rourke   Anybody seen Harve?

O'Hare   That's fuckin' crazy.

Wicklow   What's crazy?

O'Hare   All the fuckin' words in the world.

Wicklow   Does seem to be a lot of 'em, alright.

O'Hare   It's fucked-up.

Wicklow   How is it? Why?

O'Hare   As if it isn't hard enough as it is to understand people, ya know? As if it isn't hard enough already to know what the fuck some guys rabbitin' at ya, without all these other words complicatin' everything and everythin'. You know?

Rourke   Muddying the water, so to speak?

O'Hare   Yeah. Do we really need it?

Rourke   Muddying the water, an' all.

O'Hare   Do we really need all these, these, whadda ya call 'em?

Rourke   What?

O'Hare   These extra words.

Lumpy   Embellishments.

O'Hare   Huh?

Lumpy   Filigree. Verbal ornamentation. You're saying that all these extra words are just frills and frippery?

O'Hare   That's exactly what I'm saying. Frills and frippery. Do we really need 'em?

Rourke   I'm inclined to agree with ya, Marion.

O'Hare   Huh?

Rourke   I'm inclined to say 'fuck words'.

O'Hare   But you know what I mean?

Rourke   I do. I really do. Anybody seen Harvey?

Antrim   He's with Walter. On a job.

O'Hare   All these words.

Wicklow   Yeah.

O'Hare   There's too many of 'em. Fuckin' words?

Rourke   They just complicate things.

O'Hare   They do.

Rourke   Yeah, they complicate things.

O'Hare   Hard enough to communicate with people as it is.

Rourke   Complications an' all.

O'Hare   Money. Now that's language.

Wicklow   Fuckin' A.

O'Hare   That's a fuckin' language we all speak.

Rourke   That's the one.

O'Hare   That's the one makes it all go round.

Wicklow   Money.

O'Hare   That's the one.

Rourke   Dollars.

Wicklow   Bingo-bango. Gimme some of them.

O'Hare   We earn it. Deserve it. And these fucks try and deprive us of it?

Antrim   Who?

O'Hare   Government. With all their government speech and politicians. I know. I deal with these fucks every day.

Rourke   What?

O'Hare   They don't talk straight. They don't walk on the narrow.

Wicklow   Like 'law-speak'.

O'Hare   Huh? Exactly.

Wicklow   The way lawyers speak.

Rourke   Assholes.

O'Hare   Exactly.

Wicklow   All shit they say.

Lumpy   Babel.

O'Hare   Huh?

Wicklow   All the shit.

O'Hare   Why can't they just speak fuckin' English?

Rourke   Fuck English.

O'Hare   Why?

Rourke   We don't speak English.

O'Hare   No.

Lumpy   Anglo-Irish American.

O'Hare   Fuck is that?

Lumpy   What we're speakin' now. Isn't that right, Johnny?

Rourke   Speakin' straight. Speakin' true.

Wicklow   Lawyers is the opposite.

O'Hare   They use that wise-guy talk to confuse the man off the street.

Rourke   Assholes.

O'Hare   All of 'em …

Wicklow   'S like they're talkin' fuckin' Latin.

Rourke   Assholes.

O'Hare   'Blah-blah de-blah blah-blah.' What the fuck does that mean?

Antrim   Means: 'Fuck you, I got an education!'

Wicklow   Fuckin' lawyers.

O'Hare   A guy should talk straight.

Rourke   Fuckin' A.

O'Hare   A guy should say what he means.

Rourke   I agree.

O'Hare   Huh?

Rourke   Say what he means.

O'Hare   Hard enough as it is understanding people as it is.

Wicklow   Yeah. I shouldn't say this …

Rourke   What?

Wicklow   I shouldn't say it.

O'Hare   Go on. Say it.

Wicklow   I spoke to a guy straight off the boat, ya know, from back home?

Antrim   Ireland?

Wicklow   No. Fuckin' Poland.

Rourke   Whereabouts?

Wicklow   The fucking Republic of Cork.

Rourke   Jeeez. A Cork man?

Wicklow   Straight off of the fuckin' boat. Yesterday. I was doin' the Hudson shake.

Rourke   How'd that go, by the way?

Wicklow   Pretty good. So, he asks me for a light … I swear to God, God forgive me, I couldn't understand a fuckin' word.

Rourke   Yeah?

Wicklow   It was just noise. (*The musicality of a Cork accent.*) Waaww, waw-waw-waw-waawww!

Lumpy   Poor bastard.

Wicklow   It was just noise. Waaaw-waw-waw.

Antrim   They probably said the same of your folk.

Wicklow   What?

Antrim   When they washed up here.

Wicklow   Hey. We're Dubliners. Born and bred.

Antrim   Like I said.

Wicklow   Fuck you.

Lumpy   We created the 'new' English.

O'Hare   Huh?

Lumpy   American. **Rourke**   That's right.

O'Hare   Huh?

Lumpy   'So long'. Know where that came from?

Rourke   Wait'll you hear about this.

O'Hare   What?

Rourke   This is great.

O'Hare   What?

Lumpy   'So long'? Comes from Irish Gaelic: '*Slán.*'

Beat.

O'Hare   Get outta here.

Rourke   John fuckin' Wayne. 'So long!'

Lumpy   *Slán.*

O'Hare   Jesus H. Christ. He's fuckin' right!

Lumpy   Sucker. You know where that comes from?

Antrim   What?

Lumpy   Slang word, 'sucker', comes from the Irish *sach ur*. Means 'fresh, well-fed fellow' or 'fat cat'.

Wicklow   Get the fuck?

Lumpy   'S true.

O'Hare   Who would a' thought.

Rourke   Crazy, huh?

O'Hare   I use that word all the time.

Antrim   Me too.

O'Hare   Every fuckin' day of my life.

Rourke   It's Irish.

O'Hare   I don't know about yous, but I'm feeling a small pang of pride here.

Rourke   Without even knowing it, you been speaking Irish all your goddam life.

Laughter.

O'Hare   All my life.

A noise outside and they all instantly look to the door. It opens and **Gulliver Sullivan** *walks in – a charismatic man who has*

aged well and dresses flawlessly. Those seated stand, except
O'Hare*, in deference to their boss. He motions for them to sit
with a benevolent smile.*

Sullivan   Gentlemen, I apologise for the early meeting but we
have important matters to discuss. But, before we conduct our
business, I'm going to introduce you to someone. Now I want you
to be civil and watch your language.

*He motions to someone beyond the doorway. A sixteen-year-old
boy enters in scruffy denims. He has unruly hair and big, serious,
unfathomable eyes.*

Sullivan   This is my nephew, Bobby.

They all mutter a greeting to the boy.

This sorry lot here are my employees. Come on in, Bobby, they
won't bite.

The boy shuffles forwards.

This here is Antrim O'Malley. Don't shake his hands, Bobby. God
knows where they've been. Greet him with your eyes, Daniel.
Now there's a smile. That there is Billy Wicklow. Beside him is
chief Marion O'Hare, NYPD.

O'Hare   Except I don't work for him, kid, we're business
associates.

Sullivan   That's what I let him think.

Laughter. Not from **O'Hare***.*

Sullivan   The big fella there is Tom Lumpy Flannagan, Jesus
Mary and Joseph, Tommy. Is it my imagination or have you put on
weight?

Lumpy   I have, Mr Sullivan.

O'Hare   Needs to eat more apples.

Lumpy   Apples?

O'Hare   They're a fruit. You eat 'em.

Sullivan   What's happening, Tom?

Lumpy   It's the sedentary lifestyle, Mr Sullivan.

Sullivan   It's the cakes, Lumpy. It's the *cakes*. And this? This reprobate is Johnny 'The Fox' Rourke. Bit of a ladies' man.

Rourke   I'm a magnet, Mr Sullivan. I can't help it.

Laughter.

Sullivan   You're a rogue.

Rourke   That I am.

Sullivan   Come see me afterwards, Johnny. Nice shoes. OK, fellas. Now listen up. Bobby here is over from Belfast. The old turf. Belfast, County Antrim. He had a little trouble there back home and his mom thought he might be better over here for a while. Maybe just for the summer until things cool down. And I want you to make him feel welcome. He's one of my family so treat him as such. But what am I doing? He's nearly a grown man he can speak for himself. Bobby?

Bobby *looks at* **Sullivan**.

Sullivan   Anything you'd like to say?

Bobby *looks at them all in silence. He shakes his head.*

Sullivan   Man of few words. I like that.

They laugh.

Sullivan   Man of few words.

Lumpy   Taciturn.

Sullivan   Hm?

Lumpy   Taciturn. Means 'man of few words'.

Sullivan   Yes.

Silence.

Sullivan   Welcome to Brooklyn, Bobby.

Blackout.

Scene Two

Sullivan*'s place.*

Sullivan *sits behind a large antique desk, a black Bakelite telephone within easy reach.* **Rourke** *stands in front of the desk, grinning.*

Rourke   How much?

Sullivan   A hundred thousand.

Rourke   A hundred grand? In cash?

Sullivan   Hundred-dollar bills.

Rourke *whistles.*

Sullivan   Tax-free.

Rourke *looks at him.*

Sullivan   That was a joke.

Rourke *laughs, perhaps obediently.*

Sullivan   I talked to him last night. He called me.

Rourke   So he's buying a truce?

Sullivan   You could say that.

Rourke   Marconi's bowing down to you.

Sullivan   Let's not get too carried away. 'It's a token of our new understanding.' His words. We're not allies all of a sudden. We're not climbing into bed with the Italians. We are just agreeing to stop trying to kill each other. Marconi's getting old. I guess he's tired of looking over his shoulder. It's his wish to die peacefully in bed and with the knowledge that his sons will outlive him.

Rourke   When's he payin' up?

Sullivan   Today. Tomorrow. He'll send two of his men when he has the money together.

Rourke   OK.

Sullivan   Now listen to me, John. Are you listening?

Rourke   I am.

Sullivan   Until I say otherwise there is to be no further conflict with the Italians. I want the men to know this. For the foreseeable future we are now at peace with Marconi and his men. However unpalatable that may be. All grudges are forgotten. All debts are paid. If I accept this offering into my hands it is a bond and I will not on principle break that bond. My word is iron. Anyone who jeopardises this arrangement will pay severely. Anyone screws it up is history. *Anyone.* We can't afford a war with the Italians.

Rourke   We'd kick their ass.

Sullivan   There would be a high body count, yes, but they outnumber us four to one. No. To survive we have to adapt. Now, on pain of death this peace will be upheld. Do I make myself clear?

Rourke   Yes. Yes, Mr Sullivan.

Sullivan   Good. Tell the boys. Do not mention the money. You hear me? That's between you and me. But you tell them my orders. Marconi offered a truce. End of story. And be sure to tell Walter and Harvey. O'Keefe, Ryan and Joey too. No more yahoos. I want this ceasefire operational from the moment I finish this sentence.

Pause.

Rourke   Understood.

Sullivan   Good.

Pause. **Sullivan** *studies* **Rourke**.

Sullivan   How are you?

Rourke   Me? I'm good.

Sullivan   Yeah?

Rourke   Yeah. Couldn't be better.

Pause.

Sullivan   When was the last time you were in church?

Rourke   When was the last time? In church? I dunno. Richy's funeral?

Sullivan   I mean of your own free will.

Rourke   I dunno. A while?

Sullivan   You should go.

Rourke   Yeah?

Sullivan   Yes.

Rourke   OK then. I will.

Sullivan   Good.

Pause

How is sobriety?

Rourke   Good. Thinkin' straight. Thinkin' true.

Sullivan   Good.

Pause.

How are the guys?

Rourke   They're good.

Sullivan   No rumblings?

Rourke   Not that I can hear.

Sullivan   Good. Keep an ear out.

Rourke   Sure.

Pause.

Sullivan   I rely on you, Johnny. You're my left hand. I trust you. Don't disappoint me.

Rourke   I won't.

Sullivan   I know.

Blackout.

Scene Three

The Hudson River. Docks.

The deep, mournful wail of a foghorn. The sound of water lapping against concrete.

Lights up on:

Chief **Marion O'Hare**. *He is dressed in a large black police-issue coat, his hands buried deep in the pockets. He is singing 'Danny Boy' quietly to himself but he is not the best of singers and his heart isn't in it.*

Sullivan *approaches silently behind him.*

Sullivan   You're scaring the fish.

O'Hare *starts.*

O'Hare   Jesus. I didn't hear you comin'. You alone?

Sullivan   What's the rumpus?

O'Hare   All this shit with the moon. City's gone crazy. I mean, why the fuck would anyone wanna go up there in the first place? It's crazy. You gonna watch it?

Sullivan   I'm busy.

O'Hare   I gotta. The boys wanna watch it. Wife bought a new TV set. Month's fuckin' wages.

Sullivan   Why am I here?

Beat.

O'Hare   Couple a' things.

Sullivan   Shoot.

O'Hare   Hennessey.

Sullivan   Jim Hennessey? What about him?

O'Hare   He's mouthin' off.

Sullivan   What's he saying?

O'Hare   I'm embarrassed to tell ya.

Sullivan   Tell me.

O'Hare   He's an asshole. He's getting real cocky.

Beat.

He's saying things. In public, ya know?

Sullivan   No. I don't know. Tell me.

O'Hare   I dunno, Gulliver.

Beat.

Sullivan   Speak.

Beat.

O'Hare   He's sayin' you're on the way out. Can you believe this? He has the balls to say this. He says the Italians are takin' over and the Irish are on their way out. He said … an' this is in Joe's Bar, ya know, full a' cops, he says this in front of everyone, he says, and forgive me for sayin' this 'cause it's unkind and untrue. He says 'Sully's an old-school muck-savage. A ditch-digging immigrant. He hasn't got the balls or know-how any more to stand up to the Italians.'

Pause.

Sullivan   Go on.

O'Hare   He says the Irish gangs is over. He said 'Sullivan's a dinosaur and I ain't paying another fuckin' dime to 'im.' That's what he said. Thereabouts. Didn't say it to me but I was there. He was speakin' loud. I heard some of it, so I swear on my fuckin' life, that's what he said.

Sullivan   You didn't hear all of it?

O'Hare   Not all of it, but I heard what I had to hear.

Pause.

Sullivan   Who was he talking to?

O'Hare   He was talkin' loud.

Sullivan   Who?

O'Hare   Couple of guys I didn't recognise. And another guy was one of Marconi's.

Sullivan   Marconi. You're sure about this?

O'Hare   Yeah. Name's Manfreedee or somethin'. I dunno, they all sound like dishes off of a menu to me.

Beat.

I hate being the bearer of bad tidings an' all that.

Beat.

I just thought you should know.

Pause.

Sullivan   You and Hennessey have never been the best of friends.

O'Hare   I hate him, the lippy fuck. But what of that?

Pause.

Sullivan   What's the other thing?

O'Hare   Huh?

Sullivan   You said 'a couple of things'.

O'Hare   Yeah.

Beat.

Sullivan   Well?

O'Hare   Harvey.

Beat.

Harvey Marr.

Beat.

A fuckin' postman?

Beat.

What's that about?

Beat.

Guy's off his nuts. I mean a *postman*? How am I gonna explain this away? It isn't easy. Makes things difficult. Sorrow's good. He's good at his job. In, out, everything clean, but people ask questions. A junkie or a black kid maybe, but a postman? Poor bastard's only probably goin' about his business. People like postmen. Postmen are people.

Sullivan   Now he's cinders. Anybody report him missing?

O'Hare   Not yet.

Sullivan   A lonely guy.

O'Hare   We don't know.

Sullivan   Witnesses?

O'Hare   Nobody come forward yet. Nobody's sayin' anything, but that doesn't mean they didn't see anything.

Pause.

Sullivan   Let's play it by ear. It'll go away.

O'Hare   If it doesn't?

Sullivan   Make something up.

O'Hare   Like what?

Beat.

Sullivan   He was pushing drugs on his post round. A local gang whacked him. End of story.

O'Hare   And Harvey?

Sullivan   Leave him to me.

O'Hare   He's a loose cannon.

Sullivan   He had a bad day.

O'Hare   He's a liability.

Beat.

Sullivan   Don't make me explain myself to you.

Pause.

Sullivan *produces a thick brown envelope and passes it to*
O'Hare*.*

Sullivan   Go buy your wife a hat.

O'Hare *weighs the envelope in his hand.*

O'Hare   This all?

Sullivan   Don't get greedy, O'Hare. It's a deadly sin.

O'Hare *puts the envelope into his coat pocket. He pauses as if to
say something, then thinks better of it and leaves. For a moment*
Sullivan *is left standing alone.*

Wicklow *appears silently from the shadows and arrives at his
side.*

Sullivan   Prospect Heights. 589 Vanderbilt Avenue. He lives
alone. Use your feet.

Beat.

Wicklow   He have a name?

Sullivan   Hennessey. *Blackout.*

Scene Four

A tenement rooftop garden. Night.

*The muted sounds of the city: the low hum of traffic, car horns, the
distant wail of police sirens.*

Lights up slow to reveal a rooftop garden, tenderly cared for.

Sullivan *and* **Bobby** *stand looking out and up at a full moon.*

Sullivan   'We choose to go to the moon in this decade and do the
other things, not because they are easy but because they are hard.'
An Irishman said that eight years ago in the state of Texas. His
name was John F. Kennedy and he was president of the greatest
country in the world. A true pioneer. From Ireland, to America,
to the moon. That's quite a journey. I thought him a great man.
Others disagreed. They put a bullet in his head and sent him to
God.

Pause.

There will come a day, Bobby, when God will judge me. It'll be
swift as I imagine there will be quite a queue. And in those brief
moments of appraisal, in those seconds of recognition, I believe
my Lord God will see necessity in my actions. I believe that he
will say '*This man did what he had to do.*' God forbid I become
a man who is haunted by his actions. No. My conscience is clear.
I have done and will continue to do what has to be done. I'm not
a good man, I'm not a bad man neither. I'm not a genius, but I'm
not stupid. But I'm true to my word. My word is iron. And I act as
the situation requires me to.

Silence.

They continue to look out …

This city is changing. Different world from when I was a boy. You
know what getting old is? Getting old is slowly losing everything
that you're familiar with.

Silence.

He suddenly stamps his foot. It makes a dull thud.

You hear that?

He stamps his foot again.

Try it.

The strangeness of this request makes **Bobby** *smile
self-consciously.*

Sullivan   Go on.

Bobby *tentatively stamps his foot.*

Sullivan   Again. Harder.

Bobby *stamps his foot harder.*

Sullivan   Feels good, doesn't it? You know why? Under
your feet? That's turf from Kildare. Horse country. There's an
energy in it. I had it shipped over from home. Little bit of home.
These trees? Apple tree from County Armagh. Apple country.
Ecclesiastical capital of Ireland. Ash tree from Fermanagh. That's
a blackthorn from Letterkenny, County Donegal. That's a sapling
oak from County Cavan. Don't know where that is, but it's
somewhere in the middle. Lavender from County Clare. Put this
under your pillow, helps you sleep. Laurel tree from Hillsborough,
County Down. Nasturtiums from a window box in Derry City. The
walled city. This is my little bit of home. My little piece of Eden.
This is home.

They look out into the night.

Sullivan   You know what Ireland is, Bobby?

Bobby *looks up at* **Sullivan** *with an unreadable expression and
after a moment slowly shakes his head.*

Sullivan   Ireland is where the wind blows it.

Pause.

You miss it?

A small nod from **Bobby**.

Sullivan   You leave Ireland, Bobby, you never really leave it.
It's always there. It's like the moon. Always with you, even when
you can't see it. It's like it's got a pull on you. I know a lot of men
here who pine for it and they've never even been there.

Pause.

You cold?

Bobby *shakes his head.*

Sullivan   You want my jacket?

Bobby *shakes his head.*

Sullivan   C'mon. Take my jacket.

*He takes off his jacket and drapes it around **Bobby**'s thin shoulders.*

Sullivan   There you go. That's better. We gotta feed you up.

Pause.

Don't lie to your family, Bobby. Blood. Honour your blood. Be true to it. You do something wrong, somethin' keeps you awake at night, somethin' makes your brain go gurgle? You go to the church and you confess. Not everything. Sometimes you have to be economical with the truth, for your sake and whoever it is that's listening. But you sit there and you dump it in the confession box. That's what it's there for. It's a laundromat. The Irish American Catholic's laundromat of the soul. That's what it's for. I'm not criticising it. I value it. It's the rock upon which I have built my life. Without the church the Irish would be a defeated people long ago. It gave us succour when we suffered. The Irish race have suffered. Maybe more even than the Jews. They teach you about the famine back home?

Bobby *nods.*

Sullivan   Then you know what I'm talking about. A nation of exiles. Adversity. But we are a resilient people and I have come to believe that in exile a man finds his true nature. Look at what we have achieved. We built this country with our bare hands. Nearly broke our backs doing it. Once we were thought of no better than slaves. They called us pale Indians. White Negros. Now they call us Governor, Senator, President. How about that? Sixteen presidents of Irish descent. We number half the NYPD and we practically founded the FBI. 'S true. The Irish made America. Then all the others started pouring in. But enough of that. What I'm saying, Bobby, is … you're home. And don't let anyone ever disrespect you because of your heritage. You pop 'em in the kisser and then remind them that America is what it is today because of an exodus from the old country a hundred years ago. They disrespect you again? You put 'em down for good. Sometimes, words are not enough. You hear me, Bobby? You hear what I'm telling you?

Bobby *nods.*

Sullivan   And always keep your shoes clean. Good shoes are important. We are who we are from the ground up.

Pause.

Your mother ever talk about me? She ever tell you what I do?

Bobby *looks at him.*

Sullivan   I am a peacekeeper, of a kind. I'm a business man first but I also keep the peace. Ten blocks that way and about twenty blocks that way. That's a lot a' ground. I have men who work for me, some of whom you have met, and they help me do what I have to do. Some of them are policemen, some civil servants, some of them straight off the boat, and some of them are politicians. Yes, even politicians. They come to me because, like I said, sometimes words are not enough. I do what the police and the politicians can't or won't be seen to be doing. I do the unseen. I just try to keep things running smoothly. It ain't easy. The nature of man dictates that things never always run according to plan. There's always a kink. Always a bubble that needs smoothed out. What's needed is an iron hand. And that I provide. A civic duty. And I profit from it.

Pause.

He takes out his wallet and opens it. It is thick with money. He takes a twenty-dollar bill from the wallet and holds it out to **Bobby**.

Sullivan   This is the only money I'm ever going to give you, Bobby. The rest ... you have to earn.

Bobby *looks at the money.*

Sullivan   Go on, take it.

Bobby *takes the money.*

Sullivan   The world can be an ugly place, Bobby. Man's nature
makes it so. You're nearly a man, so the sooner you learn that
the better. I know that you came from a troubled place. You saw
things. You'll see things here … But hear and believe this: all that
I do is for the greater good. You hear me? I seek the *light*, Bobby,
for in *darkness* we dwindle.

They look out together for a moment, up at the moon.

Hey.

Bobby *looks at him.*

Sullivan   You wanna steak?

Bobby *smiles briefly.*

Blackout.

Act Two

Scene One

An apartment. Prospect Heights. Day. Darkness.

Heavy breathing. Muttered curses. The unseen labours of several men. The sound of something being kicked repeatedly.

Another sound: becoming discernible, the reverential tones of a news commentator reporting live on the Apollo 11 moon landing.

Lights up slow on **Rourke** *and* **Bobby**. *They sit on a threadbare sofa downstage right in front of a television perched on a wooden stool. The flickering light from the TV screen illuminates* **Rourke**'*s face: intense concentration, a barely contained, childlike excitement.*

Bobby *is beside him. Only the back of his head is visible. He is looking over the back of the sofa, upstage into the darkness. He seems captivated, riveted by the spectacle of what we can hear but cannot yet see.*

The quiet sound of kicking continues through the following. **Rourke** *does not take his eyes from the screen.*

Rourke   Jesus …

Beat.

Jesus Christ …

Beat.

Jesus H. Christ …

Pause.

Shit me … You see this, Bobby? This is history. Right here. Right now. This is huge. You'll remember this. Mark my words. Like the day they shot Kennedy. Forty years from now you'll remember where you were when man first set foot on the moon. With your Uncle Johnny. Man's gonna walk on the *moon*. Can you believe

it? Man's gonna walk on the moon and we're gonna *watch* him! I
can't decide which is crazier. We're goin' to another world. Buck
Rogers. Captain fuckin' Kirk. After this? Mark my words, Bobby,
after this, nothing will be the same again. The world changes from
this day on. From here on in. This is the greatest moment in the
history of, of, of man! Soon as he steps out up there … Boom!
Man loses his virginity. That's kinda what it is. We're about to lose
our cosmic virginity. (*Grinning.*) How about that? You know how
many people are watching this? Three billion. Around the world.
That's half the population of the planet. This is history. You wanna
know something funny? Man flying the Command Module? The
little ship circlin' the moon's gonna bring those guys back home?
Know what his name is? Nobody else seems to have picked up on
this but it doesn't escape me. I notice these things. The man flyin'
the Command Module is called, get this, Michael Collins. (*Laughs.*)
How about that? An Irish revolutionary in space. Flyin' round the
moon! Mike Collins. Stranger than fiction. They gotta be related.

In a sudden explosion of irritation **Rourke** *glances back into the
darkness.*

*He snaps back to the TV as lights come up slow upstage and
discover what is holding* **Bobby**'s *attention.*

*Three men are revealed darkly. They surround the prone shape of
a curled-up body, a lifeless thing animated in jolts by their kicking
feet. They go about this methodically, with no sense of passion,
only a slow, steady dedication to their work.*

Rourke   Guys! Fuck me!

Wicklow   What?

Rourke   We're watching this here!

Wicklow   Well, we're workin' over here.

Rourke   Keep the noise down, can't ya?

Antrim   This is business.

Rourke   Why can't you use a bullet like any other decent human
being?

He returns to the TV.

Assholes. Bobby, don't look at that, look at this.

Bobby *looks briefly at the TV, but in moments his attention returns to the action upstage.*

Lumpy *stops kicking and steps back from the others, clutching his right arm. He has a half-eaten hotdog in one hand. The others stop.*

Wicklow   Whatcha doin'?

Lumpy   My arm hurts.

Wicklow   You unfit fat fuck. (*To* **Antrim**.) His arm hurts.

Antrim   Fuck his arm. My feet hurt. Isn't he dead yet?

Wicklow   Oh yeah. He's dead ages ago.

Antrim   Then why are we still kickin' 'im, then?

Wicklow   Mr Sullivan wants him to suffer.

Lumpy   Well, he's double dead so let's call it quits.

Wicklow   What, are we keepin' you from your food?

Lumpy   My arm hurts.

Wicklow   Probably havin' a heart attack, you fat fuck.

Antrim *laughs.*

Lumpy   Stop callin' me that.

Wicklow *laughs.*

Lumpy   I'm serious! You're giving me a complex.

Wicklow   I'll give you complex right up your big fat ass, you bucket of blubber.

Antrim *suddenly looks down at the body.*

Antrim   You hear that?

Wicklow   What?

Antrim   He made a noise.

Lumpy   Him?

Antrim   Yeah.

Wicklow   Probably air escaping.

Antrim   No.

Wicklow   Punctured lung.

Antrim   No, it came from his face.

Wicklow   You sure?

Antrim   Yeah. Where his face should be.

Wicklow   Did he say something?

Antrim   Yeah. Maybe.

Lumpy   What he say?

Antrim   How the fuck should I know?

Wicklow   Listen and see if he's breathing.

Antrim   I ain't getting down in that shit.

Wicklow   C'mon, you're already bloody.

Antrim   Only my feet.

Wicklow   You're the one heard him.

Antrim   Maybe I imagined it.

Wicklow   Do it.

Antrim   Fuck.

Antrim *gets down and listens.*

Wicklow   Well? **Antrim**   Shhh! **Rourke** *glares at the TV.*

Rourke   What is that? Is that something? Is somethin'
happening? (*Beat.*) I wish something would happen. (*Beat.*) The
moon. Can you imagine it? Walking on the moon. Pure white.

No air. No sound. No cars. No garbage. No blood. Least not yet anyways. Pure as virgin snow. Like the Antarctic. Only in space. (*Beat.*) The space age they're callin' it. In our lifetime. And it all starts here. It's a good time to be alive, Bobby.

Antrim *stands.*

Wicklow   Well?

Antrim   He's still breathing.

Wicklow   Fuck.

Antrim   Tough old bird, I'll give 'im that.

Lumpy   What do we do now?

Wicklow   We finish the job.

Antrim   With our feet?

Wicklow   Unless you wanna spoil your manicure? C'mon, you fuckin' micks.

Resigned, they begin to kick the dying man again.

Rourke   It's happening! Something's happening. What is that? It's all fuzzy and shit. I can't make that out, can you? Bobby, what is it? Is that the side of the space ship or somethin'? Is that what it is? All I can see is white. This picture's fuckin' terrible. People pay taxes for this? Picture's fuckin' – What is that?! Well, it's movin' whatever it is. Looks like a big fuckin' marshmallow. Is that a man? Is that –

He calls over his shoulder.

It's a man! It's a man! Guys! Guys! They're doin' it! They're about to do it! Watch this, Bobby. You'll be tellin' your grandchildren about this some day. Listen …

The TV crackles and the sound fades out.

Hennessey, you cheap piece of shit.

He swiftly thumps the side of the TV and the sound crackles back.

Armstrong (*voice-over*)   … OK … I'm about to step off the ladder …

Rourke   Holy shit! Here we go! He's steppin' off ! (*Warning the TV.*) Don't make me hit you again. Guys! He's stepping off the ladder! Keep it down! He's about to do it!

Beat.

Armstrong (*voice-over*)   … leap for mankind.

Pause.

Rourke   What'd he say?

Pause.

Rourke   Was that it? Leap for mankind? A leap? Jesus Christ. And that's it? Did we miss something? Christ. He must a' said somethin' before that and we missed it. We missed it! (*Over his shoulder.*) You selfish cocksuckers! What did he say, Bobby? Did you hear?

Bobby *shakes his head.*

Rourke   'Leap for mankind'. Underselling it a little, ain't he? A leap? Greatest moment in history? A leap? We must a' missed it. Shit.

The other three amble over with a box of tissues. They stop around the back of the sofa and begin wiping blood from their shoes with the tissues. **Rourke** *continues watching the TV.* **Bobby** *continues to stare at the dead man.*

Lumpy   They do it?

Rourke   Yeah.

Lumpy   What they say?

Rourke   Leap for mankind.

Wicklow   Huh?

Rourke   He said 'Leap for mankind'.

Lumpy   Is that it?

Rourke   It's all I caught. He probably said something before that but I couldn't hear it over your fuckin' shenanigans.

Wicklow   That was business.

Rourke   It was barbaric.

Wicklow   Sullivan wanted him to suffer.

Rourke   Barbaric. And why couldn't you make him suffer in the next room?

Beat.

Antrim   It's got a carpet.

Rourke (*mimicking*)   'It's got a carpet'. You think he cares any more? Ya prick. We gotta friggin' kid sittin' here. No offence, kid. You're givin' him the wrong impression. We're not savages.

Lumpy   Sorry, kid.

Antrim   Yeah, Bobby. Sorry.

Rourke   You wanna apologise to him for spoiling his enjoyment of the greatest moment in human fuckin' history.

Wicklow   What was that?

Rourke   A man just walked on to the moon, you shithead.

Wicklow   Nothin' to do with me.

Rourke   Fuckin' baboon.

Wicklow   Well, business is business. And you should a' been doin' your bit, Johnny.

Rourke   In hundred-dollar shoes?

Wicklow   Should of worn boots.

Rourke   Boots? With this suit?

Wicklow   Stop bein' a fag.

Rourke   Fuck you. Bunch of baboons.

Wicklow   We're professionals.

Rourke Hooligans, the lot of ya. Ignore them, Bobby. Savages. No sense of propriety. You follow my lead. Man needs a sense of propriety.

Bobby *is looking at him now, ashen-faced.*

Rourke   You OK, kid?

Bobby *suddenly lurches forward and vomits on* **Rourke***'s feet. Pause.*

Rourke *looks up at the three men while* **Bobby** *recovers.*

Rourke   Now look what you did?

Bobby *stands unsteadily and leaves.*

Rourke   You'll be OK, Bobby. Happens first time to everyone.

Antrim   Yeah, Bob. Happened to me.

Bobby *has gone.*

Rourke   Hundred-dollar shoes. Gimme those fuckin' tissues.

Blackout.

Scene Two

Tenement rooftop garden.

Sullivan   How's the boy?

Rourke   Bobby? He's good. He's good.

Sullivan   You're showing him the ropes?

Rourke   Yeah.

Sullivan   You're looking out for him?

Rourke   Like he was my own brother.

Sullivan   You make sure he eats.

Rourke   I'll take him for a burger.

Sullivan   Get him a milkshake. A cheeseburger. Kid needs calcium. He's got to grow.

Rourke   Cheeseburger it is.

Sullivan   It's early days but I'd like to see him stay on a while.

Rourke   Yeah?

Sullivan   I like having him around.

Rourke   He seems like a nice kid.

Sullivan   It's nice having family around.

Rourke   Funny, I don't remember you ever telling me you had a sister?

Sullivan   I didn't.

Beat.

Who knows? He might even want to come into the business. You know, he's the image of my mother.

Rourke   Yeah? He looks a little like you.

Sullivan   You think?

Rourke   Yeah. Round the eyes.

Pause.

Sullivan   He say anything to you?

Rourke   Like what?

Sullivan   Has he spoken to you?

Rourke   No. He's quiet as a mouse.

Sullivan   I think he has intelligence. You can see it in his eyes. He watches. He listens.

Rourke   What happened to him, back home?

Sullivan   His mother thinks he's probably better off here. And I'm inclined to agree. Lot of trouble kicking off over there.

Rourke   Same as it ever was.

Pause.

Sullivan   You talk to Harvey?

Rourke   Yeah.

Sullivan   How is the old dog?

Rourke   Sheepish.

Sullivan   He sober?

Rourke   Pretty much.

Sullivan   I can't talk to him when he's drinking. He has to understand that.

Rourke   I think he does.

Sullivan   We all have our cross to bear, John. Harvey's is a bottle of bourbon. Mine seems to be Harvey, but I can't keep turning a blind eye every time he goes on a rampage. Makes me look weak.

Rourke   It'll blow over.

Sullivan   Send him up.

Rourke *leaves.* **Sullivan** *is left alone. Distantly we hear men's laughter. Then, softly,* **Harvey** *begins to sing 'The Auld Triangle'. He enters upstage and approaches* **Sullivan** *slowly, singing. He arrives at* **Sullivan***'s side and after a beat* **Sullivan** *joins him in the song. He sings the harmony, gently, restrained. They finish the song and continue to look out in silence.*

Harvey   How are you, ya little bastard?

Sullivan   I've been better.

Harvey   You and me both.

Sullivan   I haven't seen much of you.

Harvey I been busy. You know, this and that.

Sullivan   How's your daughter?

Harvey She's clean. Pretty much.

Sullivan   And ... ...

Harvey Maggie? Oh, she's her grandaddy's little girl alright.
Real fiery. She'll do OK. You know, I seen more of her growing
up than my own daughter. I gave her a little doll an' all, ya know?
Candy and shit.

Sullivan   You're doing OK by them.

Harvey Yeah, well ... some things you just can't fix.

Sullivan   You did good by me, Harvey. You looked out for me. I
owe you.

Harvey You don't owe me nothin'.

Sullivan   I do and it's said.

Pause.

Harvey Is that an oak leaf ?

Sullivan   Five years old, from County Cavan.

Harvey Cavan, huh? Right in the middle. Your nasturtiums are
looking good.

Sullivan   Well, they'll grow anywhere.

Harvey They look good.

Beat.

Ya can eat 'em, ya know? ... Like in a salad. They're peppery.
Nutritious.

Sullivan   I didn't know that.

Pause.

Harvey I fucked up.

Beat.

I fucked up. I was drinkin' bourbon. My brain was on fire. But it'll never happen again. This is the last time. As true as I'm standing here. This is me. Never again.

Pause.

Sullivan   OK then.

Harvey   OK then …

Pause.

Harvey   Walter's downstairs. He's singin' 'Onward Christian Soldiers' to Bobby. Kid's lookin' at him like he's a talkin' mushroom. What you gonna do with him? Bobby. Ya gonna keep him on?

Sullivan   Maybe.

Harvey   You sure about that?

Sullivan *looks at* **Harvey**.

Sullivan   I want you to observe this truce with the Italians. You break it … I can't protect you. I mean it.

He means it.

Harvey   I let you down, I'll put a cap in my head myself.

Pause.

Oh yeah, I got you somethin'.

He produces a small paper packet and offers it to **Sullivan**.

Harvey   Take it. It's a gift.

Sullivan *takes the packet and opens it, watched by* **Harvey**.

Harvey   It's real gold. It's a tiepin. You put it on your tie. It's Cuchulain. You know? The greatest Irish warrior … You better like it. Pawned a medal for it.

Sullivan   You shouldn't have done that.

Harvey   Well I did and it's done. What, you don't like it?

Sullivan   I do. Thank you, Harvey.

Harvey   Ah, don't be gettin' all mushy on me. Here, let me fix it for ya.

*He puts it on **Sullivan**'s tie.*

Harvey   There ya go.

Sullivan   How do I look?

Harvey   Like a million dollars.

The moment is held while offstage, eight voices sing in perfect harmony:

'All around the banks of the Royal Canal
All around the banks of the Royal Canal.'

Scene Three

A diner.

Rourke *and* **Bobby** *sit opposite each other in a diner booth. Red leather seats and red-and-white checked plastic tablecloth. They are contained by a kind of sixties Formica nostalgia. A hooded red lamp illuminates their small table.*

Rourke   We watched the moon landing today in my mom's place. OK? She's a nice old lady. Wears a hair net and curlers an' all. Says she was born with her hair too straight. Donegal woman. She liked you.

Pause.

We watched the moon landing at my mom's place. In fact, tell you what, she gave us both a piece of her famous pumpkin pie. How about that? Wasn't it delicious?

Bobby *is staring out the window.*

Rourke   Hey. Bobby, you gotta look at me here.

Bobby *looks at him.*

Rourke   That's better. OK, so we were at my mom's today. She made us pie. She made us tea. Good old-fashioned God-honest Irish tea.

Pause.

What I'm saying … I'm just saying we don't need to tell your uncle about … you know? Might upset him. Let's just keep it to ourselves. It's not lying. It's … an omission. Something left out. Like garbage. Somethin' you leave out then forget about.

Pause.

Bobby, you gotta talk to me here. You're lookin' at me with those big serious eyes. You're doing intensity. I knew a lotta guys did intensity. They're all dead.

Beat.

Seriously though, you gotta open up a little. The silent thing gets a little creepy after a while to be honest with ya.

They study one another in silence. Nothing from **Bobby***.*

Rourke   What? You're lookin' questions at me, might as well speak 'em.

Pause. Nothing from **Bobby***.*

Rourke   How's your stomach?

Bobby *looks at him.*

Rourke   You wanna eat?

Bobby *nods.* **Rourke** *rises.*

Rourke   What you want? Cheeseburger and fries, milkshake?

Bobby *nods.*

Rourke   Back in a minute.

Rourke *leaves to order.* **Bobby** *is left alone. He picks up the salt shaker. Sets it down. He opens his mouth and closes it. He*

*continues to do this perhaps to amuse himself. He then takes out
the crumpled twenty-dollar bill* **Sullivan** *gave him and flattens it
neatly on the tabletop. He holds the bill up to the light and mouths
the words written there: 'In God We Trust'. He folds the money
and puts it back in his pocket.*

Rourke *returns to the booth with two burgers, fries and Cokes.*

Rourke   Here ya go. Cheeseburgers.

*He shares out the portions. He takes a quarter of whiskey out of
his pocket and empties half into his own measure of Coke, then
begins eating his burger.* **Bobby** *watches him. When* **Rourke**
*catches his eye he looks out the window. This continues for several
moments in silence.*

Rourke   What?

Bobby *shrugs.*

Rourke   Aren't you gonna touch your food?

Bobby *nods.*

Rourke   I been comin' here for years. Coffee's good. Always
been good. Puts hairs on your tongue. These burgers just slide
down. Gotta warn you though, they slide outta ya too.

Pause.

Bobby   Mr Rourke?

Rourke *freezes halfway through a bite of his burger.*

Rourke   Bobby?

Bobby   That man. Who was he?

Beat.

Rourke   He was … He was just a guy.

Bobby   What did he do?

Rourke   What did he do? Oh he was … He was a bad man. He
was stealing money off of your uncle Gulliver. Bad mouthing him,

you know? Disrespecting him to others behind his back. He was a bad mouth and a thief.

Bobby *picks at his fries.*

Rourke   I don't know if Mr Sullivan has explained this to you, but on the streets here we live by a code. Ya know? You stay by the code. Everybody knows that. You go outside of the code and shit all over it and where's the code any more? Ya know? Where do we go then? Flaunting rules, willy-nilly, soon there's gonna be anarchy. You need structure. A sense of propriety. You need rules. A code. Even chaos has friggin' rules. You don't need a fancy education to work that out. *The National Geographic.* Worth a read. That guy? He flaunted the rules. He deserves to be dead. I'm sorry though, Bob. I'm sorry if it upset ya. I am. You didn't have to see that.

Bobby   See what? We were at your mum's place.

Rourke *looks at* **Bobby.** **Bobby** *holds the look.* **Rourke** *nods.*

Rourke   Yes, we were.

They eat.

Bobby   You think they're still up there?

Rourke   Who? The astronauts? Nah. They only got so much oxygen to last or some such thing. No, they're on their way back home. They planted a flag. They're comin' home. Returning heroes. Lucky bastards.

They eat.

So, why you been so quiet?

Bobby *shrugs.*

Rourke   Huh?

Bobby   Just.

Rourke   What?

Bobby   Just.

Rourke   Just what?

Bobby   Never knew what to say.

Rourke Jesus, kid, no one knows what to say, they just say it. I mean, listen to those goons today. They just open their mouths and shit falls out. They don't make sense half the time.

Bobby   My mum says, 'Say less, learn more.'

Rourke   Yeah? Clever lady. So what have you learned so far?

Bobby   Are you a gangster, Mr Rourke?

Pause.

Rourke   Now that you're talkin' to me you might as well call me Johnny.

Bobby   Are you a gangster?

Rourke   What do you think?

Pause.

Bobby   The other men. They do what you tell them to do?

Rourke   Yeah. I'm kind a' second-in-command, I suppose. Kind a' like Mr Spock. My dad and Mr Sullivan were good friends. Dad died and … well, he looked out for me.

Bobby   Who looked out for him?

Rourke   Harvey Marr. Brooklyn legend. Decorated war hero. Last of his kind. Did for Sullivan what Sullivan did for me.

Bobby   Is he a good man?

Rourke   Your uncle? If it wasn't for him I'd probably be dead in a gutter with a knife in my guts years ago. He taught me somethin'. 'Self-worth' he calls it. He's as good as you get. True to his word. My word is iron.

Bobby   He said that.

Rourke   And he means it. He means it.

They eat in silence. Then …

Bobby   I'm sorry about your shoes.

Rourke   Don't mention it, kid.

*They continue to eat in silence as the lights fade on them.
Blackout.*

Scene Four

Sullivan's *place.*

A phone rings in darkness, then finally is silent.

Lights slowly up on **Sullivan** *and* **Rourke**. **Sullivan** *sits behind his
desk, a black Bakelite phone to his right.* **Rourke** *stands before
the desk. The door behind* **Rourke** *is slightly ajar.*

Sullivan   Sit down.

Rourke   Bobby's outside.

Sullivan   Close the door.

Rourke   What about Bobby?

Sullivan   Close the door and sit.

Rourke *goes to the door, closes it and takes a seat in front of*
Sullivan's *desk.*

Rourke   Everything OK?

Sullivan   No. Everything is not OK.

Rourke   OK.

Pause.

Sullivan   Have you been drinking?

Rourke   What? No.

Sullivan   Look at me.

Rourke *looks at him.*

Rourke   We were at the diner. We had burgers, fries and Cokes.

Sullivan   Don't take him into bars.

Rourke   I didn't.

Sullivan   He's too young.

Rourke   I wouldn't.

Sullivan   His father was a drunk. I don't want Bobby to follow him.

Rourke   We were at the diner.

Sullivan   Is he alone out there?

Rourke   Yeah.

Sullivan   Bring him in.

Rourke   You want him to hear this?

Sullivan   He might learn something.

Rourke   You sure?

Beat.

Rourke *goes to the door and beckons.* **Bobby** *enters. He seems to stand taller than before.*

Sullivan   Hello, Bobby. Why don't you wait by the door? Myself and Mr Rourke are going to have a business conversation. You're welcome to listen in.

Bobby *sits and* **Sullivan** *returns his full attention to* **Rourke.**

Sullivan   I received a phone call.

Rourke   From who?

Sullivan   Marconi.

Rourke   What did he want?

Sullivan   Well, he wasn't calling for a chat.

Rourke   Was it about the money?

Sullivan *nods.*

Rourke   Well, what did he say?

Sullivan   He said he sent it.

Rourke   When?

Sullivan   He said that he sent it over yesterday.

Beat.

He was phoning to inquire if I had received it and why I hadn't contacted him.

Rourke   You didn't get it?

Sullivan   No, I didn't.

Rourke   Shit.

Sullivan   Indeed. It gets worse.

Pause.

He said the two men who were delivering the money have gone missing.

Rourke *laughs nervously.*

Rourke   Well, that's convenient.

Sullivan   How is it?

Rourke   He's lying.

Sullivan   He gave me his word.

Rourke   And you believe him?

Sullivan   His word of honour.

Rourke   And what's that worth?

Beat.

Sullivan   It was his two most trusted men: Manfreedi and Mickey No-No.

Rourke   So they ran.

Sullivan   Unlikely.

Rourke   Yeah. Maybe they were pissed at him or somethin'.
They take the money and run.

Sullivan   For a hundred grand? I don't think so. Two connected
men don't disappear indefinitely for that kind of money. It's
diminutive. A million maybe. No. They didn't run.

Pause.

Rourke   Alright. So, assuming Marconi sent the money with
these goons and assuming they didn't run off with it, where does
that leave us?

Sullivan   I told Marconi, if there was foul play whoever was
responsible would pay with their life. I swore to him. I gave him
an oath.

*He studies **Rourke** in silence.*

Sullivan   Did you mention our conversation yesterday to
anyone?

Rourke   What? No.

Sullivan   You're sure?

Rourke   I told the boys about the truce with Marconi, like you
said, but I never mentioned the money.

Sullivan You're sure, John?

Rourke I swear on my life.

Pause.

Sullivan   What's your opinion of O'Hare?

Rourke   Mary? Honestly?

Beat.

Rourke   He's an asshole.

Sullivan   Why?

Rourke   He's dumb as shit.

Sullivan   Appearances can be deceptive.

Rourke   You think he plays dumb?

Sullivan   Maybe.

Rourke   He's too stupid for that.

Sullivan   He is Chief of Police.

Rourke   So he's good at kissin' ass.

Beat.

Sullivan   Do you trust him?

Rourke   I dunno, Mr Sullivan.

Sullivan   Should I trust him?

Rourke   You once told me to trust no one. Except family.

Sullivan *nods gravely.*

Sullivan   Just keep him at a distance. Be wary of him. Be casual, but be wary.

Rourke   OK.

Sullivan   In the meantime, it's in our interests as well as Marconi's to find these two men. If they can be found, I want the truth from them. They were driving a white Buick Riviera.

Sullivan *pushes a piece of paper towards* **Rourke***, who picks it up.*

Sullivan   That's the registration number. We're not doing this through the cops, so find other means. Put O'Keefe on to it. Ryan back from Chicago? Send him out too. If they are out there and breathing I want to be the first to talk to them. Understand?

Rourke *nods.*

Sullivan   Watch your back.

Rourke *leaves.*

Sullivan   Bobby, I need you to keep a low profile for a while, OK? No going out by yourself, even to the corner store.

Pause.

Bobby   Uncle Sullivan?

Sullivan   Bobby?

Bobby   I don't like him.

Sullivan   Who?

Bobby   The man you were just talking about. The policeman. I don't trust him.

Sullivan   Why do you say that?

Bobby   I don't like the way he looks at you.

The lights slowly fade.

Music: 'Born on the Bayou' by Creedence Clearwater Revival.

Blackout.

Act Three

Scene One

The Shamrock bar.

Lights up slow stage right on a man strapped to a wheeled swivel chair, head slumped, unconscious. He has his back to us. Around him the floor is splashed with drying blood.

Several feet away, opposite and facing the anonymous man in the chair, **Lumpy Flannegan** *kneels, slumped and motionless as if asleep or deep in prayer. A half-eaten hotdog lies on the ground beside him.*

The lights slowly reveal **Wicklow** *and* **Antrim**, *who stand stage left at the jukebox. They drink bottles of beer and share a joint. Casual.*

Wicklow Thirty years he gets. For choppin' up his wife. They put him in for life but he's out in thirty years. They put him in Penn State. He comes out a fuckin' automaton. Know what that is? A robot. Nothin' in his eyes. Dead inside. How he got his name: Sorrow. Empty. Looks like he just shat a cat. Now, to prepare him for the world outside of his incarceration they teach him a trade. A good idea. Huh? Except that they teach him butchery. OK? They teach a guy who chopped up his wife into tiny little fuckin' pieces how to use a machete properly. Go figure. So what have we got? So now the guy's an artist. Best butcher in the city. But no one will employ him. On account of his homicidal tendencies. One night he's sittin' here drunk at the bar contemplatin' all manner of suicide and who, who should walk in?

Antrim Who?

Wicklow Harvey Marr. Drunk as funk. Bingo-bango. The rest, my friend, is history. Sullivan's got himself a professional waste-disposal unit. Practically provided and paid for by the government. So, you see? The law? It's a joke. Doesn't work. The justice system? Fuck it.

Antrim   Yeah.

Wicklow   Tell me about it.

Antrim   What's the matter with him, anyways?

Wicklow   I just told yous.

Antrim   No. Harvey. He's crazy, right?

Wicklow   He drinks too much. Legendary. Back in the day, on the streets they called him Drum Belly.

Antrim   Why's that?

Wicklow   Used to take punches in his stomach for drink. A real iron man.

Antrim   Jeez.

Wicklow   Did a lotta drugs. Got one of his nuts shot off in the war.

Antrim   Guy's crazy.

Wicklow   His left one.

Antrim   A postman?

Wicklow   Go figure.

Antrim   I like 'im an' all, but he's nuts. Postmen are people.

Wicklow   He asks you to go for a drink with him, don't.

Antrim   Why?

Wicklow   Don't oblige him.

Antrim   Why?

Wicklow   You'll regret it.

Antrim   Why?

Wicklow   He asks me. Two beers in, he shoots a guy.

Antrim   Who?

Wicklow   Huh?

Antrim   Who was the guy?

Wicklow   I dunno. Neither does he. He's just some guy. He shoots him in the knee and shits in his car.

Antrim   No.

Wicklow   Yes.

Antrim   The guy's car?

Wicklow   Yes. The driver's side.

Antrim   Fuck.

Wicklow   Exactly. He must a' been drinkin' beforehand.

Rourke *enters with* **Bobby** *in tow.* **Rourke** *instantly sees the man in the chair and freezes.*

Antrim   Hiya, boys.

Rourke   What is this?

Wicklow   What?

Rourke   Bobby, go wait in the car.

Bobby   I wanna stay.

Rourke   Bobby –

Bobby   I'm staying.

Rourke   What in the name of Christ is happening here?

Wicklow   What?

Rourke   What am I seeing?

Wicklow (*indicates the victim*)   This? Sullivan's orders.

Rourke   He ordered this?

Wicklow   Yeah.

Rourke   Bullshit. Bobby wait in the car.

Antrim   Let 'im stay. Kid's seen worse.

Rourke (*to* **Antrim**)   Shut up. (*To* **Wicklow**.) Sullivan ordered this?

Wicklow   Yeah.

Rourke   He told you to do this, in person?

Wicklow   Yeah. What's the problem?

Rourke   What's the problem? The problem? Lemme see. What's the problem? (*He points at the man in the chair.*) He's the Chief of fuckin' Police!!

Wicklow *stares at* **Rourke** *blankly.*

Wicklow   So?

Rourke   You don't see a problem?

Wicklow   He's an asshole. Even you said.

Rourke   Christ!

Wicklow   What?

Rourke *quickly gathers himself.*

Rourke   Is he dead?

Antrim   Not yet.

Rourke   This is fucked-up.

Wicklow   You wanna beer?

Rourke   Why did Sullivan order this?

Wicklow   Didn't say.

Rourke   Well, what did he fuckin' say?!

Wicklow   Hey, don't get grumpy.

Rourke   Tell me, William.

Wicklow   He said invite the Chief round for drinks in the bar today. Lock the doors, rough him up and ask him what he knows about the money.

Rourke   The money?

Wicklow   Yeah. The money.

Rourke   What money?

Wicklow   He didn't specify. He just said to ask him what he knows about the money.

Rourke (*to himself*)   What the fuck would he know about the money?

Wicklow   What money?

Rourke   What?

Wicklow   You know somethin' we don't?

Rourke   Jesus.

Wicklow   Huh?

Rourke   Bobby. *Over here.*

Wicklow   Huh?

Rourke   He say anything?

Wicklow   Huh?

Antrim   Has this got somethin' to do with the Italians?

Wicklow   Shut up.

Rourke   What did he say?

Wicklow   Who?

Rourke   The man you have tied to the chair, fuckwit!

Wicklow   Don't use that tone with me, Johnny. I'm getting tired of it.

Rourke   Yeah? Oh, I'm sorry. Fuck you! You're an idiot. Both of ya. Do you know what you have done here?

Wicklow   Mr Sullivan's orders.

Rourke   Can't believe this. He tell you to stick a gun up your ass and pull the trigger, you do that too?

Antrim   Ours is not to question why, Joh –

Rourke   Shut up. (*To* **Wicklow**.) What did he say, O'Hare?

Wicklow   Oh, he said plenty.

Antrim   He's got a real dirty mouth on him. The language / you could a' toasted marshmallows with.

Rourke   Did he fess up?

Wicklow   Denied all knowledge of any money but what Sullivan gave him in an envelope yesterday. Know how much he got? Two grand. When am I gonna see that kinda money? I do more for Mr Sullivan than that tub of horseshit. I got bills. I got pressing matters. I gotta a cousin needs a … an operation or somethin'.

Rourke (*to* **Lumpy**)   Get up, Tommy.

Lumpy *doesn't move.*

Rourke   Lumpy!

Rourke *looks at* **Wicklow** *and* **Antrim**.

Rourke   What's the matter with him?

Antrim *starts to giggle uncontrollably.*

Rourke   Are you high?

Wicklow *laughs and tries to keep a straight face.*

Rourke   What?

Wicklow   Lumpy's dead.

Rourke   *What?*

Antrim   Dead. Definition: deceased. Synonyms …

Wicklow *and* **Antrim** *laugh.*

Rourke   What happened?

Antrim   Funniest thing you ever seen.

Rourke   What – Bobby, get away from him. What happened?

Wicklow   It was his turn to hit on the Chief.

Antrim   The funniest thing.

Wicklow   So he goes at it like a maniac. We'd been winding him up a little an' all, callin' him Fatty and what not, so he nearly takes the Chief 's head off. 'How'd ya like them apples, Mary?!' Boom! He's screamin': 'How'd ya like them apples?!' Then he stops, an' I thought he must a' bust his wrist or somethin' 'cause he grabs his arm and makes this little …

Wicklow *and* **Antrim** *laugh.*

Wicklow   This little squeak noise –

Antrim   Like a little fat mouse –

Wicklow   Then down he goes. Like a cow in a slaughterhouse. Lights out. I gotta say it was amusing.

Antrim   Look on his face like he just shit himself.

Wicklow   Squeak. Down he goes.

Antrim   Fuckin' priceless.

Rourke   Poor bastard.

Antrim   Like Harvey would say, 'Waste of space.' Him and Sorrow got a busy night.

Rourke   This is nuts.

Wicklow   Two grand.

Rourke   Look at ya. How could you be so stupid? How? Laurel and fuckin' Hardy.

Wicklow   Hey!

Rourke (*to* **Bobby**)   You see this?

Wicklow   Hey.

Rourke *indicates the room, the world.*

Rourke   You see this, kid?

Wicklow   I don't like your tone.

Rourke   Welcome to fuckin' Brooklyn, Bobby.

Wicklow   I don't like your tone no mores. Never did.

Rourke   Idiots.

Wicklow   I don't have to be talked to like that. I'm not gonna be talked to like that. We won't take that, will we, Danny?

Antrim *shrugs.*

Wicklow   We won't be talked to like that.

Rourke   Don't you see what you've done? This is it. You can't just sweep this under the carpet. This is serious. This is the goddam it. You hear me? This is the worst. This is FBI. We're dead men. All of us. This is it.

Wicklow   What is?

Rourke   Use your fuckin' brain, the two of ya. Jesus mother.

Wicklow   So what are you sayin'? We're in trouble?

Rourke   You have no idea.

Wicklow   It was Mr Sullivan's orders.

Rourke   Shut up. I'm thinkin'.

Wicklow *(quietly)*   His say-so.

O'Hare *groans and stirs. They all look at him.*

Rourke   Shit.

O'Hare   Mother-fuckers.

Rourke   Hello, Mary.

O'Hare   Son of a bitch.

Rourke   There seems to have been a … little misunderstanding.

O'Hare *spits blood.*

Rourke   I don't suppose if we let you go you'd forget all about this?

O'Hare   You're dead men.

Rourke   I'm inclined to agree with you.

O'Hare   Assholes, the lot a' ya. Bunch of ignorant micks.

Rourke   Jesus.

O'Hare   You are in so much trouble it's unbelievable. You hear me?

Rourke   I need a drink.

O'Hare   Immigrant fucking MICKS!!

Wicklow   Hey! Pot, kettle, fuckin' black!

O'Hare   Bastards.

Rourke   Shut up! (*To the others.*) Look at me.

Wicklow, **Bobby** *and* **Antrim** *look at* **Rourke**.

Rourke   Ignore him.

O'Hare   Bog-hoppin', muck-savage Irish bastards.

Rourke   Whatever he says. Just …

He goes to fix himself a whiskey and ice.

O'Hare   You're all goin' down for this. You're dead men. You hear?

Rourke   Bob, you wanna Coke? Bobby?

O'Hare *lifts his head and his gaze finds* **Bobby**.

O'Hare   Hello, Bobby boy.

He stares up at **Bobby** *with a busted smile.*

O'Hare   You tell that uncle of yours ... You tell that son of a bitch I'll see him in hell.

Rourke   Shut up.

O'Hare (*to* **Bobby**)   You hear that, you little cocksucker?

Bobby *takes a step towards* **O'Hare**.

Rourke   Bob.

O'Hare   You tell him from me he's fuckin' extinct.

Rourke   Shut up.

O'Hare (*to* **Bobby**)   You too, kid.

Rourke   Bobby, get over here.

O'Hare   You're dead meat, you little Irish shit, you all are.

Rourke (*to* **O'Hare**)   You shut up. I'll make you suffer, I swear.

O'Hare   You're nothin'.

Rourke (*to* **Wicklow** *and* **Antrim**) One of yees stick a sock in his mouth.

O'Hare   You're dirt!

Rourke   Shut up!

O'Hare   Ditch-digging dirt!

Rourke   Shut the fuck up!

O'Hare   Potato-eatin' white niggers!

Bobby *strides purposefully over to* **O'Hare** *and thrusts something deep into his sternum, puncturing the heart. As* **O'Hare** *thrashes briefly against his binds,* **Bobby** *stabs him savagely and repeatedly in the chest. Only when* **O'Hare** *is still does* **Bobby** *stop. The boy drops something metallic and bloody to the floor. The others stare at him in dumbfounded silence.* **Bobby** *uses his left hand to wipe a drop of blood from his cheek. Then with his bloodied right hand he repeats this action, covering his face with blood.*

Rourke   Christ, Bobby.

Bobby   He shouldn't have said those things.

Rourke   Jesus.

He goes to **Bobby**. *Uses a handkerchief to pick the metal object from the floor.*

Rourke   Where'd you get this?

Bobby   My mum.

Rourke   A knife?

Bobby   A letter-opener. For opening her letters.

Rourke *wipes the blood from the weapon.*

Rourke   What does this read?

Bobby   'Titanic'.

Rourke   It says 'Titanic' on it.

Bobby   You know? The big ship that sank.

Silence.

Antrim   You know what the ironic thing is?

Rourke *looks at* **Antrim**, *a murderous look.*

Blackout.

Scene Two

Sullivan's place.

Sullivan *is seated behind his desk.* **Rourke** *paces around the room like a hunted animal.*

Rourke   … And you know what the *ironic* thing is? You wanna know what the ironic thing is? O'Hare's father *drowned* on the *Titanic*. What are the odds? Huh? What are the fucking odds!?

Sullivan   Johnny –

Rourke   I'm a nervous fuckin' wreck. You're pullin' the world out from underneath me. I don't know what's up and what's down any more. Jesus. I don't know what's back and forwards. Who's who? What's what? What the hell were you thinking?

Sullivan   Simmer down, Johnny.

Rourke   What the hell were you *thinking*, Gulliver?

Sullivan   It was necessary.

Rourke   Necessa – What have you done?

Sullivan   What had to be done.

Rourke   Jesus …

Sullivan   He couldn't be trusted.

Rourke   I feel sick.

Sullivan   You're part of the wheel that's spinning, Johnny.

Rourke   What does that mean?

Sullivan   You're spinning.

Rourke *looks at* **Sullivan** *with a danger in him.*

Rourke   I never thought I'd say this. But I doubt you.

Sullivan   It's only fools don't question. Allow me to explain. Relax. You breathing again? Good. Now, listen to me. I have reason to believe that Chief O'Hare intercepted the money.

Rourke   'Reason to believe'?

Sullivan   I have my sources.

Rourke   Who?

Sullivan   That's on a need-to-know basis.

Rourke   Well, I need to know.

Sullivan   No, you don't.

Rourke   Then what am I?

Sullivan *looks at him, unreadable.*

Rourke   What am I? Huh? Just a lackey? Is that what I am to you? Another one of your goons? Your footsoldiers? Am I like Wicklow? Like Danny fuckin' Antrim? You told me I was your left hand.

Sullivan *looks at him, unreadable still.*

Rourke   You told me you trusted me.

Sullivan   Johnny, your father was a good friend.

Rourke   Then why don't you talk to me before you take these leaps?

Sullivan   Leaps?

Rourke   This. These. These giant leaps. These fuckin' … these rash decisions?

Sullivan   I think. I decide. I do. And I've been doing this since before you were born.

Pause.

Sullivan   No one will come looking for us. O'Hare will be buried under Hennessey's floorboards. It's public knowledge they didn't like one another. Hennessey killed O'Hare and chose to disappear. Tomorrow the cops get an anonymous tip-off. It's all sewed up. Watertight.

Beat.

Rourke   What about Bobby?

Sullivan   What about him?

Rourke   He killed a man today.

Sullivan   His father did the same thing at his age and he didn't turn out so bad.

Rourke   You said he was a drunk.

Sullivan   He was. He cleaned himself up.

Rourke   Then why's the kid so screwed-up? What's he doin' over here?

Sullivan   Bobby has seen worse than Hennessey's death.

Pause.

Yes. He told me. He's blood.

Beat.

He's got a warrior's heart. The trouble he was involved in. He came home to find his father beating his mother. He knocked him unconscious with a firearm and kicked him to death.

Rourke   His own father?

Sullivan   Stepfather. His real father didn't know he existed until a couple of weeks ago.

Pause.

Rourke   You?

Sullivan   I only knew his mother one night. I'm not proud of that. But now maybe I can make amends.

Rourke   Jesus.

Sullivan   Bobby doesn't know any of this yet.

Rourke   Jesus.

Sullivan   When the time is right.

Rourke   He's a killer.

Beat.

He's a killer, Gulliver.

Sullivan   Natural born.

Rourke   He's your son.

Sullivan   Like I said. I haven't turned out so bad. Have I?

They look at one another. An uneasy silence.

The telephone on **Sullivan**'s *desk rings loudly.* **Sullivan** *doesn't move.* **Rourke** *finally looks at the phone, then at* **Sullivan**.

Sullivan *smiles and motions vaguely towards the phone.* **Rourke** *reaches for the receiver and picks it up.*

Rourke   Rourke …

He listens for a few moments then hangs up.

Rourke   O'Keefe and Ryan found the car.

Sullivan   The money?

Rourke *shakes his head.*

Sullivan   The two men?

Rourke   They got one of them. Mickey No-No.

Blackout.

Scene Three

The Shamrock bar.

Lights up on the bar. A dark slick of blood in the middle of the floor. O'Hare's blood. A dishevelled-looking man in a crumpled white suit sits unbound on the swivel chair where we found O'Hare earlier. His head shakes briefly for a moment then stops. A nervous disorder. This is **Mickey No-No**.

The bodies of **Lumpy** *and* **O'Hare** *lie off to the side in shadow.*

Wicklow *leans by the door watching* **No-No**.

Wicklow   Wop.

Pause.

Hey, rubber neck.

No-No *glances nervously at* **Wicklow**.

Wicklow   Fuck you lookin' at? *Pause.*

The sound of footsteps. The door opens and **Sullivan** *enters followed by* **Rourke** *and* **Bobby.** **Sullivan** *removes his coat and hands it to* **Wicklow.**

Sullivan   He say anything?

Wicklow   Nothin'. Every now and then he shakes like he's on spin.

Sullivan   You been nice to him?

Wicklow   Oh yeah. Real hospitable. They found this fuck under a sewer bridge in New Jersey.

Sullivan   Watch your language William, we have a minor present.

Wicklow   Sorry, kid.

Sullivan *walks over to* **No-No.** *He studies him for a moment in silence.* **No-No** *stares mutely at the pool of blood around his feet.*

Sullivan   Hello, Michael.

No-No *continues to stare at the blood.*

Sullivan   You hear that?

Silence.

That's your heartbeat.

Beat.

Bobby, come over here will you?

Bobby *walks over and stops by* **Sullivan**'*s side.* **Bobby** *stares at the blood without looking at* **No-No.**

Sullivan *indicates* **No-No.**

Sullivan   Bobby, would you trust this man?

Bobby *and* **No-No** *look at each other briefly.* **Bobby** *nods his head.*

Sullivan (*to* **Bobby**)   Thank you. (*To* **Wicklow**.) William, why don't you take Bobby for an ice cream.

Wicklow   Sure thing.

Bobby *takes one last look at* **No-No** *then exits with* **Wicklow**. *Pause.*

Sullivan *dips the tip of his shoe into the blood and begins the slow process of writing a word on the floor in O'Hare's blood. He speaks quietly and calmly as he does this.* **No-No**'s *head begins to shake.*

Sullivan   You know whose blood this is? I believe you were acquainted. Police Chief Marion O'Hare. You see, what happened was he ceased to be of use to me. In fact, the man ceased to have any usefulness to society whatsoever. All he did was take. Take, take, take. Never satisfied. Beware the man whose appetite is never sated. He'll eat you up. Every last bit. Yum-yum-bubble-gum. And then? Then he'll most probably devour himself. It's a terrible trait in the Irish. Hunger. We never forgot it. We were oppressed and denied for so long, now we feel entitled to everything, and more. Creatures of excess. One day it'll be our downfall.

Sullivan *has finished writing the word in blood. He steps back. He walks behind* **No-No** *and views his work.*

Sullivan   Can you read that? What does it say?

No-No (*quietly*)   'Honesty'.

Sullivan   I'm sorry? You're going to have to speak up.

No-No   'Honesty'.

Sullivan   That's right, Michael. It says 'Honesty'. It's the best policy.

He takes a chair and places it in front of **No-No**.

Sullivan   I'm on the brink of a war here, Michael. Very messy. Now. Clean it up. Answers. What I require from you is the truth. Plain and simple. Give me facts. Explain things as they happened.

I ask a question, you answer it. It's very simple. Tell me the truth and as a reward I will allow you your life.

No-No's *head shakes uncontrollably.*

Sullivan   But, I warn you, Michael. I'll know if you're lying. It's a knack I have. Do I make myself clear?

No-No *can't help but shake his head.*

Sullivan   Is that a yes or a no, No-No?

No-No   That's a yes, Mr Sullivan.

Sullivan   Good man. Then let's begin.

Sullivan *sits facing* **No-No**, *crosses his legs, leans back and smiles.*

Sullivan   How well did you know Chief O'Hare?

No-No   I just had a drink with him.

Sullivan   You drank with him?

No-No   Once. In Joe's Bar. Marconi introduced me.

Sullivan   Marconi introduced you to O'Hare?

No-No   Yes.

Sullivan *looks at* **Rourke***: 'I told you so.'*

Sullivan   What did you talk about?

No-No   I dunno. The moon? Everybody was talkin' about the moon.

Sullivan   Did O'Hare know about this delivery? The money. Was it mentioned?

No-No   I dunno.

Sullivan   Did O'Hare take my money?

No-No   No. I don't know.

Pause.

Sullivan Where's my money, Michael?

No-No I … I … I don't know.

Sullivan Not a good start.

No-No I don't know where it is, I swear.

Sullivan Where's Manfreedi?

No-No I dunno.

Sullivan 'I dunno. I dunno.' What do you know?

No-No Nothin', I dunno nothin'.

Sullivan That's not true, Michael. Everybody knows something.

No-No I got kids …

Sullivan Why did you run, No-No?

No-No I panicked. Please, Mr Sullivan –

Sullivan Ah-ah. Let's keep this professional. Why did you panic?

No-No Manfreedi. He didn't come back.

Sullivan Back? From where? Expound.

No-No Huh?

Sullivan He 'didn't come back'?

No-No Yes. I mean, no. He didn't. I was driving, see? I'm in the driver's seat, waiting.

Sullivan Where was this?

No-No Couple a blocks from here.

Sullivan When?

No-No Yesterday. Before lunch.

Sullivan Go on.

No-No So I'm sittin' there, listening to the car radio and I'm waitin' on Manfreedi comin' back.

Sullivan   Manfreedi was delivering the money?

No-No   Yeah, the package. He's gone, I dunno, maybe a minute? And then …

He starts to shake.

Sullivan   It's alright, Michael. You're nervous. That's understandable. In your position I'd be terrified. Take a deep breath.

No-No *breathes deep.*

Sullivan   That's good. Take another one.

No-No *breathes again.*

Sullivan   Good.

Sullivan *breathes deep.*

Sullivan   Good. And another.

No-No *breathes again.*

Sullivan   It's all in the breath.

Sullivan *breathes again.* **No-No** *breathes again.*

Sullivan   There we go.

No-No   Thank you.

Sullivan   Don't thank me. Now. Manfreedi has the package.

No-No   Yes.

Sullivan   My money.

No-No   Yes.

Sullivan   He's gone a minute. And then?

No-No   He's gone maybe a minute and then, then I think I hear gunshots.

Sullivan   You think?

No-No   Radio's on. I'm singin' along to it.

Sullivan   What's the tune?

No-No   Huh?

Sullivan   What's the tune? What are you singing along to?

No-No   'Raindrops Keep Falling on My Head'.

Sullivan   That's a nice tune.

No-No   It is. It's the best day of my life. My wife …

He starts to weep. **Sullivan** *watches him.*

She gave gave birth to a baby boy yesterday. I got two daughters. It's my first boy.

Sullivan   Congratulations. You heard gunshots …

No-No *recovers.*

No-No   They just sounded like little pops.

Sullivan   How many?

No-No   I dunno.

Sullivan   How many?

No-No   Maybe two. Maybe three.

Sullivan   Then?

No-No   I turn off the radio. I listen but there's nothin'. I waited maybe one minute. Maybe two. Manfreedi didn't come back. That's when I panicked. I got outta there. I just drove around. I couldn't think straight. I was thinkin', 'How bad is this?' I'm thinkin' how bad is this gonna look for me, ya know? Maybe people thinkin' that I stole the goddam money, ya know? But I didn't. I swear on my mother's life. Manfreedi had the money. He didn't come back. I waited. But he was … he was *gone*. I just drove around. I couldn't see no sign of him. There weren't that many people around, ya know? I looked everywhere. Everywhere. I was lookin' everywhere for the colour of the uniform, but he was gone.

Sullivan   Uniform?

No-No   Yeah. It was Manfreedi's idea. He was paranoid the FBI were watching him. They been all over Marconi, ya know? So as not to draw attention, he made the delivery in disguise, you know? His idea being, 'Who's gonna look twice at a postman?'

Rourke   A postman?

No-No   Yeah. The money was in a postman's sack …

Silence.

Sullivan *stares at* **No-No**.

Rourke *slowly lowers his head.*

Sullivan *opens his mouth but no words come out. Subtly the man's entire nature seems to change. It is like his whole being seems to quietly exhale. He slowly pulls himself to his feet, takes a deep breath and then suddenly, violently releases it in a terrifying howl of rage:*

Sullivan   YOU GOTTA BE FUCKING ME!!

Music: 'I Wanna be Your Dog' by The Stooges.

Blackout.

Epilogue

Darkness.

A church.

The lights slowly fade up to reveal **Harvey Marr** *sitting in a church pew in his pork-pie hat. He talks out, looking up at a crucified Jesus only he can see.*

Harvey   You gotta help me out here. I'm at the end of it. You gotta answer me this question. I need to know. I been losing sleep over this. OK …

Beat.

Is it chimpanzees or gorillas eat their own shit?

Beat.

He explodes with laughter, a maniacal shuddering sound that quickly becomes ugly and desperate. The laughter swiftly subsides and becomes a kind of low moaning. The mouth smiles but the eyes betray a man who has given up the fight.

How was I to know he wasn't a postman? How? What is he doin' dressed as a postman? Who delivers a hundred grand in a mail sack? What was he thinkin'? What? How could I recognise him? He had a bullet in his face. Fuck deserves to be dead. Fuck 'im. Fuck me! I'm an idiot! You're an idiot, Harvey!

Pause.

I'm at the end here. You hear me?

Pause.

I said it.

Pause.

You want me to say it again? I'm sorry.

Pause.

I'm sorry. Before Jesus and all his apostles, before you and all

your heavenly angels … I'm sorry. I'm not askin' for my life.
That's a given gone. I let down my pal. Only friend I ever had. I
accept what's comin'. I embrace it. I intend to pay my dues. My
life's worth nothin' anyways. I'm not askin' for that. I'm askin' for
forgiveness. Blessed Virgin Mother Mary forgive me and deliver
me up when the time comes. I see the error of my ways. I see 'em
all. I see 'em laid out in front of me. I been a bad man. Yes. I'm
not denying it. No. I lied and cheated and extorted and bullied
and stole and killed. I killed more men than I care to remember.
There's nothin' about the devil I don't know. But this is me. Here
I am. This is me. Right here. Harvey Anthony Ignatius Marr. This
is me. Offering up a prayer for the better of two eternities. I'm
here. I ended up right here. I could a' been with a hooker or gettin'
loaded in a bar, or gettin' loaded in a bar with a hooker, but I'm
not. In my final hour I find myself standing here. I'm right here.

Pause.

I'm right here. Harvey 'Drum Belly' Marr. The Fightin' Irish. The
end of an era. I'm right here.

Pause.

You want me to get down on my knees? Is that how it works? OK.

*He gets down on to his knees. He takes off his hat and clasps it to
his breast with both hands. He looks up at Jesus.*

*In the brightly lit church doorway upstage two figures silently
appear in silhouette.* **Sorrow** *and* **Rourke**.

Rourke *walks quietly forward and stops a respectful distance
behind* **Harvey**, *who is unaware of him.*

Harvey   I'm listening. I want you to speak to me. Please.
I'll hear you. I'm listening. I want you to say something. Say:
'I forgive you.'

He listens.

A long silence.

Then …

Rourke   Harvey.

Harvey *opens his eyes.*

Rourke   Time to go.

Pause.

Harvey   Walter with you?

Rourke   He's waiting outside.

Harvey *nods to himself.*

Harvey   Will you do me one last thing, Johnny? When you're done, send me home. The old turf. Even if it's just my heart. I wanna go home.

Rourke   Sure, Harve.

Harvey *crosses himself and stands.*

Harvey   They come back?

Rourke   Who?

Harvey   The moon men. They get back OK?

Rourke   Yeah. This mornin'.

Harvey   We're a miracle. That's the shame of it.

He looks up one last time.

Never said a word.

Rourke   Who?

Harvey   Not a word.

He places his hat back on his head, then walks upstage and disappears into the light.

Rourke *takes one brief look up at Jesus then follows him.*

Lights fade.

Music: 'Oh Happy Day' by the Edwin Hawkins Singers.

Blackout.

Planet Belfast

Rosemary Jenkinson

Planet Belfast was first performed at The Metropolitan Arts Centre (MAC), Belfast, on 19 February 2013 with the following cast:

Danny	Conor Grimes
Claire	Tara Lynne O'Neill
Martin	Paul Kennedy
Alice	Abigail McGibbon

Director	Michael Duke
Designer	Ciaran Bagnall
Video Artist	Conan McIvor
Dramaturg	Hanna Slättne

Scene One

Open plan kitchen/living room. **Martin** *is on the computer.*
Blur's 'Song 2' is playing loudly. **Alice** *comes in carrying a*
homemade shopping bag and some files. **Martin** *switches off the*
music.

Alice   Sorry. Sorry.

Martin   (*kissing her*) How was the Assembly?

Alice   Oh, you know. Braindead as usual. But, great news, Sinn
Féin are definitely voting no.

Martin   Great! (*pause*) On what again?

Alice   The vote on green underwear – what do you think? The
field trials of GM potato!

Martin   Alright! Alright!

Alice   In six weeks' time? I've only been telling you about it for
weeks.

Martin   Well, that's great, isn't it?

Alice   Terrific. Of course I'll have to support them on cross-
border initiatives.

Martin   Well, it's nice you're back-scratching.

Alice   Co-operating.

Martin   In cahoots.

Alice   It's just politics, Martin –

Martin   Sexy bedfellows.

Alice   Oh, fuck off. Why do you always – ?

She sighs.

Martin   Why do you always not finish why do you always?

Alice   (*from the fridge-freezer*) Martin, there's no *ice*.

Martin   I know. Panic. The Arctic Circle is shrinking as we speak –

Alice   Hah, hah.

Martin   I'm sorry. I forgot.

Alice   You *always* forget. Drink?

Martin   No, I'm saving myself.

Alice   You didn't eat the blueberries either.

Martin   I did.

Alice   What? Two?

Martin   No, at least five with my walnuts and yoghurt.

Alice   But yoghurt's a total … counteractant.

Martin   Well, I'm not going to graze on nuts and fruit like I'm a fucking squirrel.

Alice   People used to all the time, you know.

Martin   Oh, yeah and they lived in a cave and worshipped the stag. Forget it, Alice.

Alice   (*taking a different tack and stroking his head gently*) It's all for a reason, love. I'm not harping on at you for the good of my health.

Martin   (*disgruntedly*) No, just mine.

Alice   We both want this, don't we? (**Martin** *doesn't answer*) Don't we, love?

Martin   Yes.

Alice   So, it's just a little bit of assistance to mother nature, nothing cranky, nothing creepy.

Martin   But we're going to the hospital for checks.

Alice   That doesn't mean you can't follow your diet, Martin.

Martin   What do you want me to do, stand in a fairy ring, salute the sun god and eat five kilos of blueberries. Great, then you'll have twins!

Alice   God, so fucking annoying you are!

Martin   (*surprised*) Me!?

Alice   Everything's such a big deal to you. Food, babies, everything … (*thinks*) What did you mean by saving yourself?

Martin   What?

Alice   Just there. You said you were saving yourself.

Martin   Yes. For tonight, Alice.

Alice   What?

Martin   She's coming here. I told you.

Alice   Who?

Martin   Claire Summerton.

Alice   Oh, God! She can't come here. I've got all this (*her files*) to greenlight. I'm in the chamber first thing, then I've a really important GM meeting with the independent Unionist. I have to cut a deal, all I need is one more vote.

Martin   Well, as long as you don't tell him you're shagging Sinn Féin.

Alice   It's important, Martin.

Martin   But I told you two days ago.

Alice   It's not in my diary, is it?

Martin   Oh, right, so I have to go through your PA to book five minutes with you, is it?

Alice   I'm an MLA, Martin. I'm on message, you can't just –

Martin   Alright, alright, I'll cancel her.

Alice   Well, it's not like she's a good friend, is she? Jesus Christ, you picked her up off Friends Reunited!

Martin   She contacted me.

Alice   Friends Reunited!

Martin   The way you say it, it's like some child porn site.

Alice   Well, at least child porn wouldn't be as sad.

Martin   It's not sad. It's –

Alice   Isn't it enough to read history without you trawling the past in your private life too?

Martin   It's interesting.

Alice   How?

Martin   Remember Bouncer?

Alice   Bouncer … was he fat?

Martin   No, Alice, he was fucking skinny. *Bouncer*, of course he was fat.

Alice   Look, I don't care, Martin. Would you just please cancel her?

Martin   A compromise. (*gets out his mobile*) What about tomorrow, are you free then?

Alice   (*checking her diary*) I think so …

Martin   Or shall I phone your PA first? God, we do nothing together socially any more.

Alice   We went to that charity do last week.

Martin   Yes. Me hovering round like your pimp while you worked the room.

Alice   You were fine.

Martin   Martin McGuinness thinks I'm your bodyguard.

Alice   Does he fuck! It was a great do.

Martin   It's just we used to go out always, me and you.

Alice *doesn't answer.*

Martin   Shall I say to her tomorrow then?

Alice   Alright, but not here. Let's go out. Somewhere nice.

Martin   Mmm … The Whitefort? The Red Hand Supporters Club?

Alice   Café Vaudeville.

Martin   No, they have scantily clad dancers there. You don't want to be snapped with them, do you?

Alice   Good point. What about Muriel's?

Martin   (*happy*) Muriel's! Gay, liberal chic – perfect! (*to* **Claire***'s voicemail*) Hi, Claire, listen, I'm sorry to cancel at this short notice but Alice can't make it tonight, so I'm suggesting tomorrow night at Muriel's if you're still free. Let me know. Bye.

Alice   Done?

Martin   Done.

Alice   Claire Summerton … I always wished I was Claire Summerton. All sun-shiney. No wonder she was voted 'most likely to succeed'.

Martin   Alice McFee succeeded.

Alice   Became Alice Nixon.

Martin   Nixon's not bad.

Alice   Nixon. Name of a highly disgraced president.

Martin   Could have been worse. Alice Bush? Alice Blair?

Alice   (*laughing*) True. Claire didn't say what she does, did she?

Martin   No.

Alice   Something's gone wrong, the wheel's come off. Why else go back to the past?

Martin   (*insulted*) I go back.

Alice   Oh, Martin, you're a historian, for God's sake. It's nearly excusable.

Martin   True.

Alice   No. I wonder what she wants …

Martin   You make it sound sinister.

Alice   Sure that cousin of yours. He only wanted a job in Stormont. Him with his NVQ in networking.

Martin   Well, there was no harm in it.

Alice   But why did you have to say *I* can't make it?

Martin   Mmm, let's see. Because it's the truth?

Alice   Like I'm always the difficult one.

Martin   You are always the difficult one. But only because of your job.

Alice   (*unconvinced*) Mmm.

Martin   (*puts the vodka bottle in bin, starts laughing to himself*) Hey. Remember that protest when Claire squirted that peeler in the gub with the fire-extinguisher?

Alice   I do. It was brilliant.

Martin   She was always great fun. Wasn't she?

Alice   (*snuggles up to Martin*) Talking of fun, Martin …

Martin   I thought you had all that (*the files*) to greenlight.

Alice   (*soft*) Let's put it on amber. Yeah?

Martin   Okay. (*she kisses him*) But I warn you I may be lacking in the blueberry department.

Alice   I'm sure you'll do just fine. Remember to put the rubbish out, won't you?

Martin   I'll do it now.

He goes out with the rubbish.

Alice   (*shouting out to him*) Ah, that's why Blur was on. Reliving the oul days, eh?

The sound of **Martin** *falling and swearing.*

Alice   What's happened?

Martin *limps back in angrily.*

Martin   I fell. Face-first in the wormery. That hurt! No, why the fuck can't we have some proper fucking lighting out there instead of that eco-shit? Can't see a thing out there. Fuck sake, I'm sick of your green crap, living like fucking troglodytes, I'm so sick of this fucking SHIT! Don't fucking laugh at me … no, don't laugh …

He starts to laugh too.

Martin   Have I manure on my face?

Alice   Just a bit.

Martin   Christ.

Alice   Now you really are a caveman.

Martin *lumbers around like a caveman chasing* **Alice.**

Martin   Ugh! Ugh! Ugh!

Alice   (*laughing*) No, quit it!

He grabs **Alice** *up roughly and carries her out towards the bedroom.*

Scene Two

Claire'*s flat.* **Claire** *is sitting at her computer. Her mobile goes.*

Claire   'Lo … (*leaps up like it's someone important*) Tony! Yep, yep. Onto it … No, I can't make the heads-up. No, I know. I know I'm result deficient. I *know* and I'm working on it. Sure I got an in now. I'm going to be the one to make sure this contract goes ahead, I know how massive, yep, am working on it as we speak. (*taps a few PC keys*) Is this the pitter-patter of tiny keys or what?

Downtime? No way, it's uptime … Yep, I'm well aware of the current job market, Tone, but you know I'm the best, Tone. All means necessary, I know. Righ', righ', catcha.

She rings off. Starts typing with a new urgency and resolve.

Scene Three

The Centre for Trauma's office. **Danny** *is showing* **Martin** *round.*

Danny   So, Martin, I'm your first port of call if you've any problems whichsoever, and if I'm not here, you report to Eimer. And if she's not there, you report to Billy. Not that we're hierarchical. We run on a tight ethos of mutual regard.

Martin   I can see that, Danny.

Danny   Yes, we're very inclusive. Feel free to use the milk in the fridge. I'd steer clear of the yoghurts if I were you, a wide berth, eh?

Martin   Oh, I'd never touch –

Danny   You know what the ladies are like with the yoghurt pots, eh? Not that it's a gender issue, Martin, just a fact in this office.

Martin   Good to know, Danny, good to know.

Danny   Right. And here are the archives.

Danny *slams down a box on the desk. A huge plume of dust comes out.* **Martin** *coughs.*

Danny   History. Gets you right in the lungs, doesn't it?

Martin   Certainly does.

Danny   Could always get one of the ladies to run their wet-wipes over it?

Martin   No, it's fine.

Danny   (*of the computer screen*) See that? Eighteen and a half inches. I don't even get that, do I?

Martin   It's great.

Danny   Tell your wife that when you get home.

Martin   I certainly will.

Danny   And the blinds. If someone comes here to tell us their story, blinds down, eh?

Martin   Privacy at all times, yes.

Danny   Martin. (*bites his lip*) Can I just ask … ?

Martin   Fire ahead.

Danny   What's your story?

Martin *looks blank.*

Danny   You know? The conflict.

Martin   Oh. Nothing. I didn't, not personally.

Danny   (*shocked*) But you're meant to have.

Martin   Oh, well, I was kind of affected by it all – sure we had a bomb scare in our street once and …

Danny   All of us here have a story.

Martin   And a boy in our school was killed by a bomb if that's any good.

Danny   Any good?

Martin   No, what I meant was –

Danny   This boy was a friend of yours?

Martin   Well, yes … we were on the same bus. Not the bus that was bombed obviously.

Danny   So you once vaguely knew a boy who was killed.

Martin *looks embarrassed.*

Danny   No, don't worry about it, it's fine.

Martin   I just …

Danny   It would be better empathy-wise to have your own story, but not everyone had a part to play, did they? But you are an expert at the archives, I believe.

Martin   Of course. Two years ago I read all the famine archives.

Danny   Ah, yes, your book.

Martin   Yes.

Danny   There was some debate over whether you'd be suitable for this post. You understand this organization doesn't like any controversy.

Martin   No, no. I assure you.

Danny   Head down, eh? Head down, chin up.

Martin   That's it.

Danny   Though I do admire anyone who puts their head above the wall and gets it shot off. Not literally. Metaphorically.

Martin   Well, thanks, Danny.

Danny   Yes, we're all a bit controversial here. You do realise you're only here because of ...

Martin   Yes.

Danny   Yes?

Martin   Alice.

Danny   Celebrity wifestyle, always a winner, Martin.

Martin   Indeed.

Danny   Mm. But you couldn't have been that long at the famine archives. Sure all the victims died.

Martin   Oh, we spun it out.

Danny   You *spun* ... ?

Martin   No, no, I mean I was thorough. Thorough, I meant.

Danny   Martin, relax. I'm not cross-examining you.

Martin   No, I didn't think that.

Danny   We've cultivated an atmosphere of mutual regard.

Martin   I can see that.

Danny   (*points*) Look at this, Martin.

Martin   Er.

Danny   *This*.

Martin   (*reads off a poster*) 'The past is not a shared place but this office is'.

Danny   I wrote that.

Martin   Very good!

Danny   Like it?

Martin   Love it.

Danny   Truth recovery. The secret is in the word *recovery.* Yes?

Martin   Yes.

Danny   (*rummaging about on top of the filing cabinet*) And now I've the most important member of our team for you to meet.

Martin   Oh?

Danny   (*whips out a teddy bear*) Meet Verity!

Martin   (*enthusiastically*) Oh, your mascot.

Danny   Well, I prefer to think of her as more integral than that. The *bear*-ing of the truth?

Martin   Love it. (*shakes the bear's hand*) Pleased to meet you, Verity.

Danny   You don't need to shake her hand, she's a stuffed toy, isn't she?

Martin   Sorry, but I –

Danny   No, *I'm* sorry. You do what you want.

Martin   *Bear* with me, eh?

Danny   Nice one, Marty-boy. No, what I want you to do with Verity is when the truth gets too much for you, when the living history comes too … *live* for you, reach out to her, *hug* her, hold her.

Martin   Yes. I will.

Danny   Picked that up in a conference in South Africa. Had a bear called Nelson.

Martin   Mandela.

Danny   Well, it wasn't going to be Nelson fucking McCausland, was it? Right, any questions, Martin, before I unleash you on these?

Martin   I think you've covered …

Danny   That door is into the Room of Remembrance. (*opens it and heavenly music floats out*) Listen. (*swirling his arm round to the music, pulling it in like it's sweet air*) Enjoy the facilities. Have one of the facials upstairs.

Martin   I can?

Danny   (*closing the door*) We're all fully entitled.

Martin   Oh, and, Danny, when I've transcribed all the stories … ?

Danny   Yes, Martin, this is where it gets really exciting. In eight weeks' time we're gonna have this mega launch called 'Reflections'. I'm thinking gauze and spotlights. Stories that'll make Anne Frank's look like a picnic. The voices of victims ringing out. Lots of bigwigs, politicians … Your wife'll come, won't she?

Martin   Of course she'll be coming.

Danny   Fantastic. (*checks his watch*) Right, I've gotta budge on here. Got an anti-hate conference in the Merchant to go to. Good luck!

Martin   Cheers, Danny. Danny?

Danny   (*turning*) Yes?

Martin   What's *your* story?

Danny   (*pause*) Me? I was born into a hardcore Republican family. Just to give you a taster, my Da was part of a punishment team that shot my Ma. So, you can see how it might have turned me a wee bit.

Martin   Christ. That's terrible.

Danny   I spent five years in prison for bomb-making at nineteen.

Martin   God.

Danny   I was highly skilled. And do you know what I made the bombs out of?

Martin   No.

Danny   Yoghurt pots. (*clicks at him*) Slán for now, kid.

Danny *leaves.* **Martin** *shakes his head. Turns back to his computer. Pulls the first file out of the box, blows off the dust.*

Scene Four

Muriel's. **Martin** *and* **Alice** *are arriving in Muriel's upstairs, drinks in hand. Black Eyed Peas' 'A Good Night' is blaring out.* **Martin** *takes off* **Alice***'s coat.*

Alice   There's no seats up here either.

Martin   There were a couple of stools at the bar.

Alice   Martin, I've been on my feet all day. I'm not going to perch like some budgerigar in a cage.

Martin   Do you see her?

Alice   (*trying to be subtle*) A quarter to two. Is that her?

Martin *looks.*

Alice   No, a quarter to two, you eejit.

Martin   (*finally following her glance*) Look, I only do digital.

Alice   Would that be her with the book?

Martin   Her there?

Alice   Shhh.

Martin   Hardly. She was far nicer than that.

Alice   You never know. She could've aged badly.

Martin   Wishful thinking, Alice.

Alice   Claire!

Martin   (*in a whisper*) Don't. It's not her.

Alice   She's looking.

Martin   Only because she knows you from TV. I'll check downstairs.

Alice   No, don't go. You're my bodyguard, remember?

Martin   Who do you think you are, Indira Gandhi? Alice – you haven't even asked me yet.

Alice   What?

Martin *looks at her.*

Alice   (*covers her face*) Oh, God, your new job.

Martin   Yes.

Alice   I'm so sorry, love. How was it?

Martin *grunts non-committally.*

Alice   Really that bad?

Martin   ·Felt like I was on some youth training programme. I mean, I'm a real author. I may be in a dry patch, but …

Alice   All authors have to get out into the real world.

Martin   The real world. A trauma centre is not the real world, Alice. There's dolphin music howling in the background, holistic facials, they even have this Vibroson, they call it, this giant vibrating machine. Great, your Dad got wiped in the Troubles, a quick half hour's jiggle in this machine'll sort you out, there you go brand new.

Alice Well, it was you wanted the job.

Martin I know. I thought all those Troubles stories would get me flowing again. They only hired me because of you.

Alice No. (*checking, pleased*) Really?

Martin Really.

Alice Well, you can always leave. I mean, I'm earning well.

Martin Thanks. That's not emasculating in any way, Alice.

Alice Right, well, let me *re*masculate you by wee wifey serving her man with a soothing drink.

Martin Yeah, but you bought it.

Alice (*checks her mobile*) That's Glynis. She's done the finishing touches to the Farmers' Union speech, but big problem. I knew it, how can I kiss Sinn Féin's backside with the all-Ireland rhetoric while kissing up to my independent Unionist?

Martin Become a contortionist?

Alice It's like having a threesome without any of the fun. I'd better run round and check it.

Martin What? Now?

Alice I'll only be a sec.

Martin *groans.*

Claire *walks in, carrying her drink.*

Alice Don't moan. Sure, Martin, she's not even here.

Martin Claire!

Claire (*kissing them*) Martin! Alice!

Alice   You look fantastic.

Claire   You two haven't changed a bit.

Martin   That's why I chose Muriel's. We look gorgeous by candlelight.

Alice   As long as the flame's naked and not us!

They all laugh.

Alice   Look, Claire, I am so sorry, but I have to motor. Got a speech to amend, but I'll be back in half an hour tops, I promise, and then we'll catch up, yes?

Claire   Speech on what?

Alice   GM crops. Terribly serious.

Claire   Cutting edge, I'd say. Just, you've done so well, your career.

Alice   Ah, nights like this you pay the price. Martin'll fill you in on it.

Martin   Yes, I'm her press officer.

Alice   Well, I must grab a cab, Claire. Back soon.

Claire   Bye.

Alice *goes.*

Claire   (*after her*) Great seeing you.

Martin   Sorry about this.

Claire   It's fine.

Martin   'Grab a cab'. Where does she think this is, New York? Belfast. The City that Never Sleeps.

Claire   Only 'cos everyone's too busy getting langered in the pub. Well, at least you're still here.

Martin   I'm her stand-in.

Claire   (*appraising him*) Not a bad stand-in.

Martin   You look amazing.

Claire   Thanks. That's down to plenty of roughage and outdoor sex.

Martin   Really?

Claire   God, you always were gullible.

Martin   Me, I believe anything, even the history books.

Claire   I know! Your famine book. Congratulations!

Martin   People tell me the photos are nice.

Claire   Come on. It got tons of reviews.

Martin   Sure. *Farming Weekly* loved it.

Claire   Aw. You pissed off the *Irish Times* though. 'Anti-Irish', wasn't it?

Martin   I know. Fuck em, eh?

Claire   Saying the Irish should actually thank the English for giving them the famine. Ouch.

Martin   (*laughs*) It's only the truth. The famine helped Ireland modernise, get rid of corruption. We were always going to shake up society, remember?

Claire   Least you and Alice did.

Martin   And you?

Claire   Public Relations. People bring their ideas, I research, package, market and promote.

Martin   It's a good job, isn't it?

Claire   A purveyor of others' ideas, that's me. A conduit of crap. If ideas are good, they sell themselves. Ideas are bad, I sell them.

Martin   Even against your conscience?

Claire   Oh, I sold my conscience years ago. But I do have a fantastic flat.

Martin   Well, it's a fair trade-off.

Claire   Hey, you can always buy your conscience back later.
Yes, I suppose I've turned out the opposite of Alice. (*pause*) Alice
through the looking glass.

Martin   You won 'most likely to succeed', remember?

Claire   Alice was *seething*.

Martin   Ffff … I had to listen to it. Here. To the past.

He holds up his glass which **Claire** *clinks.*

Claire   No. To the future. (*they clink again*) How many years are
you married now?

Martin   Twelve, thirteen.

Claire   Thought you were going to marry Steffi Graf.

Martin   (*laughing*) Christ, that's right! Steffi had legs to die
for. But, you know, it just didn't work out. She had this fetish for
baldies.

Claire   Her loss.

Martin   Totally. God, me and Alice, we're like this old married
bickering couple.

Claire   Sure you were always like that. Even back then.

Martin   We were?

Claire   We all just thought you stuck together because the sex
was good.

Martin   Hunh. Good then, not now. She wants a baby.

Claire   *She* wants?

Martin   *We* want … her decision. She even has me on this
'Fast Track to Conception' diet. Blueberries and walnuts – off
the fucking wall nuts, I tell her. And she's on the chick-peas –
between us we're giving off more gases than the Kyoto Protocol
allows in ten years! We could start a wind farm between us.

(**Claire** *laughs*) Oh, and the tupperware container is now banned from the property as apparently it causes sperm DNA damage, yes, the first sign of plastic and I have to bodyswerve it by ten feet. God forbid I drop my bic biro anywhere near my groin. Yes, and in spite of me being force-fed blueberries like a French goose, she still isn't up the duff, and just to rub it in, the worms in our wormery are breeding like hotcakes, the small apiary she's growing in the garden in her crusade to save the honeybee is bursting at the seams with new life … but us, no, not a bean. Except the recommended mung beans we put into us.

Claire   Sounds crazy!

Martin   We have to live with these energy-saving light bulbs – now there's a misnomer, *light* bulbs, it's perpetual gloom, the algae in a swamp would give off more light, I have to take out a fucking torch just to read a book, but, yes, off she is there charging, the great eco-warrioress into the new dark ages. Christ, I mean, I love history, but that doesn't mean I have to live in the fourteenth century, does it?

Claire *is laughing.*

Martin   Sorry. You'll be wondering why on earth you ever got in touch. Why did you get in touch?

Claire   (*pause*) Something was missing. It's like … to know who you've become, you have to know who you were. Oh, my God, that sounds like Oprah. Self-help-city.

Martin   (*shouts out*) Quick, someone, get her a kaftan!

Claire   God, I sounded so phony.

Martin   No, no. I'm happy to be your missing link. Alice has often referred to me as the missing link, anthropologically speaking.

Claire   Yeah. (*pause*) Martin, I'm just not sure I'm happy with myself, you know?

Martin   No man in your life?

Claire Actually … I like women now.

Martin Oh.

Claire Yes.

Martin Well, at least it gives us something in common now.

Claire Yes, fabulous, we can go out and cruise some chicks.

Martin Well, *I* can't –

Claire I'm joking! God, Martin.

Martin I know, I –

Claire A lifetime of Alice has turned you into …

Martin (*checks his mobile*) Talk of the devil.

Claire Isn't it strange how you can never hear other people's mobiles but your own?

Martin It's like your own baby crying, I suppose.

Claire She coming?

Martin Speech not right. I knew it!

Claire It doesn't matter.

Martin Claire, I'm sorry.

Claire I didn't just come for her, you know.

Martin People generally just want her.

Claire I don't.

Martin I am the man behind the woman. The rock behind the …

Claire Hard place?

Martin (*laughing*) Something like that.

Claire Go on, tell me what you're working on now.

Martin Ah.

Claire (*colluding, like it's something special*) Ah.

Martin   No, it's a Living History Project. I'm compiling stories of victims from the Troubles.

Claire   Heav-y.

Martin   Only to get some writing on the go. Today I met a bomber.

Claire   Ah, explosive stuff.

Martin   Alice thinks I'm mad but she humours me.

Claire   I imagine she has enough of the old Troubles conflict in the Assembly.

Martin   Huh, the DUP are so thick, they still think the Green Party means Sinn Féin.

Claire   Whereas she thinks globally, right?

Martin   I think up orbiting, somewhere over the ozone, more like. Sorry, sorry. I didn't mean just to be bitching about Alice all night.

Claire   Only some of it.

Martin   No, she's done some terrific stuff. Education. Ethical crops. It's just …

Claire   Look, let's get more drinks, my shout. They do great platters here, salami, olives, breads …

Martin   Blueberries?

Claire   Live dangerously, let your sperm live on the edge tonight, go on.

Martin   I can't let you pay.

Claire   Go on. You're at your aunty's. A platter and a pint?

Martin   Go on then.

Claire   (*getting up*) Yes, let's have some fun.

Martin   And maybe later we could go cruising for chicks.

Claire   Mm. Don't push it.

Martin   Claire.

Claire *stops and turns.*

Martin   Let's go wild and find out who we really are.

Claire   (*smiling*) Or who we were meant to be.

Claire *leaves.*

Scene Five

Trauma Centre. **Martin** *is sitting at his desk working when* **Danny** *comes in with a box.*

Danny   Guess what this is, Marty-boy?

Martin   Don't know. History?

Danny   That's right! Living history!

Danny *pulls out a 1980s' jumper and holds it up against himself.*

Danny   We're joining forces with our sub-sub-group to create an installation for Reflections: Everyday objects transformed by the Troubles.

Martin   Sounds great.

Danny   We're going to have videos everywhere. Objects. Lights.

Martin   Did that used to be yours?

Danny   Yes. I was the height of style.

Martin   I'm sure.

Danny   So, Martin, have you any objects from the Troubles era?

Martin   Er.

Danny   A child's bicycle – could be poignant. (*imitates the ringing of a bicycle bell*) Ching-ching!

Martin   But I didn't really have that much contact with the
Troubles, did I?

Danny   Well, you lived through part of it, didn't you? Fuck sake,
Martin, you're a victim as well, aren't you?

Martin   Yes.

Danny   Yes?

Martin   Well, not really.

Danny   Shh, Martin, you must never ever say that round here.

Martin   But it's the truth.

Danny   Martin, what is this a centre of?

Martin   Trauma.

Danny   Implying ...

Martin   Trauma.

Danny   Victims. Victims.

Martin   Ah.

Danny   So I ask again. Are you a victim?

Martin   I'm a victim.

Danny   Good boy, don't let me down. Why do you think we do
the stories? Keep it live, Martin, keep it living. Keep it up, so we
keep our jobs, right?

Martin   I won't rock the boat.

Danny   Good kid, nuff said. Strictly off the record, eh? Now
back to everyday items from the Troubles. D'you have anything?

Martin   Er ...

Danny   Fuck sake, I'm not asking you to bring in a vest covered
in gore, am I? It's more subtle than that. Symbolic.

Martin   I'll see what I can round up.

Danny   Good boy, and I'll want a first draft for Reflections end of the month. Gauze, I see gauze everywhere. A Celtic harpist or two. I'm planning to bring it to the Bloody Sunday Memorial. I want it to be bigger than Holocaust Day, bigger than the 9/11 Remembrance. I hope you're excited.

Martin   I am excited.

Danny   Good. Because I'm planning a memurial.

Martin   (*pause*) A what?

Danny   A memurial. Half a memorial, half a murial. My invention. (*taps his head*) See what comes out of here?

Martin   Wow.

Danny   A fund of ideas. For the next *fund*ing round, right?

Martin   Good thinking.

Danny   We're competing with six centres for core funding, we're under threat, so go for it. Press, bigwigs, smallfry, whatever we can use, (*clicking fingers*) ideas, Martin, ideas.

Martin   Yep.

Danny   The wife still coming?

Martin   You couldn't stop her.

Danny   Great. See why I hired you?

Martin   (*pause*) For Alice?

Danny   Ideas, Martin, ideas. And now I'm off to the Wall of Life.

Martin   What's that?

Danny   Against suicide. A vigil. And I hope it is a fucking wall. Half the time they make us stand in the middle of the road. The balloons, pure suicidal it is. I'm not committing suicide just to highlight suicide, mate, no way.

Martin   You tell them, Danny.

Danny   (*pause*) You haven't used the fridge yet, have you?

Martin   No, I thought better not.

Danny   Too right. Don't give the ladies the ammo. That fridge is the last conflict zone left in Ireland.

Martin   A cold war, eh?

Danny   Good one, Marty-boy!

He high-fives **Martin**.

Martin   This fridge is not a shared space, eh?

Martin *is laughing.* **Danny** *stares at him coldly.*

Martin   Sorry.

Danny   Everywhere here is a shared space, Martin.

Martin   Sorry. Just a wee joke.

Danny   A post-conflict haven. A designated Peace Place, okay?

Martin   Okay. I mean, I know.

Danny   Well, must hurry. Faar ye well. Slán. Bye. (*waving at Verity Bear*) Bye, Verity.

Danny *leaves.* **Martin** *goes back to his computer thoughtfully, as if an idea is brewing.*

Scene Six

Corridor in hospital. **Martin** *is carrying magazines and a plastic cup.* **Alice** *is carrying a small phial.*

Martin   You're lucky. All you had to do is pee.

Alice   Give us a look then.

Martin *passes her his magazines.*

Alice   My God! She's like a beast with two blimps.

Martin   Who needs her? I have pictures in my head.

Alice   Who of? Me?

Martin *clicks his tongue and winks at her.*

Alice   You were quick.

Martin   Nice that isn't a criticism for once.

Alice   I couldn't go.

Martin   What? Sure you're usually like Belfast Water Board.

Alice   I know.

Martin   Relax. (**Alice** *sighs*) It'll happen.

Alice   I've been pumping the fluids into me. Pomegranate and boysenberry for breakfast. Then a coffee.

Martin   Coffee is very dehydrating, Alice.

Alice   It was a grande.

Martin   Just be patient. You're always in a rush.

Alice   It didn't help, you up and down all night.

Martin   I did try to be quiet.

Alice   Up and down, up and down, but not up and down on me, oh, no.

Martin   You should've been in a coma, the amount of vodka you necked.

Alice   Hardly.

Martin   Look, Alice, I'd all these ideas in my head.

Alice   Oh.

Martin   Yes, I'm going to start writing. I've got a great idea.

Alice   Well, that's great.

Martin   You don't sound convinced.

Alice   What do I have to do? Leap all over you? I think it's fantastic!

She hugs him.

Alice   Squeeze me harder. It might push my bladder.

Martin   It's just an idea, but I think it could be huge.

Alice   Great. Go get your book deal, then you can leave that stupid job.

Martin   You really think it's stupid?

Alice   No, no. It's just a bit beneath you.

Martin   I see. Like I'm beneath you.

Alice   Not as often as I'd like, baby. No, don't be so stupid. Beneath me. Why do you always … ?

Martin   Sorry. Sometimes I just think –

Alice   I'm thrilled for you, okay?

Martin   Okay.

Alice   I want you to write. I want you to be happy.

There's silence. **Alice** *is jiggling her leg.*

Martin   Are you trying to pump it out?

Alice   The car'll be here soon. I have to meet the young activists, then give a massive key-note speech to the Farmers' Union …

Martin   Relax. This is more important.

Alice   (*pause*) The doctor said at age thirty-eight, only seventy-five per cent of women will get pregnant after three years of trying.

Martin   You don't want to listen to that.

Alice   Oh, I know. Sure I told her politicians never accept statistics.

Martin   And if there's a problem we'll deal with it.

Alice   Well, there's no problem with me, I can tell you. I'm fighting fit.

Martin   I know that, love.

Alice   Right. Time for Operation Bladder. It *will* obey.

Alice *leaves.*

Scene Seven

Later that day. 'Food Glorious Food' blasts out. **Alice** *walks out to address the Ulster Farmers' Union.*

Alice   Agriculture has always been of the greatest importance to the economy and the cultural life of Northern Ireland. Indeed, I've even heard it said that Stormont itself is like a farm. Expending a lot of manure and full of pig-heads.

Laughs from the audience.

Though personally I think it's more like a zoo.

In six weeks' time Stormont will be voting on field trials of genetically modified potato in this land. I am fully aware of the position of the Ulster Farmers' Union. I understand you want to compete commercially with the rest of the world, I understand you want the best economic deal but I assure you that the Green Party will not be voting for the toxic effects, gene transfer or low yields of GM crops.

Look at China. 'Exploding Watermelons' was the amusing headline. (*a few titters*) This is the combustible reality of GM crops and it is far from amusing. And another story about cows producing breastmilk. 'Udderly Shocking' was the headline. So I'm here to tell you that any newly created plant possessing an unstable genetic structure will not, I repeat, not ever enter this land. Green politics is clean politics.

Audience murmurs disapproval.

The price of protecting people is unpopularity and I will pay it.

I'd like to cite a few words from the book, *The Great Famine*, about the potato failure of 1848. Actually, quick plug, my husband wrote it. (*a few laughs*) Well, Westminster has slashed our salaries, you know, you have to hustle where you can.

So I quote: 'The blight was not caused by nature. It was largely caused by government officials in Ireland'. Well, I promise you, this MLA will not cause a new famine in this country, this MLA will not be bullied by the Ulster Farmers' Union, this MLA will pledge to do what's right for not just the farmers, but the people. I urge every one of you to say no and to put the you back into the UK. Say no now!

Some mild applause, mostly boos gaining in strength. **Alice** *is nodding approval at her own words.*

Scene Eight

Kitchen/living room. **Martin** *is dancing and singing to 'Girls and Boys' by Blur.* **Alice** *comes in and watches him for a few seconds, smiling to herself.* **Martin** *suddenly is aware of her and stops, embarrassed, but* **Alice** *joins him and they dance together. The track fades out. He is puffing for breath.*

Martin   God, I can't believe we used to dance all night.

Alice   Wimp.

Martin   Now I need an oxygen mask and a crutch.

Alice makes herself a drink.

Martin   Good speech?

Alice   Terrible speech, great sentiments.

Martin   You're pissed.

Alice   Hopefully. That girl Glynis cannot write jokes to save her life – or mine. The farmers should have lynched me. Fuck sake, it was like Saturday night at the crematorium. Even Bruce Forsyth is funnier than me.

Martin   Jokes aside, how was it?

Alice   They hated me. Would have set their collies on me if they could have. Pelted me with their genetically enhanced eggs.

Martin   Christ. I do worry about you, you know.

Alice   Acch. I can handle them.

Martin   You should have let me come with you …

Alice   Why, what were you going to do, poke them with your biro?

Martin   No.

Alice   Anyway, the next big chance to state my case is the press conference at Queen's. That one'll be a breeze.

She looks in the fridge-freezer for ice.

Martin   I remembered the ice.

Alice   Attaboy. So, what did she want?

Martin   Who?

Alice   Fuck sake, Martin. She. Claire.

Martin   (*pause*) She wanted to, I don't know, relive something …

Alice   Relive? You want to fucking relive, die and get reincarnated. What's her job?

Martin   PR. Consultant.

Alice   Wow. (*pause*) Probably on the dole.

Martin   Look, you just don't want to know about anyone unless they're doing worse than you.

Alice   No, Martin, of course they can be doing better than me. As long as they have a terminal disease or something.

Martin   (*laughing*) You are mustard.

Alice   Claire Summerton. She wants something. Perhaps she wants you.

Martin   More like she wants you.

Alice   What?

Martin   She likes women.

Alice   Sure she was going out with the best looking boy at Queen's.

Martin   I know.

Alice   Christ, I thought you only turned lesbo if your boyfriends were dogs.

Martin   Nice phrasing. Stick that in a speech.

Alice   I would but I need every pink vote I can get.

Martin   Oh … on your way home did you look out for that couple?

Alice   (*pause*) The what?

Martin   Y'know, the couple up the cut?

Alice   Oh Christ, not your phantom copulating couple again. I'm beginning to think you live in a Hogarth painting with everyone rutting all over the place.

Martin   They were *there*.

Alice   Well, all I can say is there's a lot more sex out there than ever happens in here. (*kisses him*) Why, do you feel like impregnating me, baby?

Martin   If you knew how unsexy that sounded.

Alice   Come on, it's great. Sex with a purpose. A pleasure *and* a purpose.

Martin   In spite of that admirable utilitarianism I'm going to pass.

Alice   (*sexy*) Aren't you feeling … vaginivorous?

Martin   Oh, for fuck sake, Alice.

Alice　Or is the word a vaginatarian? You know, like a vegetarian only choosier.

Martin　I'm not talking to you when you're like this.

Alice　(*imitates*) I'm not talking to you when you're like thith. God, you're so prissy!

Martin　Doesn't stop you salivating over me like a …

Alice　Like a what? Finish!

Martin *doesn't answer.*

Alice　Heifer in heat, wasn't it last time?

Martin　Sure you're always blootered to the eyeballs. You, you're like a cat with a fucking bell. (*imitates her carrying a glass of ice*) Clink-clink-clink round the house.

Alice　Killjoy, that's what you are, my darling. I'd have more fun with Oliver fucking Cromwell.

Martin　(*watches her pour another drink*) Incredible. All your obsessions about diet and you drink like a trooper. Drinking doesn't help you know.

Alice　It does actually. (*pats vaguely where she thinks her ovaries are*) Unclenches the oul ovaries.

Martin　Fucks the kidneys. How are you going to have time anyway?

Alice　Well, I can sneak you in now.

Martin　No, I mean time for the *baby*.

Alice　There's actually this great book called, 'How to schedule your baby'.

Martin　Oh, God.

Alice　And while we're at this, I hate that sound.

Martin　What?

He's suddenly aware that he's rapping his wedding ring against the table.

Alice   You clanking your wedding chains. Take it off if you want rid.

Martin   I don't want to … Alice.

Alice   I want a baby.

Martin   Look, we'll get it sorted. We went to the hospital today, remember?

Alice   Yes.

Martin   We'll get the results in a few days, okay, love?

Alice   Yes.

Awkward silence.

Martin   Look, Alice, you … (*hastily corrects himself*) we both need to unwind. So tomorrow after your meetings why don't we go out for some fun?

Alice   What sort of fun?

Martin   I don't know … *fun.*

Alice   A visit to the Archives of the Linenhall Library, that's your sort of fun, isn't it?

Martin   Wise up.

Alice   (*sudden enlightenment*) No, I get it. A night out with Claire Summerton. (*pause*) Martin, I have a high visibility job, I'm not fucking going out with some lesbo you picked up.

Martin   Oh, fuck you.

Martin *walks to the door.*

Alice   No, fuck you! What is it, you fancy lesbians? Is that why you won't fucking sleep with me? (**Alice** *grabs up the bottle of vodka*) Fucking stick this in your head, you fucking ball-less cunt.

Martin   Take your best shot. We can always recycle it.

Martin *leaves.*

Alice   I hate you! You're in your own selfish world! You and your washed-up sperm. Useless fucker – fucking cunt! Won't even give me the one thing I want!

Blackout. Sounds of smashing glass.

Scene Nine

Claire*'s flat.* **Claire** *comes in with* **Martin**.

Martin   It's not too late to call, is it?

Claire   Not at all, come in, come in.

She hastily clears some open files away.

Martin   (*looking around, whistles, impressed*) Is this what you got for selling your conscience?

Claire   You should see what I got for selling my body.

Martin   Lights. Real unecological lights.

Claire   I should turn them down.

Martin   No, they're wonderful. Do you think the universe cares about light waste? Stars shine as bright as they can, it's glorious, it's *nature* …

Claire   Are you okay, Martin?

Martin   No. I can feel this huge bitch about Alice coming on. God, it's gone mad. If we're not trying to procreate, we're trying to kill each other. Right now it's not sure if we'll increase the population or deplete it. Malthus would love us. Oh, Christ.

He buries his head in his hands.

Claire   (*comforting him*) You'll be okay.

Martin   She's stressed, I know she's stressed.

Claire   So are you.

Martin   Sometimes it's just like living in a Bette Davis film – non-stop melodrama, without the smoking. She's taken to throwing the glassware at me. I have to wear shoes now all the time. She storms off, I storm off, between us we whip up enough energy to fuel this city! I'm trying to bury myself in my work, bury, that's the word, for I'm not really alive any more, I'm … undeceased, *something*. No, but at least I'm writing a new book. It's exciting! Or maybe I'm doing it just to forget about Alice. (*goes to the window*) Hey, the Waterfront! The Lagan Lookout! Belfast is twinkling.

Claire   Know what the problem is?

Martin   Light pollution?

Claire   You and Alice, honey. You two just can't work together. You're the past, she thinks she's the future.

Martin   What are you then?

Claire   The present. (*pause*) Face it, you two were always incompatible.

Martin   For a while we were very compatible at being incompatible …

Claire   Environment, it's the new religion, Martin. You're living with a fundamentalist and you're not even a believer, time to fess up, *admit* …

Martin   I believe in certain parts.

Claire   That's no good. It's like saying I believe in, say, Moses but I don't believe in Jesus.

Martin   That's fine if you're a Jew.

Claire   Oh, Martin. Look, I admire her ideals but she actually believes nature is more important than humans.

Martin   Well, of equal importance.

Claire   Fuck sake, didn't that go out with the Romans? Reinventing and repackaging the Ancient, that's her vibe. And why does she even want a baby when the world can't sustain it?

Martin   No probs. She'll enroll it in a permaculture course when it's two.

Claire   She should get with the programme. Live in the Now.

Martin   Quick someone, kaftan, please!

Claire   No, I mean it, Martin, leave her in the future, let's have some real fun.

Martin   Yeah, stuff her, let's go out on the town like we used to. Alright?

Claire   That's more like it. Here's a present for you.

She throws him it.

Martin   A blueberry muffin!

Claire   Only way to eat them.

Martin   Buried in sugar and fat! I love it.

Claire   Thought you might.

Martin   Thank you, Claire. Thanks. You're ... thoughtful.

He kisses her on the cheek. It's suddenly a full-on kiss. **Martin** *pulls back.*

Claire   What?

Martin   I thought you were, y'know.

Claire   What?

Martin   A lesbian.

Claire   I never said the word. I just said I preferred women.

Martin   And?

Claire   Which means I like women now. Doesn't mean I don't like men.

Martin   Right.

Claire   I'm a bit tired of women to be honest. The sex is a bit like being frisked by airport security. I want to be taken *hold* of, you know?

She pulls him to her. They kiss. He draws back.

Martin   I can't.

Claire   Why?

Martin   No ... I don't feel anything.

Claire   Nothing?

Martin   No. This is faithful to Alice.

Claire   What about your arse?

She grabs his arse and he laughs.

Claire   Your tongue isn't faithful.

Martin   (*weakening*) Isn't it?

They kiss. She starts to pull off his shirt.

Claire   Let's get you out of this. I need visual stimulus. I have no depth, you see. No hidden depths.

Martin   None?

Claire   Do you want to see?

He helps her to unbutton her jeans.

Martin   (*finds the buttons difficult*) God, I'm all fingers and thumbs.

Claire   (*hotly*) I could find a use for them.

Martin   Yeah.

Claire   Wait. Let's get some ...

She puts some music on low. Coldplay's 'Paradise'.

Claire   To relax.

Martin   Funny. I already went today in a plastic cup.

Claire   What?

Martin   At the hospital. (*pause*) I thought of you, Claire, you don't know how much.

Claire   I've been thinking of you for years. (*touches him*) Your mind might be faithful, but your dick certainly isn't.

Martin   (*worried*) Oh, God.

Claire   Relax. I'm better than a plastic cup.

Martin   Are you sure?

Claire   I'm much better than a plastic cup.

Martin   No. About this.

Claire   Don't think.

Martin   Okay. But I hope you didn't think I was blaming Alice just to get you into bed.

Claire   I didn't.

Martin   It's not her fault. She has to fight so hard. The Assembly hates her. They're fucking dickheads, sure that Sammy Wilson won't even acknowledge climate change.

Claire   Shh. Leave it now.

Martin   Sorry. It's just I can talk to you.

Claire   I've missed you.

Martin   Yes.

Claire   That day I first saw you. Freshers' week. And these girls were trying to get you to join this croquet club or something ridiculous, and you didn't even realize we were all crazy about you.

Martin   I never knew.

Claire   (*pause*) Grab my hair – hard.

He grabs her hair. She kisses his neck. They writhe together.

They quickly take the rest of their clothes off. **Martin** *stops at his boxers. They kiss again.* **Martin** *breaks away.*

Claire   What?

Claire *moves closer to him again. Touches him.* **Martin** *wriggles away.*

Martin   No.

Claire   Come on.

Martin   No, I can't. I really can't.

He quickly puts on his things. **Claire** *follows suit.*

Martin   Sorry.

Claire   It's fine. I just hope I haven't ruined things between us?

Martin   No, course not.

Claire   Stay a while.

Martin   I should go.

Claire   Where to? Back to the house of the broken glass?

Martin   (*laughs*) My God, in the past few days our kitchen has had more trauma than the Trauma Centre. I'm writing about it, you know.

Claire   Your kitchen?

Martin   The Trauma Centre. Not even Alice knows about it.

Claire   Why not?

Martin   Well, I've only done a rough chapter, but it's wild, and Alice can't do wild any more.

Claire   I can do wild.

Martin   If you thought the famine book was a hot potato …

Claire   (*laughing*) Great. So how about sending me a sneaky preview?

Martin   Well … (*looking at her*)

Claire   It can't be that controversial, can it?

Martin   It can. The gist of it is, Claire, we're part of a giant victims' industry. Why? The EU are still chucking money at us, the US, the UK, they're all still whacking us peace money to stop us fighting again. Southern Ireland has fiscal problems, right? No problem, start a conflict.

Claire   That's cynical.

Martin   It's a game. See the new head commissioner? Jimmy Thompson.

Claire   The newsreader?

Martin   Big bucks. We're giving him a hundred grand a year. He lives in a mansion up Cave Hill, the closest he's been to trauma is having his hair slightly ruffled in a riot, but he knows the game rightly. He's a victim, you're a victim, I'm a victim, capiche?

Claire   I'm getting the picture.

Martin   Here, I can even get you a grant for your victimhood. What did you see, the aftermath of a bomb? That'll get you a grand easy. See a mangled body? Five grand easy. It's a gift. Trip to South Africa to worship Nelson Mandela's arse? No prob. Or a mini-break to Majorca. So let me ask you. Are you a victim?

Claire   I'm a victim.

Martin   Why do you think we do the stories? Danny says to me, 'Keep it live, Marty-boy, keep it living. Keep it up, so we keep our jobs'.

Claire   Who's Danny?

Martin   My boss. Famed for a bomb in a London toilet.

Claire   God.

Martin   I know. Every time you flush you think you're about to be blown sky high. Look, it's all self-perpetuating. Trauma training – it's right up there with Belleek and Irish linen, as one of our biggest cultural industries. Its only real purpose is to make peace money. What are we on, Peace Three now? How many more fucking peaces are there going to be? It's a joke. The Troubles. It was a minor scuffle. So a few thousand died, yeah, but it's over years now. All this wallowing in victimhood. Half the stories I read probably came from the same person. The biggest criterion for getting a grant as a victim is you have to be on the dole. You get a job, hey presto, you're no longer a fucking victim, no more cash for you. (**Martin** *picks up the blueberry muffin*) What a joke. Alice doesn't know. Fuck her. She used to be so passionate about everything. So moral. And now she's just a deal-maker. Sinn Féin, for fuck sake.

Martin *leaves.*

Scene Ten

Trauma Centre. **Martin** *is at his computer. He's on his mobile.*

Martin   Just sending it through now, Claire.

He presses a button.

Martin   Right now. Wooosh-wooosh-wooosshh. Yes, that's the authentic sound of cyberspace, Claire.

Danny *comes in carrying a chocolate box.*

Martin   (*flustered*) Right, got to go. Talk later.

Martin *switches his mobile off.*

Danny   (*bringing the box to* **Martin**) Here you are, Marty-boy. Have a chocolate. They're from the Diversity is Good Convention.

Martin *looks in.*

Danny   See? The dark chocolate's for Afros, the milk's for coloureds and the white's for us whiteys.

Martin   (*taking the Caramac*) Great. Caramac.

Danny   That's for the Asians. Me, I always liked white the best. You see, even chocolate makes you reappraise your prejudices.

Martin   I suppose.

Danny   Funny thing, my Ma always liked Black Magic. Mad, eh? I'll pass them round the clients.

Martin   I haven't seen any in today.

Danny   None?

Martin   No.

Danny   It's alright. The chapati-making class will be in soon. They'll munch them up. (*pause*) I hope you're not sending anything from here.

Martin   No, no.

Danny   You're dealing with confidential, sensitive material.

Martin   I know and I …

Danny   I very much hope you're not a cause for concern, Martin.

Martin   Danny, I'm not.

Danny   Because if you are a cause for concern I'll have to ask you to leave.

Martin   I'm not a cause for concern.

Danny   Which would be very disappointing as I've told the commissioners your wife is coming to the grand launch of Reflections.

Martin   She'll come.

Danny   Good. Doves of Peace have Naomi Long, so we have to compete, Martin, compete.

Martin   With you there, Danny.

Danny   Good. Now tell me I can trust you.

Martin   You can trust me.

Danny   You have to protect all our jobs. Trauma centres, cross-com projects, you criticize us, we all fall, half of us are ex-paramilitaries. Fuck me, it's like a *Who's Who* of freedom-fighters in here. It's like Debrett's.

Martin I know.

Danny Good fella. I can trust you.

Martin You can trust me.

Danny Nobody here wants the truth, okay?

Martin Okay.

Danny Great, and now I can trust you, here's something for you.

Martin What is it?

Danny Funding application.

Martin Ah.

Danny Now, I know it seems daunting, but after the first one, you'll start skittering them out. That's life now, Martin, constant accountability, am I right?

Martin It's ten pages!

Danny Buzzwords, Martin, Commitment, Community, Client, Creativity. Ca … Can you think of any other c words?

Martin Er.

Danny Now, don't be filthy, Martin.

Martin Look at this. 'In five hundred words … '

Danny I've already given you four. This is why we hired you, Martin, sure this is a breeze compared to your book, more like a quick gust, it'll take you no time, right?

Martin Right.

Danny Good fella. Just emphasise how busy we are, right?

Martin Right. But …

Danny What, Martin? (**Martin** *hesitates*) Express.

Martin   Doesn't it ever concern you that hardly anyone turns up, I've only seen one person ever in the Room of Remembrance …

Danny   Shh …

Martin   No, I'm going to speak up. And most of the people who ever use the therapies are the staff. Doesn't that concern you?

Danny   In a word, no. All the staff are victims. Don't you understand? Billy – ask Billy his past. He only got the job to stop him laying hoax bombs everywhere.

Martin   Oh.

Danny   Give him a battery and some wires and he's like fucking MacGyver. Yes, and I wouldn't touch his yoghurts if I were you.

Martin   Well, I didn't mean to …

Danny   This is not a numbers game, Martin. If we can help one person …

Martin   I know, I know and you're right, Danny.

Danny   (*eats a chocolate*) See what you're making me do? I don't even fucking like chocolate.

Scene Eleven

Stormont. **Alice** *and* **Claire** *enter* **Alice**'s *office.* **Claire** *looks around.*

Claire   So here we are. The corridors of power.

Alice   I wish. Just lackeys of Westminster, that's us.

Claire   Well, you've done brilliantly.

Alice   You know how?

Claire   How?

Alice   Female genitalia. Simple as.

Claire   (*pause*) You used your sex … ?

Alice   God, no. I just mean they needed a woman in government to make up the numbers.

Claire   Oh, God, I thought …

Alice   No, no. I just meant I was a woman. I'd never sleep my way …

Claire   No, no, course not. But I think you're underselling yourself. You got in here on talent, end of.

Alice   Thanks. Thank you. Look, I was sorry about the pub last week.

Claire   Oh, it's fine.

Alice   A whole night on how to make GM crops palatable.

Claire   Bit of salt?

Alice   (*laughs*) Believe me. Extremely boring to the layperson. And my assistant is hopeless at writing jokes.

Claire   Actually, that's exactly what I wanted to talk to you about.

Alice   Jokes?

Claire   (*pause*) GM crops.

Alice   Oh.

Claire   Yes.

Alice   Oh.

Claire   Maybe Martin told you I was in Public Relations.

Alice   He said something …

Claire   Right now I'm working for Amtrex.

Alice   Ah. The biotech firm.

Claire   Exactly.

Alice   Who coincidentally will provide the seeds for the trials here.

Claire   They're doing well. They own half the rice, cotton and soya in India and China and –

Alice   You don't have to go on. They're scum. Profiteers.

Claire   Just business.

Alice   They're probably developing some spacecraft right now so as soon as they've raped the planet, they can fuck off.

Claire   Alice, nine billion people to feed by 2050. Grow the GM, we don't have to knock down the Rainforest. Take your pick. You're intelligent. You got a first in biology, didn't you?

Alice   2:1 actually.

Claire   Shame. So unless we find a planet to harvest by 2050, we're screwed, yeah?

Alice   Look, I don't really have time, Claire, to debate –

Claire   No debate. I'm not going to bore you with facts, Alice. I've got something here harder than facts. Hypotheticals.

Alice   Go on.

Claire   If … *if* an unknown company was to get in contact …

Alice   Like Amtrex.

Claire   Like Amtrex. Good girl. If an unknown company was to approach, say, a government minister …

Alice   Like me.

Claire   Like you. You're *good* at this.

Alice   I've been approached before.

Claire   And they asked her – or him – to endorse a certain paper concerning field trials …

Alice   Go on, Claire.

Claire   They could actually offer this minister a role as an eco-adviser.

Alice   Impossible. You can't go from the moral high ground to the gutter.

Claire   But she – or he – could monitor morally what they're doing. This hypothetical company is very open.

Alice   Yes. About everything but their science.

Claire   Look, we're already with you on climate change. It's eroding the land, you're right, and that's why we need GM.

Alice   You really came here expecting me – her – to change her vote?

Claire   Of course not. Just let the independent Unionist go. She'll still come out in roses, like she's done her best.

Alice   Right.

Claire   Later, if she chooses us, she could spend time at home with her husband, raise a family …

Alice   Right.

Claire   Get rid of the dark rings under her eyes …

Alice   Look, I was up at the crack for London today.

Claire   Pursue her own environmental interests. *Imagine.*

Alice   I've enjoyed this little game, but let's finish it here.

Claire   Game?

Alice   No, it's been amusing. As I said, I've been approached before. I keep thinking: is this the girl who once stormed the Students' Union and squirted a peeler in the eye with an extinguisher? Was that just a game to you then?

Claire   Who knows? Can't remember.

Alice   Try. Go on.

Claire   (*pause*) It was against student grant cuts.

Alice   Exactly. You did it for money.

Claire   No, I already had my grant. I was protesting for future generations. And I was having fun, squirting peelers in the eye.

Alice   Well, let me tell you, if you think I am selling out this land's future to Amtrex scum –

Claire   Hey, cool it, it's not like you're signing a peace treaty with Hitler here. Who are you, guardian of the planet? Rape the planet, hardly, it's consensual sex, nature and business, it's natural chemistry, honey-bee. The crops *will* happen. You think you're the future, Alice, fact is, you're the past. You're like some Luddite stopping progress. It's going to happen anyway, just *accelerate* it.

Alice   Pestilence, disease, world famine … mean *anything* to you?

Claire   (*shrugs*) Scaremongering?

Alice   Let me tell you what we're dealing with. In Africa and China, cancer rates have soared, reproductive and immune system disorders have tripled …

Claire   Where's your proof it's GM?

Alice   And Amtrex has made these seeds impossible to germinate on their own just so every year the poorest farmers have to buy new ones. That is how low you are.

Claire   And your organic seeds are gobbled up by the first plague of insects. That is how pie-in-the-sky you are. Think of it, an end to famine.

Alice   There is no end.

Claire   You think Sinn Féin is going to support you for much longer?

Alice   Yes. I do.

Claire   The Irish government are about to approve GM. Won't be long before Sinn Féin is bought by the idea that it's good for an all-Ireland economy.

Alice *gets up.*

Alice   It's been nice meeting you again.

Claire   Let's stop the hypothets. Let me tell you why you will come on board.

Alice   Huh, you've no dirt on me.

Claire   When you go home tonight, ask Martin.

Alice *sits back down.*

Alice   Ask him what exactly?

Claire   You know, I admire you. This is the most inward-looking part of the world, yet you look outward. Christ, we could win the Olympics in navel-gazing. No, sphincter-gazing, sure our heads are up our own arses. But not you. No, you shunned the narrow green and orange politics of this piss-hole of a place.

Alice   What has Martin done? *Tell* me.

Claire   And in spite of (*pats her under-eyes to denote* **Alice***'s dark rings*) this, you're the best-looking minister here. What was that Stalin said about how he always gave government posts to the deformed and ugly because they were the most ruthless? You'd've thought Stalin was working at Stormont! Edwin Poots, Sammy Wilson … Well, it's been nice to chat. Up here on Blueberry Hill.

She gets up.

Alice   Claire. I will never come on board. Never.

Claire   Oh, don't sound so Protestant. Where there's a way …

Alice   There's no way.

Claire   Speak to Martin. First.

Alice   You speak to me. *You.*

Claire   Call me in the morning. Maybe I can help you with a new speech.

Alice   Get out.

Claire   I'm quite good at writing jokes.

Claire *leaves.*

Alice *paces the room, visibly upset.*

Alice   Claire Summerton.

She pulls a compact out of her bag, checks the area under her eyes. Outside the office, **Claire** *takes out her mobile and calls her boss.*

Claire   Tone. Yeah, I'm in the hallowed home of corruption itself. Yep, I think we've secured her. No, I *know* we've secured her. No, this time I'm not the u in failure … yes, she was a friend, but not now … you have to be a bit unethical to be ethical, don't you? … no, it wasn't a Machiavelli quote, one of my own, Tone. Yep, her hubby's a bigger embarrassment than Iris Robinson. Thanks, Tone. Bye, Tone, bye.

She clicks her mobile off. She lets out a giant sigh.

Scene Twelve

Trauma Centre. **Danny** *opens up* **Martin***'s computer, reads off it.*

Danny   Oh, Marty-boy.

He holds his head.

Danny   I knew it, didn't I, Verity? I knew it. A writer.

Danny *walks out.*

Scene Thirteen

Living room/kitchen. **Martin** *is reading.* **Alice** *comes in carrying files.*

Martin   How was London?

Alice   Perfect. I told our select committee I think we've the GM vote in the bag.

Martin   Well, that's great, isn't it?

Alice   Flight home I was crammed in by a fatty. Send her on a crash-diet, please. Fuck sake, we nearly did crash. They had to send ten normal people to the back as ballast.

Martin   (*laughing*) Poor Alice.

Alice   Poor Alice is right. I took the brunt of it. Other side they could hardly get the drinks trolley past her. Her arm was so big it was stuck out like a crossing signal.

Martin   (*makes her a drink*) What's your poison?

Alice   Strychnine. No, GM crops.

Martin   Wee vod?

Alice   I thought I broke the bottle throwing it at you.

Martin   You did, darling, but I thoughtfully replaced it.

She watches him.

Alice   You're being nice.

Martin   Alice, we've been arguing far too much lately. I just want us to get along.

Alice   She said she'd just had a baby.

Martin   Who?

Alice   Her in the plane. Her of the giant ham hocks. She said she was on holiday in New Zealand the night she conceived. Right during orgasm there was an earthquake.

Martin   Was it not just her breaking the bed?

Alice   It's not fair. Medically she's everything wrong, but she gets to have a baby. Me, I've done everything right.

Martin   That's the way the cookie crumbles.

Alice   She would know. Darling, why don't we go to an earthquake zone? Haiti!

Martin   (*laughing*) Wonderful. It'd beat Portrush.

Alice   Ah, Portrush! The Haiti of the north coast.

Martin   (*looks at* **Alice** *closely*) You alright? You seem a bit …

Alice   What?

Martin   Overbright.

Alice   Well, that's probably my alcohol problem.

Martin   I didn't say you had an alcohol problem.

Alice   It's you actually have an alcohol problem.

Martin   Me?

Alice   Well, you have a problem with my alcohol, so if that's not an alcohol problem …

Alice *pours another drink.*

Martin   Alice, are you okay?

Alice   I met Claire this evening. (*pause*) After my flight got in.

Martin   Oh.

Alice   I thought you'd be more surprised.

Martin   Why? Sure she said she was all for catching up.

Alice   Catching out, more like.

Martin   What do you mean?

Alice   Anxious are we?

Martin   No. Just asking.

Alice   She lied about her job.

Martin   Public Relations.

Alice   No. Works for Amtrex.

Martin *shrugs, not knowing it.*

Alice   Big multinational GM crops machine. We had quite a chat. She wants me to help her move them into Northern Ireland.

Martin   At which point you told her to fuck off, right?

Alice   God, I told you she wanted something.

Martin   What a devious ...

Alice   Of course she wanted something.

Martin   Alice, I didn't know. (*pause*) Well, we'll not be seeing her again.

Alice   Unfortunately I might.

Martin *stares at her.*

Alice   Speak to Martin, she said.

Martin   What?

Alice   Did you sleep with her?

Martin   No.

Alice   Because I wouldn't blame you if you did. I'll understand.

Martin   (*sceptical*) Oh, sure you would.

Alice   I mean, I work with men, I can't say I'm never tempted. But I would never because of my career first and you second. You second, I have to tell the truth here.

Martin   I did not sleep with her.

Alice   Because I have to know the extent of what we're dealing with here.

Martin   I didn't. She ... kissed me.

Alice   I thought you said she was a lesbian.

Martin   I kissed her back.

Alice   Yes, that's a very odd sort of a lesbian.

Martin   I don't think she's anything ... she's nothing.

Alice   She's one fucking hell of a nothing right now.

Martin   She's so slippery. You can't get hold of her.

Alice   You presumably did.

Martin   Alice.

Alice   Did she photo you? Did she?

Martin   I don't know.

Alice   Oh, God, MLA's husband in affair with Amtrex high-flyer. I'll be laughed out of the vote.

Martin   Ignore her. You could destroy ... you can't.

Alice   Bastard. I could *kill* you right now.

Alice *lifts up the vodka bottle to throw it at him.*

Alice   Might as well go for it.

Martin   Alice. No.

Alice   (*setting it down*) No, it would be churlish to break it just after you bought a new one.

Martin   Not to mention the waste.

Alice   Don't push me, pal.

She opens the fridge, takes out a melon.

Martin   No, not the melon.

Alice *throws it from one hand to another.*

Martin   Put down the melon now.

Alice   It's not a melon, you moron. It's a cantaloupe.

Martin   Put it down.

Alice   Fucking bastard!

She hurls it at him, just missing him. He runs at her, grabs her hands.

Martin   Stop it! Stop it now!

Alice   You fucking creep! I don't even get to ruin my own political career! It's you who does! Useless fucker!

Martin   Calm down!

Alice   Why didn't you tell me? At least I could have had some fun first. I could have slept with the whole Assembly, me, the new porn-queen of Stormont, frolicking naked, sowing my wild, organic oats. Say no to GM, say yes to S & M! In fact, I should have slept with Claire myself. Let's face it, she has bigger balls than you, so I'd have more chance getting preggers with her than with you.

Martin   (*softer*) Calm down.

Alice   (*long pause*) I'm calm – as I'll ever be.

Martin   Now step away from the fridge.

Alice   What is this, NYPD Blues?

Martin *lets her go.*

Alice   Let's just get back to you and Claire, shall we?

Martin   I didn't have sex with her, Alice.

Alice   Friends Reunited. What did that mean to you, darling, reunite in the same bed?

Martin   Alice.

Alice   No, no, I'm really trying to work out your thought process, Martin. What did you think it was, shag.com, fuckyouroldfriends. com?

Martin   Alice, I did not!

Alice   Do you swear you didn't? (*he doesn't answer*) Because if you swear, I will weather this whole thing through …

Martin   I swear. I nearly did.

Alice   (*not quite trusting*) Okay.

Martin But …

Alice But?

Martin It's the book, Alice.

Alice What book?

Martin Only the one I tried to tell you about. I emailed her a chapter.

Alice Show me.

Martin *passes her a copy from beside the computer. She reads it.*

Martin It's about the Trauma Centre. The whole farce of it. Hundreds of thousands of quid going in and they only have about ten victims who they keep as victims. Not allowed to be cured, because if they are cured, it's the end of the cash.

Alice (*horrified*) It's like you're a Holocaust-denier! A Troubles-denier! Denying the trauma!

Martin I haven't published it.

Alice You gave it to Claire. Sinn Féin'll go mad. They'll pull the GM deal.

Martin I'm so sorry.

Alice *looks at him.*

Martin I'm going to sort this out, Alice, who does she think she is? She's … no one.

Alice Oh, she's quite a someone. She's fabulously gifted at blackmail. At this rate I'd heartily recommend her to the DUP.

Martin (*pulling on his coat*) I'm going to speak to her now. She's not going to destroy your career, no way.

Alice You know where she lives?

Martin Yes. I've … been there.

Alice I see.

Martin   What's that supposed to mean?

Alice   (*picks up the melon*) I'm going to feed this to the worms. You see, there'll be no waste.

He touches her back lightly. She shivers.

Martin   I'm going to take this problem away, Alice. Don't you even think another thing about it, okay? Okay?

Alice *doesn't answer.*

Martin   Okay?

Alice   Don't even bother coming back unless you sort it.

Martin *goes out.*

Scene Fourteen

Claire's flat. **Martin** *arrives outside the flat, rehearsing what he's about to say.*

Martin   We were friends, so surely that counts for something. (*rubs his forehead*) No-o-o. (*resets himself firmly*) Listen to me, Claire. (*stops*) No, sound like a fucking headmaster.

He buzzes **Claire**'s *intercom.* **Claire** *hears the buzz and presses it.*

Martin   Claire, love. It's Martin. Open up.

Claire   Martin. What are you doing here?

Martin   You know what I've come for.

Claire   (*mocking*) Aren't you insatiable?

Martin   You've threatened Alice. Come on, let me in.

Claire   Martin, it isn't personal, it's business.

Martin   But I didn't even have sex with you.

Claire   As good as. Didn't you see the camera?

Martin   Bullshit. What have you got over us, Claire, a couple of my thoughts?

Claire   Let's see. MLA's husband writes (and I quote): 'There are no victims left from the Troubles. The only so-called victims have been fabricated by money-making organizations'.

Martin   You – Claire, we were friends.

Claire   Were. Always in the past, eh?

Martin   Look, it's my book, my intellectual property.

Claire   Intellectual's going a bit far, isn't it?

Martin   God. Just how low can you go?

Claire   (*sexy*) Very. I bend to places I bet Alice doesn't.

Martin   Seducing people, blackmail, what else do you do?

Claire   I murder them, then cook them up in a blueberry pie. See? You got off lightly, Martin.

Martin   Does Amtrex know what you're up to?

Claire   I'm going now.

Martin   You mustn't do this to Alice.

Claire   But what Alice believes in is wrong.

Martin   Be reasonable.

Claire   I'm full of reason. It's you who's not. Goodnight.

Martin   I'm going to stand here all night if I have to, Claire. Hand over the fucking manuscript now!

Claire   Who are you? Al Pacino?

Martin   Claire! Claire! It's my book! Mine! What are you – why the fuck?

Martin *keeps buzzing the intercom.*

Martin   Claire?

He starts smacking it with his hand. She puts on Coldplay's 'Paradise' to block it out and opens one of her files.

Martin   Answer me, bitch!

Martin *lays his head on the intercom, gives up, turns, walks away. Sees a couple having sex in a dark entry. He watches them a moment. Suddenly they notice him and freeze with fear. He hurries away.*

Scene Fifteen

The Trauma Centre, the next morning. **Danny** *is in the Room of Remembrance, quietly immersed in archives and images of the Troubles.*

Alice *comes in, looking for* **Martin**.

Alice   Oh. I was looking for …

Danny   Alice. I know you from the TV.

Alice   I better go.

Danny   Wait. (**Alice** *hesitates*) I gave Martin a story yesterday. About one of the Disappeared. I didn't tell him it was my brother.

Alice   Oh.

Danny   At night he still comes into my dreams like some dark puppet, all froze from the bog or earth he's buried in, and the only way I can get him to leave is snap him in half, break his bones in two, crack him like hawthorn I do, and the screams of him as he falls and falls. The Disappeared. Well, he won't disappear to me and I keep on breaking and breaking him night after night. I could kill for him, my beautiful brother, I know who they are, I could drink their blood till it's pouring out of me, rip out their faces, smash their heads like paintbombs against the walls, but the one sole thing that stops me … it's here. Can you understand what that is like?

Alice   I know it's important here what you do.

Danny But does Martin?

Alice *doesn't answer.*

Danny I don't want to lose it.

Alice I'm sorry. I … went to the hospital.

Alice *looks as if she is going to cry.* **Danny** *gives her Verity Bear. She holds the bear to her.*

Scene Sixteen

Two hours later. Press conference at Queen's. **Claire** *is standing waiting on the periphery of the journalists.* **Alice** *goes up to make her speech. Applause echoes.*

Alice Good morning, everyone. Very impressive turn-out at this short notice but then of course you are all the types'd trample over your toddler to get a bit of fresh news. (*pause*) As you all know, there are only four weeks until what I believe is one of the most important votes in this country's history. Two hours ago I was coming here today to tell you why I as an MLA will be voting against the GM trials. Instead I have come here to tell you I am standing down forthwith. Due to family reasons.

I am deeply sorry to let down the voters. I apologise to my colleagues in the Green Party. The personal loss of this job is … (*she nearly cries*) indescribable.

She pulls herself together.

It's been a brief eighteen months in office but it has been quite an experience. I confess I will miss the sight of Martin McGuinness singing The Sash as he aimlessly wanders the corridors of Stormont. Before I step down, I want to say a few final words. Nature controlled by humans will destroy humans. Nature *will* rebel. I urgently call for a world-wide moratorium on releasing genetically engineered products. I urge the Assembly to strongly resist the rise of life-science companies such as Amtrex who are perfectly happy to spread disease, toxins and devastation across the earth for the sake of a quick buck.

Oh, sure I know what you all call me – Mrs Apocablip, The Nostradamus of the North … but I promise you that right now we are facing one of the greatest potential disasters the global environment has known. I urge you to say no now.

Right, no questions please. Now I am off to a new quieter life.

Beam me up, Scotty.

Alice *smiles.* **Alice** *leaves the stage. She walks down to* **Claire**.

Alice   Do you honestly think I would have ever voted for GM crops?

Claire   No, but at least I got you out of the vote.

Alice   You? It wasn't you. 'Most likely to succeed'. Yeah. Most likely to succeed at global genocide.

Alice *walks away.*

Claire   (*calls after her*) Environmentalist! Mentalist, more like! GM crops are the future and you know it!

Alice *leaves and* **Claire** *is left, alone and upset.*

Scene Seventeen

Living room/kitchen. **Alice** *is dancing to 'It's the End of the World as We Know It' by R.E.M.* **Martin** *comes in, rough and unkempt from a night of no sleep. Unseen by her, he watches her lovingly.*

Martin   Is this a private party?

Alice *turns the music off and runs to him, kissing him.*

Martin   (*surprised at the welcome*) What's this?

Alice   Where were you all night? I was so worried.

Martin   (*laughing*) You looked it dancing away there.

Alice   I only dance when I'm devastated.

Martin   I thought you'd still be at the press conference.

Alice   No.

Martin   Or Stormont.

Alice   No, not there today. (*pause*) Nor any other day. I'm fre-e-ee!

Martin   What?

Alice   I've resigned.

Martin   But … Alice …

Alice   Why? Did you sort it with her?

Martin   No, but I will. I *will*.

Alice   I've sorted everything for myself, Martin. That's what ministers do. Sort out messes. Usually other people's … but sometimes your own.

Martin   Christ sake, why didn't you tell me first?

Alice   Your phone was dead.

Martin   You just rolled over and let her win? You let me screw your life up … forever?

Alice   Martin, I didn't resign because of Claire Summerton.

Martin   But you love your job.

Alice   I loved it so much.

Martin   (*panicking*) What happened? Alice.

Alice   (*pause*) I went to the hospital. First thing.

Martin   And?

Alice   Don't worry. It's not you. You're normal. Healthy.

Martin   Oh.

Alice   It's me, love. They said my womb was an … an inhospitable environment. Me? Can you imagine?

Martin   Oh, Alice, my love.

Alice   Barren, you know? Isn't it strange? All the words for women are environmental. Never for men. (*almost laughing*) And to think I've been on those stupid bean diets, mung beans, fucking minging beans, sent from the bowels of hell by my fucking dietician, the King of the Skitters himself …

Martin   Surely this can't be it.

Alice   They said it's probably the stress. I said it was probably the sight of Peter Robinson's smug face every morning. They laughed. So, I went and resigned. Look, I've been overdoing it for years. And, yes, I have an alcohol problem. A new life I need – there may be a chance yet for me. This time it's not about me making the world a better place to live in, it's about making me a better place to live in. And with. I don't want to lose you, Martin.

Martin   You would never.

Alice   I was so scared last night I'd lost you.

Martin   Me, I was so scared I'd destroyed your future.

Alice   And we've been arguing so much.

Martin   Well, we've always bickered.

Alice   I suppose.

Martin   I've always thought of it as exercising the last little remnant of our intellects.

Alice   Keeps us young.

Martin   On our toes.

Alice   But we mustn't go too far. I don't want you treading on eggshells.

Martin   So that's what you're going to throw next at me.

They laugh.

Alice   Things will be better … I promise.

Martin   Just kinder we have to be, that's all.

He picks up the chapter of his book from the table.

Martin   First things first.

He tears it.

Alice   No way, Martin

Martin   But it's too harsh.

Alice   Yes, but if you think there's something in it.

Martin   I don't know what I believe any more.

Alice   We have to be the way we used to be. Stand up for the truth. I've failed, but you don't have to.

Martin   You haven't failed. Listen to me, Alice, we'll phone the young activists, direct action in the fields, anything.

Alice   You'll help me?

Martin   Actually I'd love to throw a spud at a peeler. Nothing too illegal. Maybe run over them with a combine harvester.

They laugh.

Alice   And no more laws round here, no more blueberries, definitely no more bluebloodyberries. God, I've been obsessed about food, haven't I? Like some sort of psycho Jamie Oliver.

Martin   On additives.

Alice   On additives. Hold me.

Martin *holds her.*

Martin   Do you remember our first night? The fancy dress party. You were dressed up as a crash victim, bandages, your head all painted red.

Alice   The embarrassment. Half the people there thought I went as a tampax. I hid in the corner.

Martin   But you still shone out. You always did. I adored you.

Alice   Not Claire?

Martin   Never Claire.

Alice   Did you sleep with her?

Martin   (*pause*) No.

Alice   Oh, Martin.

Martin   We're going to be fine. We'll live here quietly, Alice, for years. It'll be our little burrow away from the world. And we'll live on our own honey and the apple tree and the herbs and lettuce, we'll plant potatoes in the garden too, all fresh and natural, so even if the floods come or famine stalks the land, we'll be safe in our own little eco-system and we'll live here till we get old together and when you die I'll throw you on the wormery ...

Alice   What if you die first?

Martin   Then you throw me on the wormery, but we won't be sad because we'll have lived a beautiful life together, no, we won't be at all sad because our children will be just down the road, the twins.

Alice   (*laughs delightedly*) The twins!

Martin   It'll all be wonderful, even better than it used to be.

Alice   You know, seeing her again brought it all back. Sometimes I just wish it was like we were twenty again.

Martin   You do?

Alice   Always going out, hanging out at the Union.

Martin   Is Alice McFee actually saying that she misses the past?

Alice   Yeah, all the down in ones, vomiting in the plant pots, flipping the finger at peeler vans, all that life-affirming stuff.

Martin   Grab your coat then.

Alice   For where?

Martin   The Union. Sure, let's shoot.

Alice   Could I pass for twenty?

Martin   In the dark lights of the Union.

Alice   In a full burqa.

Martin   No, you look gorgeous. Let's go.

Alice   Let's! One sec but. Just have to see to my dark rings first.

Martin   Dark rings. You're perfect.

Alice *disappears into the bedroom.* **Martin** *waits for her aimlessly, checks his mobile, but there are no messages.* **Martin** *switches on the television.*

Newsreader's Voice-over … in Yunnan, Southern China. This is the first footage to be smuggled out from this remote province, one of China's biggest growers of GM rice. For months whole villages and towns in Yunnan have been in the grip of appalling starvation, malnutrition and disease. This year's crops of fruit and vegetables have failed entirely and even the rice yield has been less than expected. This villager told us that all the bees in the local hives have died and almost no flowers have bloomed. Everywhere the camera turns, fields and allotments lie in barren disuse. Some of the following scenes may be distressing to viewers.

Alice *comes back out.*

Alice   Ready! Let's relive the magic!

She stops, sees the footage.

Martin   It's started.

Alice *watches with him. A wind starts howling outside. A door bangs open.*

Alice   Yes. It's begun.

She and **Martin** *huddle together. Petals blow into the room.*

Martin   Shall I go out to the garage and put the plutonium into our spacecraft?

Alice   Yes. But where shall we go?

Martin   Straight ahead.

Alice   Some kind planet. With a sun and a moon. With better weather.

Martin   Yes.

Alice   Oh, yes.

Fadeout. Stars twinkle above. Blackout.

Desolate Heaven

Ailís Ní Ríain

For Madeleine

Desolate Heaven was first performed at Theatre503, London, on 5 February 2013 with the following cast:

Freda/Laoise/Bridie	Bríd Brennan
Orlaith	Carla Langley
Sive	Evelyn Lockley
Direction	Paul Robinson
Design	James Perkins
Lighting	Lee Curran
Sound and Music	Simon Slater

Characters

Sive,* *12 years old, female, gentle, innocent, timid*
Orlaith,* *13 years old, female, tom-boy, street-wise, confident*
Mother, Sive's Mother
Father, Orlaith's Father

The following three roles are played by one female actor in her 50s

Freda, *The Farmer*
Laoise,* *The Lorry Lady*
Bridie, *The Butcher*
–   *A physical response*
/   *The lines overlap*
(words in brackets) Irish pronunciation/translation

The roles of the Mother and Father may also be played by the actors playing Orlaith and Sive.

The play is set in Ireland

Contains a short extract from The Stolen Child *by W B Yeats.*

**Sive rhymes with dive.*
**'Orlaith' is pronounced 'Orl' (as in oral) and 'Laith' (as in 'la')
also spelt Orla.*
**Laoise is pronounced lee-sha*

Scene One

Two young girls, **Orlaith** *and* **Sive** *on a cold beach in Ireland on a 'day out' organised for young carers. It's dull and dank. Tempo is fast, they often overlap.*

Orlaith (*highly animated*) Doin' the shoppin'!

Sive Doin' the cookin'!

Orlaith Doin' the cleanin'!

Sive Collectin' the benefit!

Orlaith Collectin' the pills!

Sive Payin' the bills!

Orlaith Dodgin' the bills!

Both 'N' knowin' which to dodge!

Orlaith Or we'd have no light –

Sive No 'tricity!

Orlaith Be totally in the dark –

Sive Totally in the dark with /

Orlaith (*with a wink*) No time for all the little things little girls do!

Sive All the little things!

Orlaith (*totally exaggerated, playacting as the old townswomen to⁺*) Aaaaaahhh must be terrible hard on you altogether.

Sive (*aping her*) Aaaaaaaahhh 'tis awful altogether!

Orlaith (*hand wringing*) Awful altogether.

Sive Sure how awful could it possibly be???

Orlaith (*garbled, fast*) Y'know Auschwitz, Hiroshima and the Famine?

Sive Yeah.

Orlaith   Well way worse than all them put together!

Sive   All them put together?

Orlaith   ALL them put together!*

Sive   Is there no hope for them girls so?

Orlaith   NO!!!

Long pause.

Much slower tempo. Their voices lower in tone.

Orlaith (*darker mood, depressed by the day that's in it*)   This is total crap isn't it?

Sive   –

Orlaith   Bally-feckin'-glanna. Excuse for a beach.

Short pause.

Total arseways, girl. I'da gone go-kartin' or somethin'. Somethin' fierce y'know?

Sive   –

Orlaith   Their idea of a nice day out at the beach? Shag all to do.

Dodgy dodge-ems and dog shit. Even the bloody tide's out.

Has better sense.

(*Totally deflated.*) Jesus.

Pause.

(*Roughly, tired of getting no response from* **Sive**.)   Do you actually talk?

Sive   –

Orlaith   Hello?!

Sive   –

Orlaith   Hello, Hello, Hello, Hello, Hello???

Sive   What???!!!

Orlaith (*with a cheeky grin*)   Where's yer manners girl?

Sive (*quietly*)   Leave me alone will ya?

Orlaith   Speak when yer spoken to!

Sive   What d'ya want me to say like?

Orlaith   Feckin' anythin'!

Short pause.

Just somethin'.

Pause.

Just so I know yer here like.

Sive   I am here!

Pause.

Orlaith (*softening her manner*)   Are ya fierce shy or somethin'?

Sive (*immediately*)   No!

Short pause.

(*Softer.*)   Yeah.

Orlaith   –

What year ya in?

Sive   First.

Pause.

Sive   What year you in?

Orlaith   Second.

Sive   You fourteen so?

Orlaith   Next month.

Sive   –

Orlaith   Are you down Riordan [*pron. Reerdan*] Street?

Sive   Next one on.

Orlaith   Carroll Street?

Sive   – (*Slight acknowledgement.*)

Orlaith   I'm over on Ryanbarry. D'ya know it?

Sive (*nods 'I think so'*)

Short pause.

Orlaith   Jesus, you're a barrel a laughs/

Sive (*overlaps*)   Who's it yer lookin' after?

Orlaith   My Da.

Pause.

Sive   What's wrong with him?

Orlaith   Dunno.

Short pause.

Can't leave the house.

Sive   Why not?

Orlaith   Dunno.

Hears voices.

Panics.

That kinda stuff.

Sive   What voices?

Orlaith   His own.

I think.

Sive *gets the giggles*.

Orlaith   What you laughin' at?

Sive (*giggling more*)   'Tis funny!

Orlaith   'Tisn't bloody funny!

Sive (*doubling over*)

Orlaith (*playing along, happy to see* **Sive** *happy*)   Specially when he's shoutin' at them in the middle of the night and I can't sleep for the howlin' of him!

Sive   Howlin' of him'?

Orlaith   Never heard anythin' as brutal as my Da howlin'!

Sive   Like a dog like?

Orlaith (*loudly imitating a howling dog*)   Like Owww-woooo!!!!!!!!!

Sive (*quiet, timid*)   Owww-wooooooo!!!!

Orlaith   Louder, like Owww-woooooo!!!!

Sive   Owww-wooooooo!!!!

Orlaith (*with a growing affection for* **Sive**, *coaxing her out of herself*)   Empty yer lungs, girl! Empty yer lungs!!

Sive (*letting herself go completely*) Owww-woooooooooooooooooooooo!!!!!

Orlaith *and* **Sive** *collapse laughing. Hearty and warm. Neither of them are used to letting go this much. Ice is broken.*

Sive   Where's yer Ma?

Orlaith (*mood changes, darker*)   Fuck knows.

Sive   Really?

Orlaith   Really.

Pause.

Sive   My Mam …

Orlaith   Bedbound?

Sive (*nods*)   In a crash, two years ago.

Pause.

(*Almost too scared to say it.*) She's very angry.

Orlaith   'Bout what?

Sive   Everythin'.

Orlaith   You gotta Da?

Sive (*defiantly*)   Course.

Orlaith   What's he do?

Sive   Stays away mostly.

Orlaith   Don't see him?

Sive   – (*Shakes head*)

Orlaith   Wanna see him?

Sive   I want him to come home.

Orlaith   Why?

Sive (*with a shrug*) Just 'cos.

Orlaith   Just 'cos what?

Sive   Just 'cos!

Orlaith   That's baby talk.

Pause.

Sive   I'm –

Short pause.

Orlaith   Yeah?

Sive   Lonely on my own with her.

Pause.

Y'know?

Orlaith (*bravado*)   Nah.

Short pause.

Yeah.

Lonely on my own with him.

Pause.

Orlaith (*sees* **Sive** *is getting low in mood, changes mood*)   Hey, Sive! Tide's comin' in!

Sive   Ah, brill!

Orlaith   Took its feckin' time.

Sive   'Twill be like a proper day out now!

Orlaith (*trying to be 'tough', but can't help smiling*) Yer easy to please.

Sive   Haven't been on a day out in ages.

Orlaith   Me neither.

Sive   My Mam's not up to it.

Orlaith   My Da's not up to it.

Pause.

That tide'll bring waves.

Sive   Big waves?

Orlaith   Giant ones.

Sive   To take us away?

Orlaith   Where's it you wanna go?

Sive   Away from here.

Pause.

Orlaith   I'd take you away.

Sive   –

Orlaith   I would.

I'd take ya 'way from here.

And her.

Sive   –

Orlaith   I promise.

Sive   People are always promisin' stuff they never do.

Orlaith (*mocking*)   Well boo-hoo you!

Sive   Well they are!

Orlaith   Stop believin' them so.

Sive   Alright, I will!

Orlaith   Glad to hear it!

Short pause.

Hey, Sive.

Sive (*flat, not really a question*) What …

Orlaith   I'm cuttin' out.

Sive (*perking up*)   What?

Orlaith   I'm hittin' the road.

Sive   Watcha mean?

Orlaith   You comin'?

Sive   Whatcha sayin'?

Orlaith   Are ya comin' or are ya not?!

Sive   Sure I can't!

Orlaith   Course ya can!

Sive   Where'll we go?

Orlaith (**Orlaith** *thinks*)   Heaven.

(*Big smile.*) Good enuff for ya?

Sive   But my Mam?

Orlaith   Yeah?

Sive   And yer Da?

Orlaith   Yeah???

Sive   She can't use the loo or the stairs or cook or dress herself or anythin'!

Orlaith   Yeah???

Sive   Doesn't know 'bout the bins, only I know 'bout the bins.

Orlaith   Sive.

Sive   Yeah?

Orlaith   Feck the bins.

Scene Two

The home of **Sive** *and her invalid* **Mother** *who is bedbound.* **Sive** *has just come home from school.*

Mother   Is it you?

Short pause.

Love?

Short pause.

Is it you?

Sive (*off, breathless from carrying a weight*) Yeah, 'tis me.

Mother (*not hearing her*) Sive?

Sive   Yeah, 'tis me, Mam.

Mother   Bit late back today?

Short pause.

Bit late, love?

Sive   Sorry Mam.

Mother   Are ya alright?

Sive   Yeah –

Mother But you're a bit late like?

Sive Had to get yer prescription.

Mother What are you sayin'?

Sive (*louder*)   Had to get yer prescription, Mam.

Mother   Ah Jesus, yeah.

Sive   And the bed-sore stuff.

Mother   Jesus yeah, I forgot.

Sive   I didn't know the one I had to get.

Mother   Jesus, Mary and Saint Joseph, how much more of this shite am I gonna havta shovel inta this hole to get a bit a' ease?

Sive   How d'ya make the fridge colder, Mam?

Silence.

Mam?

Mother   What is it?

Sive   How d'ya make the fridge colder?

Mother   What in the name of God are ya doin'?

Sive   It needs to be colder, for this new cream –

Mother   Isn't there a knob?

Short pause.

Sive   Is it on the outside or the inside, Mam?

Mother   Eh, is it on the right?

Sive   Yeah, but the outside or the inside, Mam?

Mother   Am … (*She's trying to remember.*)

Ah … Is it the …

Sive   Which side, Mam?

Mother   Right, Sive.

Short pause.

'Tis on the right I think.

Sive   Right?

Mother   At the top?

Sive   Does it have numbers on?

Mother   It should. Yeah.

Pause.

Sive   Found it.

Mother   Ah, come in to tell me all your news, Sive.

Sive   Just hang on a sec.

Pause.

Sive   Mam, they didn't take the green bin.

Mother   Christ, not again!

Sive   It's still outside. Chock-a-block.

Mother   Did ya not check the thing?

Sive   Said the seventeenth. That's today isn't it, Mam?

Mother   No idea.

Sive   Took the black one last week, so it shudda been this one this week.

Mother   Does the thing not say?

Sive   Why can't they just take 'em all each week? I read the thing and put it out and it's still bloody there /

Mother   That's environmentalists for ya /

Sive   'Tis totally crammed full and smellin' and everythin'.

Mother   That's what that feckin' lot want to reduce us to. Sittin' in our own shite. And to what end? I mean, who'll benefit from any a this carry-on?

Sive   I might /

Mother   I'll be dead and gone.

Pause.

Mother   How was school anyway?

Sive   – (**Sive** *is still bogged down by the uncollected bin.*)

Mother   Did Devlin ask ya 'bout your essay?

Sive   –

Mother   Sive, would ya answer me?

Sive   He said next week would be alright.

Mother   Oh good.

Sive   But no later.

Mother   No later?! Who does he think he is?

Sive   It's fair enuff, Mam.

Mother   No later or what? Is he threatenin' you?

Sive   Course not.

Mother   Better not be /

Sive   Sure amn't I already a week late with it?

Mother   Tellin' you, a workin' child, what he wants and when he wants it! Typical man, totally selfish.

Sive   Devlin's alright, Mam /

Mother   Domineerin', bullyin' pricks the whole fuckin' lot a' them.

Sive   It's his job /

Mother   That's men all out. Keep well away from 'em girl, I'm tellin' ya.

Sive   Mam, it's alright OK?

Mother   No man will ever tell you what to do as long as I draw breath, do you hear me?

Sive   I do, Mam, I do.

Pause. Things settle.

How's the back?

Mother   No change.

Sive   Is the new stuff havin' any effect, d'ya think?

Mother   Sure I can hardly tell anymore …

Sive   When will ya be up and about again, Mam?

Mother   I don't know.

Sive   By the summer maybe?

Mother   I don't know, Sive.

Sive   For my birthday?

Mother   We'll see, Sive.

Sive   That 'ad be brill.

Mother   We'll see.

Short pause.

I wouldn't hold out too much hope.

Short pause.

Sive (*direct address*)   She's gotta crushed pelvis and a shattered spirit.

Mother   Bedbound for two years.

Sive I've a Da –

Mother Fucked off first chance he got.

Sive Haven't seen him for two years –

Mother Couldn't fla* (*Fuck.) me anymore – back's done in.

Sive She hates him –

Mother And what I see of him in you –

Sive And me –

Mother That cuntin' bastard.

Sive He was alright to me.

Mother I never wanna see that prick again.

Sive I want ta see him, just like it us'ta be. Me lyin' there 'tween 'em in the bed and them ticklin' me 'til I was screamin' my head off.

Mother If he ever even so much as darkens that door again –

Sive Come back Da.

Mother I'll fuckin' annihilate him.

Scene Three

The home of **Orlaith** *and her* **Father**. **Orlaith** *has just come home from school. Her* **Father** *is lying on the couch.*

Orlaith Back, Da.

Pause.

Da, I'm back!

Father (*who has been asleep*) Ah … how's my sweetheart?

Short pause.

Orlaith (*cheekily*) I'm not yer sweetheart. I'm nobody's sweetheart me.

Father   My girl doesn't do sweetheart, does she?

Orlaith   No, Dad. She doesn't!

Pause.

She somewhat roughly pushes up his legs on the couch so she can sit on it with him.

Father   So, is the world still turnin' out there or what?

Orlaith   That's all it's doin', Da.

Father   School any good?

Orlaith   Same ole ding dong.

Father   You learnin' anythin'?

Orlaith   No! But had a great laugh with the lads at dinnertime tho', down the field. I'm the head a' the gang I am.

Father   Sure what'll that teach ya?

Orlaith   Life skills, Da, life skills!

Father   Jesus, but you've an answer for everything, Orlaith.

Orlaith (*she flashes him a big grin and slaps him, playfully but roughly, he winces 'like a girl'*)

Father   I opened the window earlier. Listenin' to the birds singin' …

Orlaith   Gay.

Father   Nah, 't was lovely, like they were in conversation or somethin'. Such delicate music they make.

Orlaith   Yer sad, Da! (*Playfully punches him.*)

Father   Are they singin' to each other or talkin' to each other or what?

Short pause.

Orlaith?

Orlaith   What?

Father   Do'ya think they're singin' or talkin' or what?

Orlaith   Who?

Father   The birds

Orlaith (*'Have you lost your mind?' look.*)   What birds?

Father   Ah, forget it.

Orlaith   Already have!

Father   You are anaful girl, d'ya know that?

Orlaith   I am, but ya love me all the same, don't ya?

Father   Well, yer not the worsta them.

Orlaith   I'm the only one you've got, Dado! Only one you've got.

Pause.

Father   Did you have English today?

Orlaith   Yeah.

Father   Who were ya doin'?

Orlaith   Heaney.

Father   Heaney?!

Orlaith   Yeah.

Father   Feck Heaney, Yeats is the man.

Orlaith   Yeah but /

Father   The only one ya should be readin'

Orlaith   Well, we won't be tested on *him* will we?

Father   What's the education system in this country comin' to?

They look at each other – a nod of recognition and a smile.

Orlaith/Father   'Tis comin' to shite, ta shite 'tis comin'! *Pause.*

Orlaith (*serious*)   Have ya moved?

Father   –

Orlaith   Da? Have ya moved?

Father   Didn't have the mind to, love.

Orlaith   But you said you'd try /

Father   I know, love, I know.

Orlaith   'Twill only get worse if ya don't try, Dad, the doctor said so –

Father   I'm just not up to it, love.

Orlaith   You havta try, Da!

Father   I will try, Orlaith –

Orlaith   Yeah, but when?

Father   Don't you be worryin' yerself /

Orlaith   When are ya goin' to try?

Father   I'll make an effort tomorrow.

Orlaith   – (*Weighted with worry for him and herself.*)

Father   I'll tell ya what –

Pause.

(*He knows he is lying as he says it.*) I'll move tomorrow.

Short pause.

If I'm up to it.

Orlaith (*upset, changes the subject, suddenly charged with defiance*)   I'll put the tay-tties on. Fish fingers alright for ya?

Father   You're an angel.

Orlaith   –

Father   I'd be totally lost without ya, Orlaith.

Orlaith (*ignores this*)   Ready at half-six so.

Father   Ya know that, don't ya?

Orlaith   –

Father   Totally lost.

Orlaith (*under her breath*)   Not so lost ya couldn't find yer way.

She leaves the room.

Father   'Come away, O, human child
  To the waters and the wild
  With a fairy hand in hand
  For the world's more full of weeping than
  You can understand.' (*Yeats*)

Scene Four

3am. **Orlaith** *is at the town fountain.* **Sive** *is on her way to meet her.*

Orlaith   Three o'clock in the morning at the town fountain.

Sive   I'm scared to death.

Orlaith   Been preppin' my escape for days.

Sive   Wantin' to go –

Orlaith   Can't wait.

Sive   But panickin' everytime I think about it.

Orlaith   Collected the benefit. Walked home. Da asleep on the couch, same as ever. Made the dinner. Fed Da. Ate my dinner. Cleaned the house. Mopped the floor. Gave Da his pills and finally, checked his breathin' before slippin' out 'n' away.

Sive   The district nurse was there when I got home from school, spent an hour showin' me a new exercise to help ease my Ma's pain –

Orlaith   Three-fifteen at the holy fountain.

Sive   And here's me knowin' I won't be around to help her do it.
My shoes fill with guilt.

Orlaith   She's late /

Sive   I'm nailed to the ground /

Orlaith   Where is she? /

Sive   My head is spinnin'

Orlaith   What if she doesn't come?

Sive   My stomach is sick.

Orlaith   She forgotten 'bout me?

Sive   Will I? Won't I? Will I? Won't I? Will I?

Orlaith (*overlapping with* **Sive**)   Will she? Won't she? Will she?
Won't she?

Sive   And I'm out that door,
Boltin' through the streets,
Heart like a bass drum,
Big bag slung on my back
Weighin' me down –
Packed too much –
I start to run.
The load gets lighter
I keep runnin' –
Burst by burst brings more brilliant briskness.
No lookin' back now,
No thinkin' back now!

Orlaith   Three-thirty am, she appears.
Half-runnin', Half fallin'
Outta breath – pantin' away.

Sive   Runnin' for my life /

Orlaith   She runnin' for her life.
She's runnin' to me.

Sive   Bass drum in my mouth.

Orlaith   Bass drum in *my* mouth.

Sive   And she's there. Leanin' back 'gainst the holy fountain, lookin' cool.

(*Out of breath.*) Were ya worried that I wasn't comin'?

Orlaith (*bravado, cowboy cool*)   Nah.

Sive (*regarding the fountain*)   Yer not supposed to lean 'gainst the holy fountain. 'Tis a sin.

Orlaith   Is it now?

Sive   Ya know it is.

Orlaith   I don't feckin' care.

Sive (*amazed by her*)   You're cool out, aren't ya?

Orlaith – (*Of course I am!*)

Sive Not 'fraid of anyone.

Orlaith   Nope.

Sive   Or anythin'.

Orlaith   Nope.

Sive   Wow …

Orlaith   Roll yer tongue in girl and let's get walkin'.

Scene Five

Two days later, in the afternoon, **Sive** *and* **Orlaith** *are eating sandwiches in a golden field of hay.*

Orlaith   By daylight we're in the next town and after a day's walking 'tis evenin' and we're settled in a golden field eatin' corned beef sambos and crisps. Backs against hay bales. Comfy out.

Sive   No crusts!

Orlaith   Cut them off.

Sive   I hate crusts.

Orlaith   I know.

Sive   How did you know?

Orlaith   Yer a girlie –

Sive   – (*Confused by this answer.*)

Orlaith   Girlies can't handle crusts.

Sive (*defiant*)   I can handle crusts!

Orlaith   Bet yer Da cut 'em off for ya –

Sive   He did not. I did it myself. I'm well able to do it myself!

Orlaith   Alright! Keep yer scalp on!

Sive   –

Goes dark, then quieter.

Da *us'ta* do it for me. Totally neat like. But I'm crap at it. End up manglin' the bread 'n' everythin'

Orlaith   – (*Smirking.*)

Sive   Yer good at it tho'. These ones are totally neat.

Orlaith   I'll cut them off for ya every day so.

Sive   Will ya? (*Big smile.*)

Orlaith   If I can afford the bread.

Sive (*smile fades*)   Oh.

Orlaith (*sees the change in* **Sive**)   What's wrong withcha?

Sive   Nothin'.

Orlaith   Sive, what's wrong withcha?

Sive   –

Short pause.

Orlaith?

Orlaith   What?

Sive   Are we low on food?

Orlaith   We're out.

Sive (*panicking*)   Oh God, no!

Orlaith   That's the last sambo, girl.

Sive   What'll we do?

Orlaith   I'll think of something /

Sive   How'll we? /

Orlaith   Don't you worry about it **Sive**   But how'll? /

Freda (*'posh' British accent, coming from afar*) Who's goes there?

Sive   What's that?

Orlaith   Dunno.

Sive   A man?

Orlaith   Maybe, dunno.

Freda   I see you. Loitering about in my field.

Sive/Orlaith   Feck!

Freda   What are you up to?

Sive (*petrified, clings on to* **Orlaith**)   Oh no, Jesus!

Orlaith   Sive! Calm down.

Freda *is in her late 50s. Dressed somewhat like a 'gent of the fields', she has a no-nonsense, clipped British accent and probably a twitch. She sees the two girls. Failing the local slang terribly.*

(**Freda** *trying to be fierce but happy to have company*) Top of the morning to you.

Orlaith   Aaaaaaa –

Sive *gives* **Orlaith** *a push to make her respond.*

And to you, Missus.

Freda   Hmm. I see you've been making use of my bales.

Orlaith   Oh just leanin' 'gainst them. Havin' our sambos.

Freda   Sambos?

Sive (*offering hers to* **Freda**)   Corned beef?

Freda   I will know if just one straw is out of place.

Sive (*to* **Orlaith**)   Oh GOD! We're dead!

Orlaith   We haven't done anythin' to them, missus, promise. Just leanin' against /

Freda   It's been dashed awkward this year trying to get them all exactly the same shape with not one single straw out of place.

Orlaith   Can't have been easy –

Freda   You simply would not believe the amount of time I have to spend clipping the buggers. Year in. Year out.

Orlaith   Sounds like a big job alright –

Sive   What's she talkin' 'bout?

Freda   It isn't easy you know. Ireland is full of wanton bales!

Orlaith   You're not wrong –

Freda   Just as well I'm here to whip them back into shape. If it wasn't for me they'd let this wondrous countryside go to rack and ruin. The bales of Ireland would make for a sorry sight indeed were it not for my diligence and clippers.

Short pause. She gathers herself.

I'm Freda, the Farmer.

Orlaith   I'm Orlaith. She's Sive.

Sive (*to* **Orlaith**)   Is she a bit touched?

Freda   I heard that young lady.

Sive   Sorry /

Orlaith   You've done a mighty job on them, missus.

Freda   It really does unnerve me to see so many unkempt bales the length and breath of Ireland.

Orlaith   It must get ya down alright /

Freda   It is single-handedly responsible for giving me my high blood pressure.

Sive   You should take Diamox. Two in the mornin'. Two at night, with water.

Freda   What a very knowledgable young lady, you are. Tell me, have you girls been admiring my bales?

Orlaith   Yeah, they're very …

Sive   Neat!

Freda   I spend days on each one. Snip snip, snip sniping until they are /

Sive   They're perfect.

Freda   Exactly, until they are perfect.

Orlaith   Oh you can see the effort put inta them /

Freda   One often feels that the (*As if it's a nasty word.*) 'locals' don't fully appreciate my contribution to the glory of the Irish countryside /

Orlaith (*impatient*)   Freda, if I may say so, these are about the finest bales I've ever seen.

Freda (*almost overcome with pride*) I'm about to dine. Would you young ladies care to join me?

Sive (*overexcited*)   Yes!

Orlaith   That'd be brill.

Freda   Excellent. Come along then.

Sive (*to* **Orlaith**)   She's a looper.

Orlaith   Play along with her, Sive. We'll get a meal and maybe a bed for the night out of it.

Sive   What luck!

Freda   Chop, chop, ladies!

Pause.

Sive   Orlaith's right. There's no harm in her. Just off with the birds. Even has a big bale in her livin' room and her trimmin' away at by hand with a tiny nail clippers. We sit there amazed, watchin' her snip, snippin' away – any little stray straw drivin' her demented.

When **Freda**'s *back is turned* **Orlaith** *makes fun of her to* **Sive**. *She enjoys putting on the performance for* **Sive** *who is mortified that they'll be caught.*

She gives us pea soup and bread she's made herself – still warm from the oven and way nicer than the bread at home and she's real butter 'n' all. 'Tis so gorgeous we stuff our faces and chat away 'til night falls and she says we can settle down for the night if we want. Sittin' in front of her big open fire, she starts tellin' us a story. Course Orlaith rolls her eyes and starts messin' around but I want to hear it. We curl up together in front of the fire and listen …

Freda   There was once a poor widow woman who had a daughter called Ciara who was very beautiful but very lazy. While the widow woman worked very hard every single day at her spinning wheel Ciara just sat around doing nothing which broke her Mother's heart. One day a Prince rode by, and upon seeing Ciara said, 'Your daughter is the most beautiful girl I've ever seen but why does she look so sad?' The widow, realising her chance said, 'Oh she's not sad, she's just run out of weaving to do, she's a very hard worker and she gets sad when she runs out of work to do'.

The Prince was very impressed. He knew his Mother, the Queen, would want a girl who was both pretty and productive for him to marry and now he had found her. 'I beg your permission to take her home.' The widow woman gave her permission and the Prince gave her a purse full of coins in return. He took Ciara home to the Queen, who was so delighted to hear that she was both pretty and industrious that later that evening she pointed out the pile of fine flax on the floor and said, 'You can begin any time you like, I look forward to seeing these spun into the finest thread'.

Ciara didn't sleep a wink that night, as she tossed and turned she wished she had listened to her Mother and learned to spin. By morning she was in tears. Then suddenly, out of nowhere sprung a little fairy woman with huge feet who said, 'If you invite me to your wedding to the Prince I'll spin all of these into the finest thread ready for the Queen'. Ciara immediately said 'Yes, if you do this spinning for me you can come to my wedding!'

Orlaith   My heart is poundin' –

Sive   Orlaith kinda puts her hand on my arm –

Orlaith   Been sneakin' glances at her all evenin' –

Sive   It's shakin'. She's shakin' –

Orlaith   'Tisn't like me to be this awkward –

Sive   Inchin' her fingers down to my hand.

Orlaith   Her skin's way nicer than /

Sive   / It feels nice.

Orlaith   Neither of us lasts 'til the end of the story –

Sive   This is lovely –

Orlaith   We both fall asleep.

Scene Six

Two days later. **Orlaith** *and* **Sive** *are walking on the road.*

Sive (*brightly*)   Where we actually goin', Orlaith? Technically like.

Orlaith   Well, technically like, I'm tryin' to get us to a decent beach.

Sive   A beach!

Orlaith   Bally-feckin'-glanna can go 'n' boil its head in a pot.

Sive   Coast is miles and miles away.

Orlaith   A decent beach this time. With sand and water!

Sive   'N' how'll we get there, Orlaith?

Orlaith   Thumb it.

Sive   Jokin'?

Orlaith   No jokin'.

Sive   Jokin'?

Orlaith   You' jokin'?

Sive   But how'll we get there? /

Orlaith   How d'ya think?

Sive   Can't thumb it on our own.

Orlaith   We're not on our own.

Sive   We are!

Orlaith   We're two together.

Sive   My Mam'll kill me!

Orlaith   Forget 'bout yer Mam. Jus' you 'n' me now girl and I'm totally strong like. I'd take on anyone I would.

Sive (*impressed*)   Would ya?

Orlaith (*bravado*)   Course!

Sive   Really?

Orlaith   Ya!

Sive (*fretting*)   Ya think we'll get a lift?

Orlaith   Course we will! If you take off your top off?

Sive (*utter panic*)   What? No way! I'm not goin'!

Orlaith   Sive girl, I'm only jokin'!!!

Sive   'Tisn't funny.

Orlaith   Lighten up, will ya?

Sive   Could be a mass murderer or anythin' –

Orlaith   Stop panickin'!

Sive (*almost passing out with anxiety*)   Oh GOD!

Orlaith (*'flexes' her arms comically and straightens into a 'thumb'*)   Sure who'd mess with me, look at these muscles, girl!

Sive   Stop!

Orlaith (*playfully*)   You're a total scaredy cat.

Sive   I'm not!

Orlaith   You totally are!

Sive   Not!

Orlaith   I'm not scared of anyone now.

Sive   Wish I was like you –

Orlaith   No point bein' scared.

Sive   I'm scared of everythin'
Worried about everythin'
All the time …
Wish I was like you.

(*Total admiration.*) You're tough out.

Orlaith   I have to be. My Da's a wimp.

Sive   Don't! (*As in 'don't say it'.*)

Orlaith   He is!

Sive   Who howls!

Orlaith   Owwwwwwoooooooooooh!

Sive   Owwwwwwoooooooooooooooooooooh!

Things calm down.

Long pause as the girls wait for a lift.

All jus' flyin' past us.

Orlaith   – (*Determined.*)

Sive   Not havin' much luck.

Orlaith   –

Sive   'Twill be dark soon.

Orlaith   –

Sive (*panicking*)   What if we don't get a lift, Orlaith?

Orlaith   Jesus but yer a right worrier!

Sive   I don't want to sleep in a field again, 'twas scary.

Orlaith   Scary? Ya told me ya liked it?!

Sive   I did! But 'twas scary.

Orlaith   You're a fecker!

Sive   – (*Hurt.*)

Orlaith   Look, will ya leave it to me, Sive!

Sive   – (*Gentle sulk.*)

Orlaith (*softer*)   We'll get a lift. OK?

Sive   –

Orlaith   I'll sort it out for us, Sive. No need to be worryin', OK?

Sive   I'm tired 'n' hungry 'n' cold

Orlaith   Take my jacket

Sive   I'm worried about my Mam –

Orlaith (*more harshly than she intends*) Well don't be. She won't be worryin' 'bout you!

Sive   Y'not worried about yer Da?

Orlaith   Spent enough time worryin' about him. He'll be fine.

Sive   How d'ya know?

Orlaith   Made of stronger stuff than he lets on.

Sive   Ya testin' him, see if he'll manage like?

Orlaith   No!

Sive (*upset*)   'Cos he mighten' (*as in 'might not'*) manage! They mighten' manage without us. Maybe we should go back home, Orlaith?

Orlaith (*strongly, she's not going to allow this talk*)   Sive, I got you away from your Ma and her ravin' and we've been havin' a grand time upta now haven't we?

Sive   Yeah.

Orlaith   We'll get there. 'Twill be fine. Promise.

Sive   Don't make a promise 'n' break it.

Orlaith (*hugs* **Sive** *with one arm as she's still 'thumbin'*)   Wouldn't do that to you girl.

Orlaith *continues to attempts to stop vehicles with no luck, she looks at* **Sive** *who is shivering at the side of the road and redoubles her efforts to get them both a lift – scared that* **Sive** *will change her mind and leave her. We see her growing desperation and perhaps, fear. Then,* **Laoise***, the Lorry Lady pulls up.* **Laoise** *is from the deepest inlands of Ireland. A law unto herself. In pants* *and practical working wear. Scrubbed squeaky clean, her big red cheeks gleam at us. A woman who loves the open road and her freedom.*

Laoise   Need a lift, girls?

Sive   'Tis a woman!

Orlaith   Thanks, lady.

Sive   We're safe!

Laoise   Hop in so.

The girls hop in.

Laoise   Killrowdan any good ta ya?

Orlaith   Brill, thanks!

Laoise   Grand so.

Short pause.

You girls alright?

Orlaith   Grand, yeah.

Sive   Fine, thanks.

Laoise   Off on yer travels are ye?

Orlaith   Headin' for the coast, yeah.

Sive (*excited*)   The beach!

Laoise   Good idea, ladies.

Pause.

Sive   Didn't know girls could drive lorries?

Laoise (*amused*)   Why d'ya say that?

Sive   Ya never see any –

Laoise   Ah there's a few of us on the road alright –

Sive   Legs a bit too short or somethin' –

Orlaith   What ya talkin' about?

Laoise   What she sayin'?

Sive   Thought girls' legs couldn't reach the pedals –

Laoise (*laughin'*)   Well I've no trouble!

Orlaith Sorry missus, she's a bit thick.

Sive   I am not!

Laoise   I'm Laoise. Lorry Driver

Orlaith   I'm Orlaith, she's Sive.

Laoise   You girls campin' out back there?

Orlaith   Roundabout like.

Laoise   Been there a while?

Orlaith (*with a smile, but wise to the questioning*)   You spyin' on us or somethin'?

Laoise   Jesus no /

Orlaith   'Tis a free country ya'know!

Laoise   Sure I know it 'tis. That's what I like about it!

Orlaith   What d'ya mean by that?

Laoise   Nothin' at all.

Short pause.

So, ya havin' a nice adventure?

Orlaith   Yeeeeaaaahhhhh. (*Elongated to give impression of a fuller answer.*)

Sive   We've run away!

Orlaith   Sive! Shut up will ya!

Pause.

They're driving along.

Sive (*sniffing the lorry cabin air*)   Very lemony smell –

Laoise   I've lemons in the back.

Sive   Lemons?!

Laoise   Yeah! I deliver lemons.

Sive   I like yer little plants there all over the dashboard, yer squirty air freshener thing, yer hand wipes, hand gel, hand cream –

Orlaith   Yer well stocked, lady!

Laoise   I like things very clean girls /

Sive   And yer big string of plastic lemons all around the windscreen. 'Tis lovely.

Short pause.

'Tis pristine!

Orlaith (*with a wink to* **Sive**)   Manically pristine!

Laoise   I'm on my way to Killrowdan. Mad for lemons down there 'cos of all the fish.

Sive   Fish?

Laoise   Oh yes, bet ya didn't know every person in Killrowdan eats five lemons a day?

Sive   Five lemons a day?!

Orlaith (*with a wink*) They must be very bitter –

Laoise (*with a wink back*) Oh, they are, yeah.

Pause.

OK.

Havta stop for petrol, girls.

Sive   And she's gone for fifteen minutes. She buys us Twixs, Taytos and Tanora. Sooooo nice of her.

Laoise   There ya are now, girls. Get those down ya. Sorry I was a bit long there.

Orlaith   No worries.

Sive   Thanks for these!

Laoise   Very welcome.

Sive   Was very hungry –

Laoise   I like to have the ole chat with the Garagers. Givin' and gettin' the news like. I'd be lost without gettin' the news.

Orlaith (*suspicious*)   What kinda news?

Laoise   Things jus' goin' on 'round the place.

Orlaith   Hear anythin' interestin'?

Laoise (*forlornly*)   To be honest, I did.

Orlaith (*bracing herself for the worst*) –

Laoise   I did, indeed.

Orlaith (*buying time, trying to figure out what to say*) Did ya now?

Laoise   I did.

Short pause.

And I havta say I'm a bit surprised girls.

Sive (*innocently*)   Why's that?

Orlaith (*elbows her*)   Sive! Eat your Taytos!

Laoise (*seriously*)   Well, I thought –

Orlaith (*panic*)   What?

Laoise   Well,

Orlaith (*afraid they've been rumbled*)   Just say it!

Laoise (*blurts out*)   Well, I thought she'd been neutered!

Sive/Orlaith   What???

Laoise   Said she was gettin' her neutered after the last time.

I mean twenty-one kittens at a go's a bit much girls, do'ya not think? Took her so long to find homes for them all that those kittens gave birth to even more kittens. It's anaful situation now 'cos Masie's got eighty-seven cats to deal with.

Orlaith *laughs heartily and with much relief.*

Sive   Eighty-seven cats!

Laoise   'Tis no laughin' matter!

Sive/Orlaith (*both girls are laughing now*)   Sorry.

Laoise   'Tis great being on the road girls. The open road's the only road for me.

Sive   We're drivin' along, afternoon sun streamin' in on top of us. Lorry Lady puts on some great music and we're hummin' along, happy out. Our bellies are full and we're gettin' drowsy and then it's evening. Can't see outside anymore. 'Tis black.

Laoise   You're tired, travellers?

Sive (*sleepy*)   Yeah.

Laoise   We've still a way to go.

Orlaith (*sleepy*)   Have we?

Laoise   Settle down for yourselves. I'll tell ya a story if ya like?

The girls are too tired to respond.

When the Queen saw the excellently weaved shirts she praised Ciara and said she had a bigger pile for her to weave next. Later than evening, sitting at her wheel, Ciara's eyes were full of tears, she had no idea what she would do. This was the last thing she expected. Then a different little fairy woman with huge hips appeared and as before, she promised to do the spinning for her in return for an invitation to her wedding to the Prince. Again, Ciara agreed and the little woman set to work. The Queen was so delighted with the quality and speed of the weaving that she set her an even bigger amount to weave and said if you manage to weave this batch by tomorrow I will let you marry my son. Ciara thought about how close she was to becoming a Princess and how easily she could lose the chance forever. She cried heavy, heavy tears and then out of nowhere appeared a little woman with a huge nose who did all the work for her and to the highest standards all in return for an invite to her wedding.

Sive   I don't remember the last bit 'cos I dropped off –

Orlaith   I didn't drop off, 'cos I was lookin' at you –

Sive   Orlaith's arm 'round me –

Orlaith   Yer head dropped against me –

Sive   'Twas lovely –

Orlaith   Makin' me a blush in the dark –

Sive   Lovely –

Orlaith   This weakness in me …

Pause.

Change of tempo. Lively.

Sive   Lorry Lady drops us in the middle of Killrowdan.

Laoise   Well girls, be good and stay safe on your travels.

Sive   The place was black – (*packed full of people*)

Orlaith   Fulla de la-de-las! (*posh people*)

Sive   Lorry Lady bought us gorgeous fish and chips, took a lemon from her load and squeezed it on fresh.

Orlaith (*reacting to the fresh lemon*)   Feck!

Sive   Oooooh!

Orlaith   Bitter!

Laoise (*with a wink and a smile*)   But sweet, eh?

Sive   I dunno!!

Laoise (*Small note of seriousness.*)   Now, take my advice, girls, 'n' be movin' on from here as soon as yer done.

Orlaith   We'll not be stoppin' long, Laoise, still aimin' for the beach.

Laoise   Good women!

Sive   Thanks for the lift!

Laoise   Enjoy yer freedom girls and all it brings ya.

Sive   She slipped us a few bob, climbed up into the lorry and she was gone.

Scene Seven

Sive *and* **Orlaith** *are eating their sandwiches by the harbour in Killrowdan. Their feet dangling over the edge. Both girls content and quiet in each other's company.*

Orlaith (*looking at* **Sive** *who's looking out to sea, she smiles at her*) –

Sive   Orlaith?

Orlaith   Yeah?

Sive –

Orlaith   What?

Sive   Nothin'

Orlaith   What?

Sive   Jus' thinkin'

Orlaith   Thinkin' what?

Sive   Jus' …

Orlaith   Jesus, out with it!

Sive   Jus' wonderin'

Orlaith　Yeeeeaaahhh? (*Drawn out.*)

Sive　Why d'ya play with boys, not girls?

Orlaith　Dunno.

Always have.

Sive　D'ya not like girls?

Orlaith　They're always goin' on 'bout clothes and make-up /

Sive　I'm not /

Orlaith　'N' boys 'n' hair 'n' borin' crap.

Sive　But ya like me?

Short pause.

Orlaith (*bravado*)　You're alright.

Short pause.

For a girl.

Sive　You do like me tho'?

Orlaith　Suppose /

Sive　Do ya or don't ya?

Orlaith　I just said I did!

Short pause.

Jeez!

Sive　But why tho?

Orlaith　I don't feckin' know, Sive!

Sive　Ya don't know?

Orlaith　No!

Sive (*deflated*)　Y' don't know –

Orlaith (*more gently*)　Yer different or somethin'.

Short pause.

Don't know why.

Short pause.

Can't –

Explain.

Sive   – (*Completely confused, then, trying to change the subject.*)   Look! What's that?

Orlaith   What's what?

Sive (*pointing*)   Red thing, there –

Orlaith   A buoy. I think.

Sive   S'not a boy! Over by the pillar thing!

Orlaith   It *is* a bloody buoy, ya see 'em in the sea. Can be anchored or driftin'

Sive   Anchored or driftin' …

Sounds like us.

Orlaith   What you on 'bout?

Sive   Anchored,

Now driftin …

Orlaith   You're a loon –

Sive   *You're* a loon!

Orlaith   Loony feckin' loon!

Sive   Howlin' at the moon like yer Da!

Orlaith   Owwwwoooooooooohhh!!!

Sive   Owwwwwooooooohhhhh!!!

Collapsing with laughter and bonding ever closer. Things calm.

Orlaith   My Da won't touch me.

Sive   What?

Orlaith   Said I remind him of her …

Sive   Your Ma?

Orlaith   Who else?

Sive   That's mad.

He's mad –

Orlaith   I *know* that.

Sive   'Cos yer not yer Ma, are ya?

Orlaith   No –

Sive   Yer you like. Aren't ya?

Orlaith   –

Sive   I can't understand Ma's and Da's at all –

Orlaith   Me neither.

Long pause.

Sive   I'd touch ya …

Orlaith (*pretend shocked*)   Perv!

Sive   Notta perv!

Orlaith (*softly*)   Perv …

Pause.

The boys touched me.

Pause.

In a weird way.

Sive   I hate boys.

Orlaith   Me too.

Sive   I'm never goin' near one.

Orlaith   Me neither …

Pause.

Orlaith   Hey, want another Tanora?

Sive (*as if it's a massive indulgence*) Yeah!

Orlaith   I'll go over to the shop so. Hang on there for me.

Sive   And off she heads over to the small shop back from the harbour. Turns 'round and sticks her tongue out at me then mimes a howl. She's a loon. There's a bitta warmth still left in the day and it's lovely being here with her.

Pause.

Then she's outta the shop and over to me, boundin' back, her face fierce.

Sive   What is it?

Orlaith   Feck.

Sive   What?

Orlaith   We're on the radio.

Sive   What d'ya mean?

Orlaith   On the news. They're lookin' for us.

Sive (*petrified*)   No!

Orlaith   Can't trust feckin' anyone to keep their gob shut.

Sive (*panicking*)   I didn't say anythin' to anyone.

Orlaith   Don't mean you.

Sive   I don't want them to find us, I don't wanna go back home!

Orlaith   We're not goin' home.

Sive (*loudly*)   Oh God!

Orlaith   Put that outta yer head.

Sive   No!!!

Orlaith (*forthright*)   Sive! Stop yer squealin' or you'll be bringin' us even more attention.

Sive   My Mam will kill me!

Orlaith (*grabs* **Sive** *and holds her tight, squeezing her to calm her down*)   No, she won't.

Sive's *body melts into* **Orlaith**'s.

Scene Eight

Sive *and* **Orlaith** *are in the next town. Sitting on the steps of the church waiting for weekday morning mass to finish.* **Orlaith** *is more serious and less confident than before.* **Sive**'s *anxiety at the possibility of being found starting to show.*

Sive   'Twas only all old biddies we saw goin' in.

Orlaith   They're the ones with the money, Sive.

Sive   Under their mattress maybe –

Orlaith   What are you sayin'?

Sive (*under her breath*) Not in their pocket …

Orlaith (*agitated*)   Sive, could ya stop complainin' for one minute?

Sive   I'm not complainin'

Orlaith   You are!

Sive   I'm not!

Orlaith   You are!

Sive   I'm just sayin' that /

Orlaith   Well stop 'just sayin'' /

Sive   Won't work/

Orlaith   I'm sick of it/

Sive   Rob a granny?

Orlaith   Shut up!

Sive   We've no money, no food, nowhere to sleep 'n' they're out lookin' for us.

Orlaith (*very angry*)   I'm doin' my best!

Sive   – (**Sive** *flinches, silenced by* **Orlaith**'s *anger, reminding her of her* **Mother**'s *anger.*)

Orlaith   Well amn't I? Whatcha think we're doin' here? Waitin' for Holy feckin' Mary to appear or something?

Sive   OK!

Orlaith   That isn't gonna happen.

Sive   Sorry.

Orlaith   There's no miracles gonna happen here, girl.

Sive   I'm sorry, Orlaith.

(*upset*)   I'm sorry.

We see how timid, frail and anxious **Sive** *really is.*

Sive   Don't let them take me home to her.

Orlaith   – (*Realising the new responsibility on her shoulders.*)

I won't –

Pause.

Sive.

I won't.

Sive   – (*Pulling away.*)

Orlaith   I'm sorry for shoutin' at ya.

Sive   Shoutin' at me, yer jus' like her.

Orlaith   I didn't mean to.

Sive   I don't like it.

Orlaith   I know you don't, Sive.

Mass is over, the congregation filters out. **Orlaith** *jumps up to try and catch someone's attention. We see a desperation about her we haven't seen before.*

Orlaith   Missus! D'ya need your fence paintin'? Nice fresh lookin' fence for the summer. Protected for the winter! Missus? Fence paintin'. *Etc.*

Orlaith *repeats this several times, with less and less enthusiasm,* **Bridie** *is the last person coming out of the church. She's a sturdy woman with a kind face very brightly coloured with rouge and lipstick. She approaches them. Her make up is completely at odds with her 'farmers walk'.* **Bridie** *has a very distinctive laugh, she laughs after most of her lines whether they are humorous or not.*

Bridie   What is it yer sellin'?

Orlaith   Fence paintin'

Bridie   Face paintin'?

Orlaith   No –

Bridie   Who needs face paintin'?

Orlaith   *No, fence* paintin'

Bridie   No offence taken love. Not easily offended.

Orlaith   No, I didn't /

Bridie   Maybe I overdo the ole rouge a bit /

Orlaith   I didn't say /

Bridie   But it keeps me cheerful!

Sive (*to* **Orlaith**, *under her breath*) What's she on?

Bridie   'Tis very kind of you to offer tho'.

Sive (*still under her breath*) Is she langers or what?

Orlaith   Don't mention it.

Bridie   Very kind.

Orlaith (*seeing her chance*) Maybe there's somethin' else we could help you with?

Bridie   Like what?

Orlaith   Odd jobs?

Sive   We need money /

Orlaith (*trying to quieten* **Sive**)   She means pocket money, for sweets 'n' stuff.

Bridie   Are ye any good at paintin' fences?

Orlaith   We're brilliant at paintin' fences!

Bridie   Well, come on so, I've a grand big fence needs paintin'.

Sive   Brill!

Bridie   I'm Bridie. The Butcher.

Orlaith   I'm Orlaith. She's Sive.

Bridie   Sive? Lovely name.

Sive (*scared*)   A butcher?! /

Orlaith (*impressed*)   Wow! You cut up cows and stuff?

Bridie   I do.

Sive   Girls can do anythin' so –

Bridie (*big smile*)   Yeah, we can. Never never thought about it. Just did it.

Orlaith (*To* **Sive**.)   Don't think about it –

Sive   – Just do it!

Orlaith   That's a good one.

Bridie   Now girls, my fence needs paintin' but before we go I've got my two favourite words for ya!

Orlaith   What's that?

Bridie   Corned. Beef.

Sive   And suddenly she's whippin' us off down the main street, past all the tiny colouredy houses, pubs and little shops. Stridin' ahead strong all purposeful like 'til we come to a small purple coloured stone shop with a huge sign sayin' *Bridie The Beef Butcher* over the door.

Orlaith   We're lookin' in the window and all we can see is corned beef –

Sive   Our tongues are hangin' out for a bitta grub –

Orlaith   That's all she sells!

Sive   Corned-beef patties.

Orlaith   Corned-beef pies.

Sive   Corned-beef puddings.

Orlaith   Corned-beef porkers.

Sive   Sides a' corner-beef.

Orlaith   Shins a' corned-beef.

Sive   Heads a' corn-beef.

Orlaith   Hides a' corned-beef.

Sive   Corned-beef stew.

Orlaith   Corned-beef salad.

Sive   Corned-beef soufflé.

Orlaith   Corned-beef slop!

Bridie   Wait 'til the smell hits ya, girls!!!

Sive   Mad as a bottle of chips!

Bridie   No chips here, girls!

Orlaith   Loon!!!

Bridie   Come out the back 'til I show ya this fence of mine.

Sive   And we spend the next four hours doin' her fence. It gets cold as it gets late and our hands are going numb with it but we're singin' and laughin' away, gettin' it done as fast as we can. And just as we come to the end of the job it hits us.

Orlaith   The smell …

Sive   Lovely …

Orlaith   Oooh … starvin' …

Sive   Me too.

Orlaith   Did 'ya think there's any chance she'd / (*feed us*)

Bridie   Nice work girls!

Short pause as **Bridie** *surveys the finished fence.*

Fancy some corned beef?

Sive   And in we go to the little purple house. She's fried up a mountain of corned beef – the thick slabs slidin' into the sizzlin' golden butter. It's the best smell ever and we scoff every last bit of it down as soon as it hits the plate.

Bridie   You've done great work altogether on that fence, girls. Rest yourselves now. Stretch out there by the fire while I tell ya story.

The whole county was counting down the days to the wedding of Ciara and the Prince, and on the day the Queen spoke of how happy herself and the bride would be, after the honeymoon, spinning and weaving together for days without end. Then the guardsman walked up to the head table and said to the Queen that Ciara's three aunts had arrived and may he let them in. 'Of course!' she said and in they came, one uglier than the next. Upon seeing the three of them the Queen asked why the huge feet, huge hips and huge nose and all three responded that it was because of a life spent at the loom, spinning thread that they had developed these curious shapes. The Prince was so shocked at hearing this that he turned to his bride and said, 'I never want you to become as ugly as these three! My darling, you will never have to spin again!' And from that day forth Ciara enjoyed all the finery and luxury her life as a Princess bestowed on her and she languished once again in her lazy ways and they all lived happily ever after.

Sive   Ahhhh …

Orlaith   What??!!

Sive   Ah, that's lovely /

Orlaith   No way!!

Sive   I love happy endings /

Orlaith   No such thing!

Sive   They all lived happily ever after /

Orlaith   That doesn't happen, Sive.

Sive   It happened to Princess Ciara.

Bridie   Exactly. Could happen to you.

Orlaith   There's no Prince gonna ride up and whisk us away to a life of happy ever after.

Sive   She got lucky, we might?

Orlaith   Not gonna happen!

Sive   Maybe it 'twill?

Bridie (*to* **Sive**)   You've got faith, Sive, that'll take you far.

Orlaith (*to* **Bridie**)   You should know better than fillin' her head with that stupid nonsense.

Bridie   Those with faith never drown in the sea of life.

Sive   – (*Smug smile to* **Orlaith**.)

Orlaith   Stupid story 'n' yer a fool to believe it.

Long pause.

Things calm.

Bridie   I heard about ye both on the radio.

Short pause.

I know who ye are.

Short pause.

Orlaith   What ya gonna do?

Sive (*panic*)   Are ya gonna tell on us?

Bridie No and I won't be askin' any questions either 'cos, if I'm honest with ya, I don't want the responsibility of knowin' the answers. You're nice girls, ya remind me a bit of myself at your age. (*To* **Orlaith**.) Particularly you, and I might be a fool, but I want to help ya.

Orlaith Anyone know we're here?

Bridie   I've told no-one, but the villagers might have seen you comin' down the street with me into the shop after mass.

Sive Orlaith, we passed loadsa people, they'll all be talkin' 'n' comin' to get us.

Bridie Ah, don't be worryin' yerself love, go on out to the bathroom and splash some water on yer face – your colour's a bit high.

Sive *exits.*

Orlaith Ya gonna tell on us?

Bridie –

Orlaith I'm not goin' anywhere without her.

Bridie *is wanting to say something, but struggling to come out with it.*

Bridie Is her surname Cassidy?

Orlaith Yeah.

Bridie – (*Worst fears confirmed.*)

Orlaith   Why?

Bridie –

Orlaith   What's happened?

Bridie   Her Mother's dead.

Orlaith   What?

Bridie   Found by the Gardaí* (*Pronounced gar-dee.*) two days ago, had to break down the door to get access.

Orlaith   But how? /

Bridie   She'd fallen down the stairs.

Orlaith   – (*A million thoughts racing through her mind.*)

Bridie   They can't trace her father –

Orlaith (*mind in a haze*)   Doesn't live with them …

Bridie   I'm so sorry for your trouble.

Pause.

You'll have to tell her. You know that Orlaith, don't you?

Orlaith   Yeah. I do.

(*Not entirely convincing.*) I will.

Sive *comes back into the room. She looks very anxious and uncertain. She can't read* **Orlaith**.

Bridie (*regarding* **Sive**)   Ah, you look a bit better now. Feelin' a bit better?

Sive   – (*Nods.*)

Bridie   I sleep here above the shop these days but I've a cottage about five miles out from the village near the coast, yer welcome to it for a bit. I could drive ye both out there after night-fall.

Sive   Wow. Really?!

Orlaith   Why d'ya do that for us? I mean, ya don't even know us or anythin'?

Bridie   I know enough.

Pause.

Suppose ya remind me of myself and Beth –

Sive   Who's Beth?

Bridie (*sadly, this pains her*)   Beth, was my friend.

Sive   When was? –

Bridie   Ah, long time ago now, wish I'd the guts then to do what yer doin' now.

Sive (*innocently*)   Come with us?

Orlaith *gives* **Sive** *a look to 'shut up'.*

Bridie   Y'know, I've lived here all my life and this village has yet to accept me as the butcher. Or anything else …

Orlaith   Thanks for yer offer, Bridie. We accept.

Sive   Thanks, Bridie.

Sive *hugs* **Bridie** *warmly.*

Orlaith   We'll accept. (*Your offer, nothing else.*)

Sive   You're brilliant.

Orlaith (*jealous*)   Sive! Don't be smotherin' her.

Bridie (*With total warmth and sincerity.*) Oh 'tis lovely to be hugged. Not been hugged in years.

Orlaith   We'll not take somethin' for nothin'. We'll do some jobs 'round the place for ya.

Sive   Keep it spick and span.

Orlaith   Keep it tickin' over for ya.

Bridie   Now that sounds like a deal girls. Come on out to the car, 'tis dark enough now to steal away.

Scene Nine

Later that evening. The girls arrive at the cottage. Secluded. Near the sea. Much excitement.

Sive (*in awe of the place*)   Woooooooow! God, this is lovely, isn't it, Orlaith?

Orlaith   It sure is, girl.

Sive   Can't believe our luck.

Orlaith   Bridie's done well for herself, hasn't she?

Sive   Someone must be watchin' over us /

Orlaith   There must be money in corned beef /

Sive   With all the luck we've had.

Short pause. **Sive** *is looking around at everything in the room in detail.*

Look at the size of that fire – 'tis huge.

Orlaith   Niiiiceee.

Sive   D'ya think it's real Orlaith?

Orlaith   Course it's real, ya gowl.

Sive   Really real? Wow!

She looks around. The items are large and old fashioned. **Sive** *mistakes them for expensive, modern items due to their size.*

Big telly, fluffy rugs, massive couch.

(*Pointing to a shelf covered in competition trophies.*) Hey, look at all the trophies –

First prize – All Ireland Corned Beef Championships.

Orlaith   They all say first prize.

Sive   Imagine bein' that good at somethin'?

Orlaith (*jealous*)   Your tongues hangin' out there girl –

Sive   Bridie's amazin' isn't she?

Orlaith   'Twill shrivel up, fall off if ya don't put it away.

Sive   Must be a hundred a them –

Orlaith   Come on we gotta get the heatin' goin' here.

Sive   OK.

Orlaith   Get ourselves sorted.

Sive   Hey, 'tis like we're real grown ups!

Orlaith Check outside the back, see if there's coal will ya?

Sive *lightheartedly runs off to check while* **Orlaith** *sizes up the cottage.* **Orlaith** *stands in the middle of the room as if she doesn't know what to do.*

Sive, *excitedly, coming back into the room.*

There's peat.

There's coal.

There's sticks!

Orlaith   Brill.

Sive   Can you light a fire like?

Orlaith (*amused*)   Can you *not* light a fire?

Sive (*with a smile*)   I can plug one in!

Orlaith   Jesus! Well I'm gonna show ya. I'll show ya everythin' ya need to know.

Sive   – (*Big smile.*)

Orlaith   D'ya think there's any food?

Sive   She said there was stuff in the freezer.

Orlaith   Go and have a look while I sort this out, would ya?

Sive   'K so.

Sive *leaves the room.*

Sive (*shouting into the room*)   Oh noooo!

Orlaith   What is it?

Sive   The fridge isn't cold.

Orlaith   What?

Sive   The fridge isn't cold.

Orlaith   It's probably not on, ya gowl!

Sive   Oh.

Orlaith   Plug it in!

Sive   'K so.

Pause.

The light's workin' and 'tis hummin' –

Orlaith   Must be workin' now so.

Orlaith *goes about the room, looking at what's there in a practical way and getting it sorted.*

Sive   Orlaith?

Orlaith   Yeah?

Sive   'Tisn't cold.

Orlaith   Whatchamean?

Sive   The fridge.

Short pause.

How d'ya make it colder?

Orlaith   There's a knob on it somewhere I think –

Sive   Where tho'?

Orlaith   How'm I supposed to know!

Ya gotta turn the knob –

Short pause.

Sive   Found it! Found the knob!

Orlaith   There ya are.

Sive   Upta four?

Orlaith   Yeah. Upta four.

Sive   Within the hour we've scoffed two frozen shepherds pies and glugged a big bottle of Tanora – our lips orange from it. The fire's blazin' and we're lengthways on the sofa facin' each other. Feet facin' faces. Snug out like.

Orlaith   My belly's on fire just lookin' at her, my heart in two minds, a gammy mixture of a kinda grief for her –

Sive   This is totally brill –

Orlaith   And a kinda love.

Sive   Isn't it, Orlaith?

Orlaith   Sure is!

Sive   Just us two –

Orlaith   Place all to ourselves –

Sive   Snug and warm –

Orlaith   Bellies full –

Sive   'Tis heaven … *Pause.*

'Spose we can do anythin' we like now, Orlaith?

Orlaith   'Spose we can.

Sive   So what'll we do?

Orlaith   Anythin' we want.

Sive   Really?

Orlaith   I'd do anything for you.

Sive (*blushin'*)   –

Orlaith (*with a wink*)   But it's gotta be just the two of us. No Ma's. No Da's. No boys. No Bridie. They'd only mess this all up on us.

Just you and me now girl –

Sive   Forever?

Orlaith   Forever.

Sive   Really?

Orlaith   Why not?

Sive   Forever!

Orlaith   'N' ever!

Sive   'N' ever!!

Orlaith   'N' ever!!

Sive   'N' ever!!!

Orlaith   'N' ever!!!

Sive   'N' ever!!!!

Orlaith   'N' ever!!!!

Sive   'N' ever!!!!!

Orlaith   'N' ever!!!!!

Pause.

Sive   This is heaven?

Orlaith   Looks like it to me, girl.

Sive   Looks like it to me, too.

Orlaith *looks around the room. Twinkle in her eye.*

Orlaith   Hey, Sive!

Sive   Yeah.

Orlaith   D'ya know what I wanna know?

Sive   I don't wanna know!

Orlaith   I wanna know what Bridie's got in her cupboards.

Sive   Jeez no!

Orlaith   She'll never know.

Sive   Can't nosey 'round. She'll find out.

Orlaith   Only if *you* tell 'er.

Sive (*enjoying a chance to be bold*)   'K so.

Orlaith   Good girl!

Sive   Justa quick peep –

Orlaith *and* **Sive** *approach the side unit.* **Sive** *is tentative and gentle.* **Orlaith** *is bolder. She rummages around and pulls out several cans of different varieties of corned beef.*

Orlaith   Ha! Busy Bridie's bad secret!

Sive   What is it?

Orlaith (*laughing*)   More feckin' corned beef.

Sive (*joining in*)   What else?

Orlaith   Secret stash!

Sive   Of corned beef?

Orlaith   Of crappy corned beef!

Sive   You'd think she'd enough of the stuff in the shop?

Orlaith   Bet she scoffs this straight from the can when no one's lookin'!

Sive   YUCK!

Orlaith *reaches in further, finds a full bottle of vodka.*

Orlaith   Hey, hey, what's this?

Sive   Put it back!

Orlaith   Is there no end to Bridie's carryin' on?!

Sive   Oh God, put it away!

Orlaith   Looks innocent enuff –

Sive   Orlaith!

Orlaith   Wanna sip?

Sive   No way!

Orlaith   Go on.

Sive   My Ma would kill me!

Orlaith   There's no Ma's 'n' Pa's anymore to be tellin' us what to do /

Sive   We shouldn't! /

Orlaith   I'm havin' a sup!

Orlaith *sips from the bottle.*

Orlaith   Down the hatch!

Her face contorts from the taste, but she toughens it out.

Sive   Oh God!

(*Face wrinkle.*) Is it yuck?

Orlaith   Nah.

Badly covering up the violation of drink on her tongue.

Nahhhhh.

(*Fibbing.*) 'Tis fine.

Not my first time anyway. (*She's lying.*) Me and the lads were always swiggin' stuff –

Sive (*smitten*)   Yer so cool –

Orlaith (*holding out the bottle to* **Sive**)   Your turn–

Sive   I don't wanna get sick.

Orlaith   You won't get sick.

Sive (*getting more uptight*) I don't wanna fall over.

Orlaith   You won't fall over.

Sive   I don't wanna get the gawks and spew.

Orlaith   For feck's sake! Sip it!

Sive *takes a very tentative sip.*

Orlaith   Go on!

Sive *has less of a reaction against the drink than* **Orlaith** *did and soon takes a second and third sip.*

Orlaith   Jeez girl, gotta thirst on ya!

Sive   'Tis kinda nice.

Short pause.

Oooohh … My stomach

Orlaith (*worried*)   What?

Sive   Gettin' warm … nice …

Orlaith *and* **Sive** *continue to take sips throughout the following, becoming lively, excited and giggly at first.*

Sive   Hey, Orlaith!

Orlaith   Yeah.

Sive   D'ya know what *I* wanna know?

Orlaith   No.

Sive   Don't get lively!

Orlaith   What?

Sive   Don't get lively!!!

Orlaith   Spit it out would'ya?

Sive   OK.

Steadying herself.

What's it like kissin' a boy?

Orlaith   Oh God!!!

Sive   'Oh God!!!' what?

Orlaith   Quit askin' perv questions!

Sive   'Tisn't a perv question!

Orlaith   Why you so feckin' interested?

Sive   I'm not interested /

Orlaith   You wanna kiss a boy or sometin'?

Sive   Only askin' like!

Orlaith (*shouting around, as if there's boys in the room*)   Sive wants to kiss a boy! Sive wants to kiss a boy!

Sive   No way!

Orlaith   Do ya?!

Sive   No way I said!

Orlaith   Betcha do!

Sive   I don't!

Orlaith   Do ya?!

Sive   Keep yer hair on!

Orlaith   Well, don't ask 'cos I don't wanna talk about it.

Sive (*sarcastic*)   Sorry!

Long pause.

Orlaith (*subdued*)   I don't wanna talk 'bout it.

Pause.

I only did it so I could keep hangin' 'round with them.

Short pause.

Angry with herself, hits herself hard – in an unforgiving, controlled way – on each of the following words.

Stupid.

Stupid.

Stupid.

Bitch.

Sive   Oi! Stop it. What's wrong with ya? You'll hurt yerself Orlaith!

Pause.

Knowing she shouldn't prolong the subject but her curiosity is getting the better of her.

What was it like?

Orlaith (*can't help smiling at* **Sive**)   You don't give up do ya?

Sive (*smirk*)

Orlaith   Rough.

Sive   Tongues?

Orlaith (*she gets no pleasure from talking about this*)   Yeah.

Sive   Oh my God!!! That's disgustin'!!!

Orlaith   That's normal!

Sive   I'm never doin' that with a boy. Yuck!!!!

Short pause.

Sive   Orlaith.

Orlaith   Yeah.

Sive   Promise ya won't shout?

Orlaith   What is it?

Sive   Don't shout, alright?

Orlaith   Sive, yer drivin' me mental!

Sive   I wanna ask ya somethin'

Orlaith   Go on!

Sive   Have ya touched a mickey?

Orlaith   Yer curiosity will kill ya if I don't do it first! (*Short, matter of factly.*) Yes.

Sive   No!

Orlaith   Yes!

Sive   Feck! Really?

Orlaith   Yeah, really –

Sive   Oh my God!!!!

Orlaith   What's it to you?

Sive   What's it like?

Orlaith   Weird out.

Sive   Weirdy weird?

Orlaith   Yeah, they change size.

Sive   Boys change size?

Orlaith   No, their mickeys do!

Sive   Mickeys change size?

Orlaith   Yeah!

Sive   No way girl!!!

Orlaith   I'm not fibbin'

Sive   No waaaaay!!!

Orlaith   I'm tellin' ya!

Sive   Pullin' my leg?!

Orlaith   I am not!

Sive   That makes no sense.

Orlaith   I know!

Sive   Totally loop da loop!

Orlaith   Totally luner lune!

They fall around laughing, then playact – pretending they have 'mickeys' which expand too.

Orlaith   D'ya wanna know somethin'?

Sive   Yeah.

Orlaith   'Tis a secret right? I mean total secret!!

Sive   What is it???!!!

Orlaith   I kissed a mickey.

Sive *is hysterical, runs around, covering her ears – we can see she's fairly unsteady on her feet now.*

Oh my God! Oh my God! Oh my God!!!!

Orlaith *laughing.*

Sive   You'll go to hell in a fast car for that!

Orlaith (*taken offence*)   I didn't wanta do it!

Sive   Was it totally awful like?

Orlaith   I got sick …

Sive (*calmer*)   I thought they were yer pals?

Orlaith   So did I.

Sive   Some pals …

Orlaith   We us'ta have a great laugh tearin' up and down the main street on our bikes makin' mayhem. Then it changed. They changed. Stickin' it in my mouth 'n' everythin'.

Couldn't breathe …

Gagged.

Gawked.

They didn't stop.

They didn't care.

Short pause.

That place us'ta be where we'd play as small kids.

Pause.

Why did they change Sive?

Sive   I hate *all* boys now.

Really hate them …

Orlaith (*tough*)   But I didn't cry.

Sive   What did yer Da say?

Orlaith   I didn't tell him.

Sive   How come?

Orlaith   No point.

Sive   He'd a sorted them out.

Orlaith   My Da can't even sort out his own feckin' washin'. I did everythin' for him, y'know. Everythin'.

Short pause.

I couldn't tell him.

(*Seething.*) Next boy comes near me's gonna get his balls chopped off.

Sive   – (*Gets the giggles.*)

Orlaith   – (*Isn't laughing.*)

Sive   – (*Realises it's no joke.*)

Orlaith   – (*Hits herself again, harder this time.*)

Sive   – (*Scared now.*)

Orlaith (*getting more emotional and unhinged as she speaks*)   Why do people change, Sive? Why do they say one thing then do another? Why don't they keep promises?

Sive (*At a loss.*)   Dunno, girl.

Sive *moves up the couch and puts her arm around* **Orlaith**.

Dunno.

Sive   'Tis in the past now –

Orlaith   Is it?

Sive   Course it is.

Orlaith   Why doesn't it feel like it so?

Sive   –

Orlaith   Why?

Sive   Forget 'em.

Orlaith   How?

Sive   Look, you can be whatever you want now, Orlaith. A farmer, a butcher, a lorry-lady …

We can do anythin' we want now.

Orlaith   D'ya like that feelin'?

Sive   Yeah, totally /

Orlaith   It doesn't hav'ta end y'know.

Short pause.

If ya stay with me that feelin' doesn't havta end.

Sive   You're so brill …

Orlaith   Am I now?

Sive   Totally.

Orlaith   How 'bout a proper hug this time so?

Sive   – (*Squirming in embarrassment.*)

Sive *gives* **Orlaith** *a very quick but tight hug then retreats.*

Orlaith (*hurt – she's weighed with memories and sensitivities*) Is that it? Is that all I get for takin' you away from all your troubles?

Sive   – (*Cringing with shyness and affection.*)

Orlaith   Is that all I /

Sive *suddenly grabs* **Orlaith**, *wraps her arms around her and holds her tightly for what seems like an age. Then she suddenly separates and retreats back into herself.* **Orlaith** *is totally taken aback and not sure how to respond. But eventually gently moves back towards* **Sive**, *tentatively leans in and kisses her awkwardly on the mouth. They hold this position. They breathe as one.*

Clinging on.

Eventually they part.

Scene Ten

A few weeks later. **Orlaith** *is alone in the cottage. She's changing a plug. She seems burdened, weighed down.* **Sive** *bounces in the door with a shopping bag. She's radiant and far from the meek girl of earlier scenes. She's wearing a colourful, light dress and is more 'feminine' than before.*

Sive (*sing-song*)   Hallllllooooo!

Orlaith   – (*Distracted.*)

Sive   Orlaith –

Orlaith   I'm fixin' the plug.

Sive   You can do everythin'!

Orlaith   –

Sive   He didn't have any bread left.

Orlaith   You serious?

Sive   There's some stuff in the freezer anyway.

Orlaith   He's useless /

Sive   Or did we eat those?'

Orlaith   Hardly stocks anythin' /

Sive   Ah noooooo. We ate them!

Orlaith   Too busy chattin' up girls.

Sive   What ya sayin'?

Orlaith   Said he's too busy chattin' up girls –

Sive (*laughing*)   He gave me the eye again.

Orlaith (*not laughing*)   Watcha mean 'again'?

Sive   Y'know–

Orlaith   I don't get 'the eye' –

Sive   And a whistle as I left!

Orlaith   Perv.

Sive   Ah no, Quinn's nice.

Orlaith (*Mocking.*)   'Quinn's nice'. How d'ya know?

Sive   He's really friendly/always up for a chat, just the distraction of it.

Orlaith   He's distracted all right –

Sive   Not like that. He's just lonely /

Orlaith   For God's sake, Sive –

Sive   There in the shop every evening on his own.

Orlaith (*mocking*)   Poor him!

Sive   Fingerless gloves 'cos of the cold, hardly any customers –

Orlaith   Poor Quinn!

Sive   Tryin' to do his homework on the counter, his Da has him workin' every night –

Orlaith   You should keep away from him–

Sive   Why?

Orlaith   I'm tellin' ya, ya jus' should.

Sive   'Tis the only shop for miles Orlaith!

Orlaith   Thought you hated all boys?

Sive   He's just the shop boy!

Orlaith   An' you all dressed up for him like a fool.

Sive   I'm not all dressed up.

Orlaith   You are.

Sive   I'm not.

Orlaith   You are!

Sive   I'm not!

Orlaith   You are!!!

Sive   I'm not!!!

Orlaith   I'm tellin' ya, ya are! Half dressed. Like a whore.

Sive   I am not!

Orlaith   Like a fool –

Sive   I'm not a fool.

Orlaith   You'll be bringin' trouble on us with all a' this caper –

Sive   I went to buy bread.

Orlaith   And to give him an eyeful.

Sive   We were just chattin'!

Orlaith (*sarcastic*)   Oh really?

Sive   You're just jealous.

Orlaith   I'm jealous, am I?

Sive   Yeah.

Orlaith   Why would I be jealous?

Sive   'Cos he doesn't look at *you* –

Orlaith   I don't want that leerin' leech lookin' at me!

Sive   He wasn't leerin' –

Orlaith   Gawkin' at yer titties.

Sive   He wasn't!

Orlaith   His tongue hangin' out.

Sive   Stop!

Orlaith I'm no way jealous –

Sive Stop it, Orlaith, please! (*Quieter.*) Please!

Sive *is totally perplexed by* **Orlaith**'*s behaviour.*

Why you bein' like this?

Orlaith   I just don't want him hurtin' ya.

Sive   But he's not.

Orlaith   Not yet.

Sive *deliberately changes the subject.*

Sive   Any luck with the plug?

Orlaith (*bravado*)   'Twas a cinch.

Sive   Yer brill at that stuff. Don't know how ya do it.

Orlaith   I can do way more than most boys –

Sive   Lucky for me!

Orlaith   Ya should remember just how lucky and not go out half-dressed just to buy bread!

Sive   – (*Hurt by this but trying to make things better between them.*)

D'ya wanna go out on the bikes?

Orlaith   Are ya mad?

Sive   Why?

Orlaith   'Tis pissin' down out there!

Sive   'Tisn't too bad.

Orlaith   'N' yer half dressed.

Sive   We'll stick those coats on –

Orlaith   No.

Sive   Bridie won't mind.

Orlaith   No!

Sive   Why not?

Orlaith   I don't want to!

Sive   Maybe tomorrow?

Orlaith   No point, 'twill still be pissin' down.

Sive   Maybe it won't –

Orlaith   It 'twill.

Sive   We'll wrap up.

Orlaith   No thanks, Sive.

Sive   Would be a laugh –

Orlaith   I don't want to –

Sive   Ah, come on!

Orlaith (*much more harshly than intended*)   I said no, Sive!

Sive   What's wrong, Orlaith?

Orlaith   Nothin'.

Sive   So why are ya shoutin' at me?

Orlaith   Dunno.

Sive   That's a baby's answer –

Orlaith   It isn't!

Sive   It is!

Orlaith   –

Sive   Come outta yerself, Orlaith. Tell me.

Short pause.

Come on, shake a leg, girl!

Pause.

Are ya missin' yer Da or somethin'?

Orlaith (*without a thought, harshly*)   No.

Pause.

(*More gently.*) Do ya miss yer Mam?

Sive   Yeah.

Orlaith   A lot?

Sive   I'm worried 'bout her on her own. You?

Orlaith (*tersely*)   I told ya, I don't miss him.

Sive (*angry*)   What's wrong?

Orlaith   Nothing!

Sive   Ya want me to leave or somethin'?

Orlaith (*Sudden fear that* **Sive** *might leave her*) No Sive, no.

Don't ever leave –

Pause.

Please. Sit down?

Sive *sits down next to* **Orlaith**.

Closer.

Sive (*moving closer*)   OK.

Orlaith   Don't talk.

Sive   What?

Orlaith   Don't talk –

Sive   –

Orlaith   I don't wanna talk.

Sive   And it's then I see this light about her which I can't make out.

'Tis murky.

'Tis dark.

'Tis not of *this* world.

Orlaith   Closer Sive –

Sive   Been tip-toeing 'round her for days –

Orlaith   Closer –

Sive   'Fraid she'll start on me – we're wrenchin' apart 'n' I don't know why.

Orlaith   Hold me? –

Sive *moves to hold* **Orlaith**.

Sive   Now what I've run from seems less confusin' –

Orlaith   Tighter, Sive –

Sive   Than where I've run to –

Orlaith   Tighter, squeeze this outta me?

Sive   And now I'm scared –

Orlaith *takes* **Sive**'s *hand and slowly begins to squeeze it until it*

hurts **Sive**. **Sive** *is at first confused, then pained, then humiliated*
…

Bridie   'Come away, O Human Child –
To the waters and the wild –
With a fairy, hand in hand –
For the world's more full of weeping than you can understand.'

Orlaith   Stay away from Quinn, Sive.

Bridie (*Direct address.*)   'Tis a bockety rhyme. Like life I
suppose –

Orlaith   He'll only break ya …

Bridie   Nothin' ever really fits does it?

Scene Eleven

Two days later. **Sive** *and* **Orlaith** *are in the living room of* **Bridie**'s
cottage.

Orlaith   You're quiet these past few days, Sive.

Sive   –

Orlaith   What's wrong with ya?

Sive   –

Orlaith   Sive? /

Sive   I'm fine.

Orlaith   Good.

Sive   –

Orlaith   I love ya.

Sive   –

Orlaith   You know that don't ya, Sive?

Sive   – (*Shrugs 'I suppose'.*)

Orlaith   Not Quinn. Me. *I* love ya.

Sive   I know …

Orlaith   Cheer up so –

Sive   –

Orlaith   Big puss on ya.

Sive   –

Orlaith   Come on, we'll have the craic!?

Sive   –

Orlaith   Sive?

Sive (*suddenly, fast, panicked*)   I want to go home.

Orlaith   What ya say?

Sive (*tempers her tone*)   I think I should go home.

Orlaith   Why would'ya want to do that?

Sive   My Mam.

Orlaith   Yeah?

Sive   Worried 'bout her.

Orlaith   There's nothin' there for ya –

Sive   She needs me.

Orlaith   There's nothing there –

Sive   She's there. Da's there

Orlaith   Hidin' from you –

Sive   He's not.

Orlaith   Bet he is.

Sive   Well, I'll find him –

Orlaith   They'll only bring ya down, Sive –

Sive   She can't cope without me 'n' I want us three to be together.

Orlaith   They'll only burden ya, bind ya /

Sive   They won't

Orlaith   Listen to me, Sive /

Sive   No.

Orlaith   It will never happen.

Sive   It might –

Orlaith   It won't.

Sive   How d'*you* know?

Orlaith   Why are ya tryin' to ruin everythin'?

Sive   Not tryin' to ruin anythin'!

Orlaith   Ya not happy here with me?

Sive   Didn't say that –

Orlaith   Yer not tho'!

Sive   Orlaith, I didn't say/

Orlaith   Ya think I'm a piece a' shit or somethin'?

Sive   I never / (*said*)

Orlaith   That whatcha think?

Sive   No!

Orlaith   IS IT???

Sive   NO!!!

Orlaith   I'm not gonna let anyone take our heaven hostage. D'ya hear me, Sive?

Short pause.

Sive, d'ya hear me?

Sive (*very upset*)   I wanna go home –

Orlaith (*roughly*)   Come here!

She draws **Sive** *to her and holds her tightly, she slowly puts her hand between* **Sive**'s *legs … Through her tears* **Sive** *'melts' into her in total confusion and anxiety.*

You've gotta stay with me girl, I'll do anythin' for ya but you've gotta stay with me. Promise me.

Sive *in totally caught up in her emotions. Utterly confused.*

Orlaith   Promise me?

Sive *fights back tears.*

Orlaith   Sive?

Sive   –

Orlaith   That's it.

Sive *her body jolts …*

Orlaith   That's it.

Let it all go, girl.

Let it all go …

Scene Twelve

Sive *is alone.* **Orlaith** *is alone.* **Bridie** *is alone.*

Sive   The sparkle's gone from the air.

The lightness is gone.

Short pause.

She's been touchin' me –

Orlaith   She's leavin' me –

Sive   In ways I don't understand –

Orlaith   She's no longer with me –

Sive   In ways I don't like –

Orlaith   She's goin' back there I can tell –

Sive   In ways I do –

Orlaith   She's breakin' her promise –

Sive   I'm scared to say anythin' –

Orlaith   She's breakin' my heart –

Sive   For fear of the blackness again –

Orlaith   She said she never would –

Sive   So I tip-toe 'round her –

Orlaith   But now she is –

Sive   Tip-tip-toe 'round her –

Bridie   *Come away ...*

Sive (*brighter at the thought*) Quinn says there's a great disco in the village with as much Tanora as you can drink, 'n' as much toffee 'n' Taytos as you can scoff.

Orlaith   We go down to the beach.

Sive   Says you can feel the music thumpin' in yer chest.

Orlaith   She wants to go alone.

Sive   Says it feels mental altogether when the lights are flashin'.

Orlaith   But I stay close. Won't let her leave my side.

Sive   I want Orlaith and me to go to the disco.

Orlaith   Won't let her outta my sight.

Sive   So I drop a hint.

Bridie   *Come away O human child ...*

Sive   Tells me to stop playin' the fool and chasin' after Quinn.

Orlaith   We're at the water's edge –

Sive   She says he doesn't want me and never will.

Orlaith   Testin' the temperatures together.

Bridie   *To the waters and the wild ...*

Sive   Sure Quinn's got nothin' to do with anythin'.

Orlaith   Wadin' in, inch by inch in silence

Sive   He's just a pal.

Orlaith   She's quiet. Doesn't say a word.

Sive   Why's she turned so cruel?

Bridie   *Come away O human child ...*

Orlaith   She looks at me.

Her eyes hold mine for a minute.

Her chest stutterin' as it rises, falls.

Short pause.

It's hurtin' her to breathe.

Sive   Mrs Long at school talked about petrification. I us'ta think she was talkin' 'bout being scared or somethin' but really it was 'bout stuff gettin' hard and changin'.

Orlaith   She's goin' home.

Sive   Changin' to stone 'cos of water and minerals and things.

Hard. Tough. Rigid –

Orlaith   Where her dreams can never come true.

Sive   Like Orlaith is now –

Orlaith   Movin' on to a life without me in it.

Sive   And I'm petrified –

Bridie   *With a fairy, hand in hand ...*

Sive   Why do people change?

Why do people /

Orlaith (*overlapping*)   She turns from me and slowly inches forward into the water as my heart stiffens with pain and then I explode, bawlin' to the winds, boundin' forward, forcin' her head under the water – her long hair tanglin' 'round my fingers. I'm pushin' her down as she's trashin' beneath me. Fingers held in pleasure, now clasped in pain and my blasted heart's like a bass drum, dull in my chest. She's strugglin', puttin' up a fight as a rage bolts thru' me and finally I've the force I need to hold her underwater long enough 'til the life seeps out of her.

She stops trashin'.

Jolt by crooked jolt.

Bridie   *For the worlds more full of weeping ...*

Orlaith   My eyes squint against the settin' sun as I watch her body float away. The quiet waves now slowly takin' her to another place.

Away from here.

Away from me.

Bridie   *Than you can understand.*

Orlaith   A piece of my heart trails her body closely, further and further towards the horizon.

Towards heaven itself.

Bridie   *The worlds more full of weeping ...*

Short pause.

It's over. The water moves no more.

Bridie   *Than you can understand.*

Orlaith   When I finally turn from the shore,
   I notice my heartbeat has changed,
   There's one less beat everytime.

Pause.

I pray for rain.

Pray until moist.

The End.

The Boys of Foley Street

Louise Lowe

The Boys of Foley Street was first performed as part of the 2012 Dublin Theatre Festival as a Public Art Commission from Dublin City Council and co-produced by ANU Productions with Dublin Theatre Festival, with the following cast:

Larry	Thomas Reilly
Noely	Paul Marron
Christopher	Eric O'Brien
Tony	Jed Murray
Bomb Victim	Sinead Corcoran / Zara Starr
Macker	Peter O'Byrne
Ma	Bairbre Ní hAodha / Laura Murray
Denis	Lloyd Cooney
Kathleen	Caitriona Ennis
Bernie	Louise Mathews
Maeve	Dee Burke
Anna	Una Kavanagh

Devised and created by the company

Visual Art & Installation	Owen Boss
Producer	Hannah Mullan
Technology Design	Niamh Shaw
Sound Design	Vincent Doherty
Lighting Design	Sarah Jane Shiels
Costume Design	Niamh Lunny
Production Manager	Aidan Wallace
Site Managers	Caoimhe Regan / Fiona Keller / Jessica Curnow

Characters

Larry
Noely
Christopher
Tony
Bomb Victim
Macker
Ma
Denis

Kathleen
Bernie
Maeve
Anna
Reporter

The LAB

Audience Members in groups of four (every half hour) arrive to the LAB.[1] Two Audience Members are issued with headphones and instructed to listen from the street. The other two Audience Members are guided to a parked car (parked on James Joyce Street) where they sit in the car and listen to the same recording on the car radio. Larry approaches the car, hobbling on a crutch. He has a blue sleeping bag under his arm and a bottle of cider in his hand. He knocks on the car window.

Larry   Roll down the window. Roll down the window. What are youse listenin' to? It's crazy isn't it? You see old films; it's like looking at an old film, y'know what I mean? It's crazy and I'm saying Jaysus, y'know, that's, that was us! That was us.

The Audience remain listening. Noely waits for five minutes. He walks towards the parked car. He climbs into the driver's seat. He adjusts the rear-view mirror so that he can look at the Audience.

Noely   Are they expecting yis?

Noely *changes the CD to rave music and drives off.*

Noely   Did yis know that a teaspoon of strychnine can kill a farmyard full of rats?

He drives towards the flat.

Larry *then walks towards the two Audience Members who are standing outside the LAB, wearing headphones; he takes the headphones off the Audience and has a listen to what they are listening to.*

Larry   What are yous listenin to? It's crazy isn't it? You see old films; it's like looking at an old film, y'know what I mean? It's crazy and I'm saying Jaysus, y'know, that's, that was us! That was us.

---

[1] The LAB is a purpose-built facility for the arts, based on Foley Street, Dublin. See www.thelab.ie for more information.

Larry *gives the headphones to Front of House staff and motions for* **Audience** *to follow. He walks up Foley Street with* **Audience** *following. He stops at old pictures of Foley Street showing the LAB and surrounding area.*

Foley Street

Larry   I used to live there. That's the Foley Street I remember, not this one. See that park there, that's where the flats were, now I'm going to show yous where the interview happened, with meself, me three mates and Pat Kenny. When Kenny was here his car was broken into and his radio was robbed, it was a mini. That's gas isn't it? He never mentioned that on the radio. Over there is iPhone alley, I'll let yous make up yiser mind about why it's called that. Righ' this is where the interview happened, I was standing here, me three mates were there and Kenny was there. He was asking us about what we got up to and we were just telling him about robbing, what we used to rob, and about growing up …

Christopher *runs from iPhone alley,* **Larry** *spots him and hobbles across the road to confront him.*

Larry   Git! Git! Come 'ere you, stay there. Stay there! Where's the money?

Christopher   Gis about five minutes, and I'll have it for ye, I'm in a hurry …

Larry   You fucking scumbag you never even came up to see me when I was inside. Stand there!

Christopher   I was busy.

Larry   Busy me bollix.

Christopher   I'm in a hurry, gimme about five minutes, I'm good for it.

Christopher *backs up the street, towards Beaver Street.* **Larry** *motions to* **Audience** *to follow and pursues* **Christopher**

continuing the confrontation. As they near the laneway **Larry**
whistles, and **Tony** *approaches them from Beaver Street.*

Christopher *sees* **Tony**, *panics and runs down the laneway. They
catch up with him as he is cornered in a dead end.*

Christopher   Relax will ye?

Tony   Where you going? What ye talking to him for, talk to me.

Christopher   Gis five minutes and I'll get it for ye.

Tony   Come 'ere t'me, what are ye gonna do in five minutes?

Christopher   Will ye talk to him?

Larry   Me bollix. (*He throws crutch at* **Eric**)

Christopher   I'm good for it.

Tony   Give it to me so.

Christopher   I don't have it on me.

First Rotation Option A
Tunnel / Archway

Larry *gives* **Audience Member B** *his sleeping bag and tells them
to stand there in the laneway.* **Larry** *takes* **Audience Member A**
through gate and tells them to get into the car. While that happens,
Tony *is still confronting* **Eric**.

Tony   Where are you going? Come 'ere and say hello.

Larry *closes gate on* **Audience Member A.**

Larry   Get his phone.

Tony   Gimme your phone.

Christopher *resists,* **Tony** *gives him a slap on the head.*

Tony   Gimme your fucking phone.

Christopher *hands over phone reluctantly.* **Tony** *takes phone and gives it to* **Larry**.

Tony   What's your pin number?

Christopher   Five, four, two …

Tony   Five, four, two? Five, four, two? (*He kicks* **Christopher**)

Christopher   Five, four, two, six.

Tony   Five, four, two, six. Did ye get that?

Larry   Yeah.

Tony *takes off jacket and hands it to* **Audience Member**.

Tony   Here, hold that.

Tony *turns back to* **Christopher** *who is making a run for it.* **Tony** *slams him against the metal gate. He is laughing.*

Tony   Where are ye going? Where are ye going?

He slaps him and pushes him towards back of lane. **Larry** *starts filming the action on* **Eric**'s *phone, turns the lens on himself and puts arm around* **Audience Member** *gets a shot of them both.*

Larry   Aren't we lovely? Here – take the phone and film this.

Tony *takes off top and ties it around his waist, spreading his arms.*

Tony   Where you going? Come 'ere t'me and gimme a hug.

Christopher *makes a run for it;* **Tony** *grabs him in a headlock and starts pulling him deeper into the lane.* **Larry** *begins doing press-ups directly in front of the* **Audience Member**.

Tony   Smile for the camera.

Christopher   Turn that fucking off!

Larry   Film me. Film me I said! This is fucking deadly!

Tony *throws* **Christopher** *up against corrugated gate and slaps him around, his hands are around his throat and he starts searching his pockets, throwing the contents onto the ground.*

Christopher   Watch me medal.

Tony   Fuck your medal.

Larry *brings the* **Audience** *closer to the fight.*

Larry   Keep filmin', film that!

Tony *makes* **Christopher** *pick up money and hand it to him.* **Tony** *throws it back on the ground.*

Tony   What do ye think this is, Dunnes' fucking Stores?

Tony *pins* **Christopher** *to the gate once more, holds him there, and punches him repeatedly in the face and when he is finished he shakes punch off as he walks back towards* **Audience**.

Tony (*To* **Audience**)   Give me me jacket.

Larry *continues to make lots of noise with his crutch, jumping around and aiming it at* **Christopher**.

Larry   Scumbag, get the fucking money!

Christopher   Fuck off.

Larry   Who you telling to fuck off?

Christopher   Sorry.

Tony   Right come on, I've got to get back to the flat.

Larry *walks to* **Audience** *to get sleeping bag.*

Tony   Say goodbye to your bird/fella.

Larry *kisses the* **Audience** *on the lips. Together they walk back up the lane.*

Christopher *spits out blood and propels off wall onto corrugated gate; jumps up onto metal gate; and hangs for a moment; drops to the ground.*

Christopher   (*After them up the lane*) PRICKS! (*To* **Audience**) Gimme that fucking phone, you.

He takes phone off **Audience Member**. *After a few seconds* **Larry** *and* **Tony** *reappear.*

Tony   What d'ye say? You think I'm fucking bad? Wait till ye see what's coming after.

Larry *makes shooting motion with crutch.*

Larry   You've been warned!

Larry *and* **Tony** *leave while* **Christopher** *collects his belongings.*

Christopher   Where's me medal? Where's me medal? Here, help me find me medal. Did one of them take it? Do you have it? Me granny gave it to me, it's me lucky charm.

He continues searching on the ground. He is upset.

Christopher   Do you think they're hard? They're not hard, they're only messing about, do ye wanna see a hard man?

He takes out his phone and shows the **Audience Member** *a video of a gang rape that he was involved in.*

Christopher   I'll show ye a hard man. Do ye know him, do ye? That's me!

Second Rotation Option B

Christopher's *mother enters down the lane. She calls out his name as she walks down the alleyway.*

Ma   Christopher!!!! Christopher Phelan!!!

Christopher *ushers* **Audience Member** *inside the gate of the laneway.*

Ma   They told me you were in here.

Christopher *tells* **Audience Member A** *to get out of the car, tells* **Audience Member B** *to get in the car. Tells* **Audience Member A** *to take his phone and to tell his Ma he's not there, and pushes them out to the laneway.*

Ma   Where is he? Tell me where he is.

Christopher   I'm here Ma, I'm only messin'. What's wrong?

Ma   Get over here. What are you doing with my son? Jesus Christ look at the state of you. What happened to you?

Christopher   Get off me Ma, you're embarrassing me.

Ma   I asked you what happened?

Christopher   Nothin. Just messin' about.

Ma   Who's she/he? (*Indicating the* **Audience**) You're a bit too old to be hanging around with him.

Christopher   That's Larry's mate. What's wrong with ye?

Ma   I need ye to come home with me.

Christopher   I'm not going home, what's wrong with ye?

Ma   Your name's on the list.

Christopher   What list?

Ma   Your name's on the fuckin list for tonight Christopher. People are talking.

Christopher   Who put me name on the list?

Ma   You said it was the end of it all of this. You said you wouldn't bring any more trouble to my door.

Christopher   I haven't done anything in weeks Ma, I swear on me Nana's grave. I swear on our Maeve's life.

Ma   Empty your pockets.

Christopher   There's nothing in me pockets.

Ma   Empty your fuckin pockets, Eric.

Christopher   Look, I've nothing. Where are the kids?

Ma   At home. Take your shoes off.

Christopher   For fuck sake Ma.

She takes his shoes off, leaving him standing in the street in his socks. She picks up his trainers and examines them. She searches him.

Ma   Did they rob you? Where's your phone?

Christopher   She/He has it.

Ma   What are you doin' with his phone, gimme it.

Christopher   Gimme me phone.

*The **Audience Member** chooses who to give phone to. If they give it to **Ma**, **Christopher** has to grab it off her.*

Ma (*To **Eric***)   Gimme the phone.

Christopher   You're not getting me phone Ma.

She pushes him hard.

Ma   What are ye hiding?

Christopher   I'm not hiding anything Ma.

Ma (*Pushing him again*)   Don't fuckin lie to me Christopher. I've had it up to fuckin' here with all of this.

Silence

Ma   Come home with me Christopher.

Christopher   I'm not going home, Ma.

Ma (*To **Audience***)   Tell him to come home with me; he's not going to listen to me.

Christopher   Don't tell me what to do.

Ma   So what are you going to do?

Christopher   I don't know Ma, I'll sort it.

Ma   Sort it? How are you planning to sort it?

Ma   Don't fuckin' walk away from me.

Christopher   Go home Ma.

Ma   I need to know Christopher, what are we going to do?

Christopher   I DON'T FUCKIN KNOW !

Noely *arrives in the car.*

Noely   Get in the car, you.

There's a struggle between all three. **Ma** *tries to stop* **Christopher** *getting in the car and* **Noely** *is trying to drag* **Christopher** *forcibly into the car.* **Christopher** *eventually gets in the car with* **Audience** *and* **Noely** *drives off.*

Ma   (*Screaming after the car*) Christopher!

Second Rotation Option A / B

Audience Member A *gets told by* **Larry** *to get into the car. He closes the steel gate behind them. Large-scale projections fill the wall of the old cinema: http://vimeo.com/52181901. Inside the gate is a disused railway tunnel. Inside the tunnel is a 1974 blue Ford Cortina. The back door is open. A woman is draped across the roof of the car. She is covered in debris from a bomb. Upon sitting into the car, the* **Audience** *triggers the RFID sensor[2] which plays the soundscape and cues lighting change. Audio starts playing 'Sugar Baby Love', bomb, Taoiseach's address, news report playing over the radio followed by a long bomb noise / white noise.* **Bomb victim***: lying on top of car, head at boot and legs on top of windscreen. She slowly slides down windscreen. Movement on bonnet towards headlights, she falls head first off bonnet. She lies on top of car – her right arm alongside of back window, her left arm down by side window (access to sensor).*

---

[2] Radio-frequency identification (RFID) is a wireless non-contact use of radio-frequency electromagnetic fields to transfer data, for the purposes of automatically identifying and tracking tags attached to objects. In *The Boys of Foley Street* we created mini computers Arduinos that captured the Audience Member's movement and a sensor then triggered sound and lighting cues. There were no lighting or sound operators working on the production.

She is lying face down with legs bent to the right. Her left leg is straightened and drops down onto top of windscreen. She pushes her body down windscreen, leading with her left leg, straight and aimed diagonally towards bottom left corner of windscreen. She falls slowly down the windscreen, ending up on left side in front of windscreen, pushing with her right arm down and away from windscreen. At the same time she stretches her right leg back towards edge of bonnet, bent at the knee. She reaches with her right arm above head towards corner of bonnet, looking in same direction and at the same time slowly moves from side to back and stretching her left leg out. She drags her body across bonnet, her left arm lying on bonnet, right arm above her head. She returns her gaze towards **Audience***, moving slowly, speeding up when bomb sounds and lets her body go loose. Abruptly her body slides partially off left side of bonnet and she hangs over the front of the bonnet before falling slowly to the ground. She stands in front of the car in the headlights to deliver testimony.*

Bomb victim   First bomb, clatter of thunder, bomb, ah no thunder, must be, bomb made noise, dust, never thought, actual atrocity, first bomb.

Big big Georgian door, pushed the door, no pulled the door, big flash, window on my right, flash, flash exploded, big flash, whirlwind or something. Blasted, just blasted, everything was blasted, everything flying, falling on the ground. Electrical vibes, through my body, lightning, I never lost consciousness, didn't realise, a bomb, electrical thing, through my body, electrical shock, vibrations, shook and shook and shook, everything collapsed, everything settled, everything stopped, shaking, falling, everything settled.

On my knees, couldn't see, didn't occur, didn't panic, moaning weakly, moan louder, grabbing, hands and knees, looking, dying, didn't realise, kneeling, gravel, dirt, rubble, afraid, eventually on to my feet, I can't see, I couldn't see, I realised, I can't see, couldn't see.

A fire where the window was, just in my mind, a fire, no fire, I realised, I remember, don't let me be blind.

Dust rising, I don't know, all of a sudden, sight, ground up, into my left eye, shoe shop, demolition site, empty silence, and the dust, was unbelievable, everything was grey, everything grey, lying in the street, people were grey, grey, everything grey and bloody.

Help me, so shocked, no answers, seconds, minutes, head cut, cream trousers, cardigan, blood, right side of my face, something wrong, my eye, blood, somebody else's blood, I don't know what it is.

Reset *on* **Ma** *screaming CHRISTOPHER! or car horn beeping.* **Bomb victim***'s journey now goes towards meeting room on adjoining James Joyce Street. En route she passes* **Larry** *and* **Audience** *on Street.*

Bomb victim (*Spoken as she walks down the street towards the meeting room site*)

A fireman, I knew, the moulded feather down the back of his hat, body draped, out the window, I thought, taking the mannequins out, in case they get broken, these were living people, five minutes ago, I thought that, for years and years and years, taking the mannequins out, brought up to mind things, not break things, mannequins, important, out the window, they were people.

A guy came over, very handsome, come with me, a policeman, the shop, the lady, telling him the lady, hurt and moaning, bodies on the street, it didn't, it's difficult for me, didn't feel anything, wasn't bodies, I wasn't shocked, horrified, numb.

Car Chase

Noely *drives the car back towards Foley Street. There are road works in the centre of the road.*

Noely (*To* **Christopher***, laughing*)   You're in some fuckin' trouble.

He turns left and **Christopher** *opens the door and throws himself out onto the street, running back behind the JCB that is blocking the road from the car.*

Noely   Fuck!!!! Fuck!!! Stupid little bollox. *He turns the volume up on the car radio and rave music blares as he skids away and heads towards Liberty House flat complex. He drives into the complex and stops outside a flat on the ground floor.*

Flat

Bernie *is outside the front door smoking.* **Denis** *is standing on the balcony above the flat.* **Kathleen** (*a young child in a school uniform*) *is in the playground.* **Maeve** *is in the bathroom.* **Anna** *is lying on the living room chair. The car pulls up with two* **Audience Members***.* **Denis** *and* **Kathleen** *run down to the car. They get in to the car.*

Noely   Watch them.

He points to the **Audience Member** *who needs to go into the living room.*

Kathleen   Don't mind him, move yer feet. Here, d'yis want to go to a party?

Denis   Ye come on in and have a party.

They walk to the door of the flat.

Kathleen   What's your name?

Bernie   Who are you?

Denis   It's … (*says* **Audience's** *name*).

Kathleen   Fuck off.

Bernie   What are ye's doing?

Denis   Comin' in for a party … relax … we won't be long.

Bernie   It's my fuckin' house.

The four have walked on past **Bernie** *into the flat.* **Bernie**
*follows closing the door behind her and standing with back to
door.* **Kathleen** *has brought the* **Audience Member 1** *in to the
living room, shutting the door behind her.* **Denis** *in the hall with*
Audience Member 2 *who shows them into a small bathroom.*

Denis   Get in there, go on get in. Have a look at that. (*He points
the* **Audience Member** *towards peep holes in the wall which show
a video of* **Maeve** *being gang raped by three men*). Knock yerself
out.

Maeve *is sitting on the toilet, she is undressed and is dishevelled.*
Maeve *looks at* **Audience**.

Maeve   Am I allowed to wash myself?

Maeve *stands at sink and washes with carbolic soap. Two minutes
in* **Maeve** *turns off tap. (Audio cue from* **Kathleen** *turning off
music).* **Maeve** *takes some tissue, dries her hands, turns back to*
Audience; *she uses toilet tissue to wipe intimately between her
legs.*

Maeve   Maeve met a young girl at the GPO. She says she
wants a pen pal. She asks her to go to a party. There is no party.
Tony tells Maeve to lie down. Tony tells Maeve to pull up her
skirt. Tony gets on top of Maeve. Maeve's skirt becomes wet.
The bed becomes wet. Tony gets off Maeve. Denis does not take
off his clothes but takes out his private parts. Denis catches a
hold of Maeve's private part and feels it. Denis wets Maeve's
private parts. (*To* **Audience**) Am I allowed to put my dress back
on?

Maeve *puts dress back on. She moves as if in pain. She hands the*
Audience *a safety pin and invites them to pin her dress where the
zip has been broken.*

Denis   Are yis on your way over?

Maeve   Can you get my bag from him?

Maeve *puts bag on toilet, takes out lipstick, hairbrush, money,
safety pin. She brushes her hair with difficulty.*

Denis *enters.*

Denis   Did you get the money? Give them the money. Take it.

Rotation B *repeats as before until three-minute cue. Then:*

Maeve   Can you help me get home?

Denis *followed by* **Bernie** *go into the living room.*

Whilst the others are in the hall, **Kathleen** *sits* **Audience Member 1** *down on chair at the end of the table on the right by the window.* **Anna** *is sitting on the opposite chair.*

Kathleen *(To the* **Audience Member***)* What's your name again? *(She waits for an answer)* Do you want tea? Will you be my new friend? Here, look what I have … *(She goes to the sideboard and offers them a Big Time bar. She sits on the table facing them and swings her legs)*

Denis *and* **Bernie** *enter.*

Bernie   Here you, what's your name? What are you doing here?

Kathleen *(names the* **Audience***)*   my friend.

Denis *sits down at table. There is a bowl of cornflakes on it. He begins to eat it.*

Denis *(Calls* **Audience Member** *by their name)*   I love cornflakes. Do you like cornflakes?

Bernie   It's not a fucking halfway house.

She goes to the kitchen. **Kathleen** *mimics* **Bernie***. She stares at the* **Audience** *and puts her feet on the table.*

Bernie   Get your feet off my table.

Kathleen   It's not your table. *(To the* **Audience***)* Tell her it's not her table.

Bernie   It is my fucking table, get your feet off it now.

Bernie *pulls her feet down and she tries to get them back up but* **Bernie** *clamps her knees down.* **Kathleen** *stands on the table.* **Anna** *enters from bedroom door and stares at* **Audience**.

Bernie   I don't know what way you were reared, but you don't put your feet on the fucking table.

Bernie *and* **Anna** *catch eyes and* **Anna** *follows* **Bernie** *to the kitchen, swaying at the beads.* **Denis** *slaps* **Kathleen** *on the legs.*

Denis   Leave it out.

Kathleen   Fuck off.

She kicks the cornflakes off the table towards **Denis** *with her right leg.*

He pushes the chair back.

Denis   Fuck!

He grabs **Kathleen** *by the hips, she puts her hands on his shoulders. He lifts her off the table, sets her down.* **Kathleen** *and* **Denis** *extend right arms, grabbing each other at the elbows.* **Kathleen** *pulls him into her, he ducks to his hunkers. He goes under her legs. She lifts her left leg over him. He gets up and turns to face her. He lifts her onto the table lying on her back. She grabs both his upper arms, turns him over her onto his back on the table also. Her right hand is at the back of his neck, she propels him into the wall. She swings her legs over the table so that they are dangling.*

Kathleen (*Shouts*)   This is deadly.

In the kitchen, **Bernie** *stares at the wall.* **Anna** *comes into the kitchen dancing at* **Bernie** *and kicks the pram numerous times. She exits dancing backwards into the living room.* **Kathleen** *turns the music up load.*

Kathleen (*Shouts*)   This is deadly.

Anna *moves to living room door. She bangs it with her right hand. She kicks with her right leg and spins on her left foot 360 degrees. Repeat × 2.* **Kathleen** *has left hand on table. She propels into the*

wall, her right hand hits the wall. Looks to **Audience**. *Repeat ×*
2. **Denis***: right foot onto table, propels right to the wall, both his*
hands hit the wall. Repeat × 2. **Bernie** *is cooking (Depending on*
the time of day this can be breakfast, lunch, dinner, supper etc.).
Denis *and* **Kathleen** *meet at opposite side of the table, both hands*
on the table facing each other. He grabs both her shoulders. She
grabs his shoulders. They scream into each others' faces. Holding
hands, they rotate under each other till they reach the edge of the
table. She goes under his right arm, wraps arms around his back.
He puts his left arm across her stomach, right arm across her
back and lifts her. Her legs go straight up in a diagonal with her
head pointing towards the floor. He pivots half way and sets her
down. Her left leg first and then right. He pushes her into the wall,
they struggle with each other at the wall. She pushes him to the
floor. He collapses and stays on the floor. He watches as **Kathleen**
goes to **Anna** *who is dancing. They grab each other. They dance.*
They mosh. They scream. They headbang. **Kathleen** *then lifts*
Denis *off the ground and kisses him aggressively and pushes him*
back into the wall. **Anna** *invites the* **Audience** *up to dance with*
her. They dance. They mosh. They scream. **Anna** *grabs* **Kathleen**
to dance with them some more (c. 30 seconds). **Denis** *covers his*
ears and shakes his head. **Kathleen** *pulls away, heading towards*
the bedroom and turns down the music.

Kathleen   I have to go to school.

She picks up a bottle of vodka and drinks from it.

Denis   … My fucking cornflakes!

Denis *goes to the kitchen.*

Denis   Clean them up.

Bernie   What?

Denis *goes to the hall.* **Bernie** *curses under her breath, she enters*
the living room, lifts the chair and collects the bowl and spoon
from the floor. She goes back into the kitchen and waits until **Anna**
is seated. She returns to living room with a shovel and brush and
cleans up the mess. **Anna** *guides the* **Audience** *back to their seat.*

Anna   Sit down you.

She looks in mirror on wall. She examines hair, face, breasts. She picks up some hair clips and begins to clip hair up randomly. She watches **Audience** *in mirror.*

She sits on the table. She changes the song on record player. She dances. She takes blonde wig off the dummy and puts it on. She clips it into place. She is keeping eye contact with the **Audience**. *She moves and sits in armchair. She propels/threatens* **Bernie** *while she is cleaning up cornflakes. She propels from armchair to table beside* **Audience** *twice. She then propels from window sill to table twice. She limply turns 360 degress against windowsill twice, opening and bending her legs.*

Anna   Look At Me! … Fuckin' Look At Me!

Anna *propels from window wall to adjacent wall.She lifts her right foot and slowly places it hip high on window wall. She lets her head drop between her legs and looks at* **Audience** *through her legs. She repeats this twice. She lifts her right leg and mounts the left arm of the arm chair. She propels against chair, floor, sideboard, table, walls. She gets up on the chair placing her feet on the hand rests. She drops her head between her legs again and looks at* **Audience** *through her legs, her backside directly facing them. She drops her right arm down between her legs and bangs the back of chair sixteen times, keeping eye contact upside down with* **Audience**. *This resembles a trunk moving back and forth: elephant dance. She then stretches upwards towards roof still standing on the armrests and propels against all walls and ceiling sixteen times. She then places her right cheek against wall, raises her two hands and places them above her head, outstretched against wall. She slowly slides down the wall. She sits on the back of the chair looking at the* **Audience**, *she swivels and slides down to seated position.*

Anna   Get me me fur!

Anna *puts on her boots helped by* **Kathleen**. *They also help her on with her white fur coat.* **Bernie** *puts out cornflakes and vodka. She grabs a cigarette and stands outside the flat smoking.*

Anna   I'm goin' to sip champagne with Oliver Reed! … (*She gestures slicing her own throat. She raises both hands, in a victory position, holding them above her head*).

Anna   Where's me glasses?

Denis *comes in from hall.*

Anna   Where's me glasses?

Denis   I don't fuckin' know.

She then strikes him violently on the back of the head

Anna   Where's me bleedin' glasses?

She starts searching for her glasses upending kitchen. **Bernie** *returns to the kitchen, she cooks and cleans.*

Kathleen (*To the* **Audience Member**)   You should go.

Kathleen *goes to the bedroom she begins to inject heroin.* **Denis** *takes the* **Audience** *out of the room.*

Denis   C'mon let's get out of here, before she fuckin' snaps!

Reset
Audience Rotate

Denis *(Whispering to the* **Audience***)* you'd better not go back in there – she's a mad bitch … swear to God, touched she is. She once came after us all in the flat, we were about fourteen. We thought that she was still inside in the Joy. We'd been out on this mad bender the night before, robbed a chemist in Enniskerry and came back here. About six in the morning some of us were still strung out inside, the place was in rag order. I was all over the place, I woke up with the sound of the kitchen window coming in, some young one that I'd never met before was lying in me lap. I thought we were getting raided so I jumped up. Anna had put her fist through the window and was shouting, let me in, let me bleedin' in … blood pouring down both her arms, like out of a horror film or something. We were shitting it, no one wanted to open the door. Nobody moved 'cause we knew better. She kept on screaming that she could see us and if someone didn't let her in quick she was going to slice us all up. The stupid bitch that was lying on top of me staggered to the door and opened it. She used the glass from the broken window and just opened yer one up, her whole face was a mess, there was nothing left of it. She kept on stabbing her over and over saying we had no permission to be in her flat. She came in then and upended the table. Swear to God, I was brickin', thought I was dead, she said that no one was going home, that she was going to kill all of us and bury every one of us out the back and I am telling you, I fuckin' believed her too. She's capable of anything, that one. I was never so glad to see the pigs as I was then. Never fucked off as quickly … Sure, I once saw her embed a hatchet into her own daughter's head – right out there in front of the –

Denis *is interrupted by* **Maeve** *and brings* **Audience Member 2** *into living room, sits them in the same chair.*

Denis   Sit down there. Do you want a cup of tea?

He goes to the kitchen and makes the tea if necessary. Makes cornflakes and sits at kitchen door staring at **Audience***.* **Kathleen** *comes from bedroom with goggles on her head.*

Kathleen   Ma, Ma, are you awake? Here, look … look at me … gis a shot on your sunbed. Ma, go on, gis a shot of your sunbed …

Repeats as she goes to **Anna***, sits on her lap, kisses her all over and giggles as* **Anna** *tickles her. They both laugh hysterically.* **Tony** *enters.*

Tony   Who the fuck are you?

Tony *goes to the kitchen, gets scales and enters living room, puts scales on table, takes bag from the coat, leaving bag on table and coat on the chair. Sits and weighs bag of heroin at the table,* **Kathleen** *watches from* **Anna***'s knees. She walks around the table to* **Tony***, sits on his lap, whispers in his ear and pulls him up to dance.* **Tony** *resists. She pulls him, stands on his chair, dances for* *him.* **Tony** *grabs her into his arms, dances with her, grabs* **Denis's** *tobacco off the table, and carries* **Kathleen** *to the kitchen and sets her at the side of the sink. He rolls a cigarette, looking back at the* **Audience** *and* **Denis***. All the time,* **Bernie** *is watching them with a cigarette in her hand and tops up the vodka once. She is still except digging nail into thumb.*

Kathleen   She is watching you. Get rid of her and I'll suck your dick.

Tony   I can't get rid of her. Wait till later. Good girl.

Tony *finished rolling his cigarette and puts it in her mouth and she leaves and goes into the bedroom.* **Tony** *walks out of the kitchen and throws tobacco to the table at* **Bernie***, and goes to the scales.* **Bernie** *knocks back vodka, gets up and walks around the table smiling at* **Tony***. She seductively goes to* **Tony***, holds his face and they start to dance.* **Tony** *lifts her and she wraps her legs around him. They dance. She pulls back and looks at him.*

Bernie   What were you doing with the child? What were you doing with the child?

Tony   I wasn't doing anything.

Bernie   What were you doing with the fucking child?

Tony   What the fuck.

She bites his ear. He struggles with her into the kitchen, throws her off as she is still screaming. She repeats this for some time. **Tony** *throws her against the kitchen wall, putting his hand to his ear.*

Tony   My fucking ear, ya mad fucking cunt.

He grabs his jacket and drugs. **Kathleen** *is in the doorway laughing at him and he says 'Fuck off' at her as he leaves.* **Bernie** *stands with hands on the sink.* **Anna** *sits, having watched the entire thing.* **Denis** *is in the hallway the entire time looking in at* **Maeve***.* **Anna** *performs her movement piece again with* **Bernie** *in the kitchen cooking or making tea.* **Denis** *enters.*

Anna   Where's me glasses? (*She slaps him hard across the face*)

Denis   I don't fuckin' know.

Denis *goes into the kitchen to look for her glasses.* **Maeve** *sends* **Audience Member 2** *in to* **Denis** *in the kitchen to ask if she can go home.*

Denis   Tell her to come in and ask herself.

Maeve *enters with* **Audience** *and asks again if she can go home.*

Denis   Have you got the bus fare?

Maeve   No.

Denis (*To* **Audience Member**)   Have you got the fare for her?

Audience *may give bus fare to* **Denis** *or* **Maeve**.

Denis   Walk her to the bus.

He starts singing 'Should I Stay or Should I Go'. Everyone looks at the **Audience Member** *and laughs.* **Kathleen** *walks out with the* **Audience Members**, *followed by* **Denis** *and* **Maeve**. **Macker** *is outside the flat sitting in his car taking pictures.* **Kathleen** *runs up onto the balcony. There are a group of kids outside the door; some are on skates, others on bicycles.*

Kathleen   Do you like taking pictures of little girls? Does it get you off at night sitting in yer car? This is harassment this is, do you know that? It's fuckin' disgusting, a man your age taking pictures of young girls. Someone stop him. It's not right. You ought to be ashamed of yourself.

Kids   That's harassment that is.

Denis *pushes* **Maeve** *back into the flat*

Denis   Get back in there you. (*To* **Macker**) Fuck you.

Macker *guides both* **Audience Members** *into his car.*

Macker   Get in. You don't want to stay here, do you?

Kathleen *runs back to the car as he is getting into the driver's seat. She is very upset.*

Kathleen   Here where are yis going? Don't be going with him. I thought you were my friend? You can't just leave me here. I gave you a big time bar (*chips / toast etc., as applicable*).

Macker *starts the car and begins to drive off. Other kids follow.* **Kathleen** *runs after the car, she is hysterical.*

Kathleen   Please, Please come back. Don't leave me. You said you were my friend. Please … please.

Reset
Car (Interior)

Macker   Don't be minding her.

(*Silence as he drives down Beaver Street, heading towards James Joyce Street*)

Seen something. Put it down. Heard something? Put it down. The central committee will protect you. No names. Anonymous. Investigated. Dealt with. No police, that's why people trust us, come to us. We're helping each other to help ourselves. We deal in facts. Keep your eyes open and watch. We're a private citizen's organisation. We access the individual situation, we investigate the individual situation, we gather evidence and then we sanction each individual situation. We're wanted and we're needed; sure without door-to-door co-operation we'd be nothing.

If you have information don't be afraid to name names. Anything you've seen just put it down, just say what ya saw and the committee will investigate it. Look at yer neighbours, look at yer families, look at the person sitting next to you. Look at them … go on … really look at them and if you seen them do something, then you have a responsibility to do something about it.

Don't be afraid, names are the most difficult words to speak. For months in our meetings you'd be hearing murmurs … finally someone, usually a mother will say 'everyone knows who's doin' it' … then a name is whispered, repeated by someone else. Then shouted by someone pretending to clarify. Then pandemonium. Anyone who is named is invited to come to a subsequent meeting and give a reply. If you're innocent then you've nothing to fear. The innocent are cleared and the others are dealt with. People come to me every day sayin' this one's a pusher and that one's a pusher … no report is ignored but we won't move on that unless we have absolute proof, we have to cover ourselves. We've seen pushers accuse one another in meetings.

Every single case we proceeded against has been proved, remember that.

Macker's *car pulls up outside the CPAD* (*Concerned Parents Against Drugs*) *meeting room. He gets out and asks the* **Audience** *to get out of the vehicle on the passenger side.* **Macker** *approaches the door to the meeting room with the* **Audience**. *A* **Reporter** *is waiting at the door to the studio and asks a question.* **Macker** *opens the door to the meeting room. As he answers the* **Reporter**'s *questions, he ushers the* **Audience** *inside the room one by one.*

Macker   What I want … what CPAD wants is the day when it is all over; the day when no one fills the pushers' shoes because the detoxed addicts have thorough rehabilitation, the kids are no longer interested in heroin and the pushers have been disposed of by the law or the community. To this end, every stake-out and every tail is a potential new beginning. The end of one pursuit or individual is often the beginning of three or four others. We know who these people are, with help of people like you we keep them under surveillance, we investigate them and then we deal with them. Right that's enough; we've stuff to do here.

Macker *closes the door in her face. The* **Reporter** *waits outside, looking in the window. Inside the meeting room there are hundreds of photographs of previous* **Audience Members** *overlapping on the wall. It is the headquarters of a surveillance movement. The* **Audience** *is aware that they too have been photographed previously leaving the flat with* **Kathleen**. *Their* *picture is waiting for them on the wall.* **Macker** *moves to the top left corner of the space to the stacked fold out chairs. He proceeds to set out the chairs one by one from the window whilst talking to the* **Audience***. After four or five chairs,* **Macker** *asks the* **Audience** *to sit and continues to lay out the chairs in rows of five.* **Ma** *bursts through the doors, she is very upset.* **Ma** *delivers her speech from the edge of the chairs in the centre of the room.*

Ma   Here. You. Macker. Fuck you. Fuck you and fuck all the rest of them. Fuck the priest. Fuck Christy Burke. Fuck yis'er committee. This has gone too far. My Git's not a drug pusher. He's a kid. He turned fifteen last week for fuck sake. (*To the* **Audience**) Who put him forward? Who put his name on that list? Who? Who put his fucking name on that list? Tell me!

(Silence – she waits for the **Audience** *to speak)*

Ma   This is a load a bollix. Yous are supposed to be helping. To be doing something for this community. That's all yis hear outa yis, the community this, the community that, well who the fuck do you think are the community? I'm the community Whacker. I am! Me and my family. I have a seven-year-old and a four-year-old terrified in the flat, waiting for it to be torn apart. What have they done wrong? This is a fucking witch-hunt that's all it is. Who protects them? Answer me? How can yous stand there and tell me that I have a choice? What fucking choice do I have? Yous have taken that away from me … how can you expect me as a mother to put my fifteen-year-old son out on the streets, sure it's help he needs. I know that, that's why I came here in the first place. I stood there with you at all them meetings; talking about his problems … nodding like a bleeding sap that something needed to be done …

Macker *sits down on the chairs one row ahead of* **Ma** *on the right hand side of the room.* **Ma** *approaches* **Macker** *from behind and sits on the chair behind him.*

Ma   Why are yis doing this to me? To my family? Where's your proof?

Have yis any fucking proof? Answer me. He's not a pusher. I'd know Macker. I'd know. And I'm telling you from the bottom of my heart that he's not.

(*To the* **Audience**)

Ma   Who put him on that list? Who put him on that list? (*Back to* **Macker**) Tell me, cause I'll tear ya fucking apart. Yous should be fucking ashamed of yourselves … chasing little kids with yiser committee, why aren't yis chasing the ones who are fucking responsible? Are yis afraid? (*To the* **Audience**) Are you afraid? Why aren't yis out chasing Tony Felloni, putting his kids out onto the street? Big men aren't yis, hiding behind yer committee. Yis are huddled together, hiding behind the IRA cause yis are fucking terrified. And yous are right to be, it's a fucking epidemic … but the answer isn't bringing lump hammers and crowbars to my door. He's a kid Whacker just a little fucking kid and I'm trying my best. I've nowhere to send him. You know that. He's not a pusher. I'll swear on anything that yis want me to. It's just me … I'm all he has and he's all I have. Call them off Macker. Please. Call them fucking off, please, please, I'm begging you.

Macker *stands and turns to leave.* **Ma** *stands to block* **Macker**. **Macker** *moves her forcibly to one side. He moves towards the door.* **Ma** *follows.* **Macker** *exits the studio and gets into the car still parked outside.* **Ma** *follows him out the studio and watches* **Macker** *get into the car.* **Reporter** *leaves studio and tries to repeat her final question to* **Macker**. **Ma** *tries frantically to get into the car, she is crying hysterically now and is really upset.*

Ma   Please, This has gone too far. I'll do anythin'. Just … he's just a fucking kid. You know him. Call them off.

He pushes her away and locks himself inside the car. She continues to bang on the window. He turns up the radio and inserts the key into the ignition. **Macker** *then drives down James Joyce Street. He makes a three-point turn to come back along James Joyce Street, passing the studio and* **Ma** *runs after him screaming.*

Ma   Call them fuckin' off … this has gone too far.

*The **Audience** sit alone now in the CPAD room for c. 30 seconds.*
*The **Bomb victim** enters the meeting room, she is walking slowly*
and covered in debris and rubble. She is holding a large brick
in hand. She waits for approx. 3.5 minutes making eye contact
*directly with **Audience**. A soundscape plays, police sirens play*
*from outside in the street. (**Tony** and local TDs talking about*
how the police say that there is no heroin epidemic in Dublin).
The soundscape then blurs featuring voices from the original
recording.

Larry   It's crazy isn't it? You see old films; it's like looking at an
old film, y'know what I mean? It's crazy and I'm saying Jaysus,
y'know, that's, that was us! That was us.

*The **Bomb victim** drops the brick loudly on floor and enters*
the kitchen to wash herself. Sirens continue then silence. The
***Audience** remain alone in the meeting room. The front door is*
open onto the street. Life continues outside.